By yon bonnie banks

MAURICE LINDSAY

By yon bonnie banks

A GALLIMAUFRY

HUTCHINSON OF LONDON

HUTCHINSON & CO. (*Publishers*) LTD
178–202 Great Portland Street, London, W.1

London Melbourne Sydney
Auckland Bombay Toronto
Johannesburg New York

★

First published 1961

*This book has been set in Garamond type face. It has
been printed in Great Britain by The Anchor Press,
Ltd., in Tiptree, Essex, on Antique Wove paper and
bound by Taylor Garnett Evans & Co., Ltd., in
Watford, Herts*

Contents

Preface   7

PART ONE
AT HOME

1   Presenting Credentials   11
2   How I came to be here   17
3   Reconnaissance through History   23
4   Travellers' Tales   30
5   Lochside Diary   47
6   Through the Poets' Eyes   53
7   The Poet and Society   69
8   Our Village   76

PART TWO
. . . AND ABROAD

9   Glasgow—capital *de facto*   85
10   Edinburgh—capital *de jure*   103
11   Dundee—jute, jam and journalism   117
12   Aberdeen—the Silver City   125
13   The Highlands—atrophied attitudes   138

PART THREE
THE SPIRITUAL FABRIC

14   C. M. Grieve: the poet as leader   157
15   Scottish Nationalism: dampness in the heather   165

Contents

16   Lallans and all that   170

17   Scottish Education: system for yesteryear   180

18   Scotland's Churches: a waning influence   188

19   The Scottish Press: less and less Scottish   195

20   The National Character   203

21   The Death of Scotland?   211

     Index   221

Illustrations

Loch Lomond   *facing page* 64

Ben Lomond from Cameron Wood   65

Edinburgh: Princes Street from Calton Hill   80

Edinburgh: the Old Town from Princes Street   81

Dundee from Broughty Ferry Road   144

Aberdeen: Castle Street   145

Highland Cottage: the home of MacNab, a black-smith at Dalmally   160

Glasgow: an amateur concert   161

Preface

WHEN I first had the idea of writing *By yon bonnie banks*
I intended simply to set down the nature of the pleasures
of living on Loch Lomondside. It was then suggested to
me that a much better notion would be to survey Scotland from
my Loch Lomondside viewpoint. I decided to do both things,
dividing the appropriate sections of my book into 'At Home',
'Abroad' and 'The Spiritual Fabric'.

In the second and third sections it seemed pointless to provide
yet one more topographical survey, one more retelling of those
hoary legends that grow vaguer in outline with each successive
generation of storytellers; so I set out to examine not only
national traits and characteristics but whether or not Scotland
still stands where she stood. A few weeks after I finished the
book, a change of circumstances occurred which has now led me
to move my home down to the Borders. This gallimaufry is therefore a record of the eleven years—no insubstantial part of a man's
life—that I was privileged to spend on Loch Lomondside.

The approach I have adopted is necessarily a highly personal
one, and no doubt there will be much in these pages with which
some of my fellow Scots may strongly disagree. Many of the
critical strictures I have passed upon the Scots apply, of course, at
least as much to me as to anyone else. In my general conclusions
about Scotland's future, or absence of future, I may very possibly
be wrong. I hope that Time may prove me so: Time alone can
do so. In reaching these conclusions I have touched upon a
number of topics the discussion of which sometimes generates
heated feelings. One Scottish weakness I have not mentioned in
what follows is the Scot's capacity for taking offence. It has
always seemed to me that taking offence should be the sole
prerogative of very young schoolboys. As none of them are
likely to read *By yon bonnie banks* I very much hope that, however

Preface

strenuously my gentle readers may disagree with me, none of them will take offence.

I acknowledge with thanks help given to me by the staff of the Mitchell Library, Glasgow, and by Miss Greta Stevenson and my wife. I wish also to thank the following authors and publishers for permission to quote extracts:

Hugh MacDiarmid for permission to quote from *Scottish Eccentrics*: John Holloway and the Marvell Press for *Poem for Deep Winter*: G. S. Fraser for *Home Town Elegy*: Longmans, Green & Company and Robert Conquest for permission to quote from the Introduction to *New Lines*: Faber & Faber for permission to quote from *The Narrow Place* by the late Edwin Muir: W. & R. Chambers for permission to quote from *The Future of Scotland* by James A. Bowie.

The illustrations are all from the Mitchell Library collection and reproduced with their permission.

MAURICE LINDSAY

PART ONE
At Home

I

Presenting Credentials

ANCESTOR worship is generally thought of as a practice peculiar to the Japanese. The picture of Japan in the minds of many people is the colourfully comic, ferocious image planted there by Sir William Schwenk Gilbert, who, in *The Mikado*, makes Pooh-Bah, in a moment of extremity, apologize for present indignities to his protoplasmic ancestors.

In Scotland the cult of ancestor worship is also strong, although in recent years it has become somewhat depersonalized. There was a time when great-grandparents, and even great-great-grandparents, had their honoured place on the dining-room wall. Unfortunately, walls in the second half of the twentieth century are no longer large enough to support those prim-looking ladies and severely bewhiskered gentlemen but for whose fecundity and expansive ambitions there would be fewer of us alive today to be smugly censorious about the hypocrisies of their way of life. Many much-respected great-great-grandparents have been consigned to the flames in civic cleansing yards simply because they represent the past in a form that has become too bulky for the present to contain.

Happily, however, there are less awkward ways in which one's past can be transmitted. A convenient method is the myth, which occupies no space at all and cannot readily be proved or disproved. To have had a female ancestor who spent a night with the Bruce's cup-bearer may not seem much of a social distinction. It is at least more original than merely having had an ancestor careless enough to get himself caught by Claverhouse's high-born rowdies while taking part (probably rather tunelessly) in an open-air conventicle among draughty Lowland hills.

Since the descendants of the Picts and Scots first came together

to make up a more or less unified Scotland the country has
been peopled by romanticists: by men and women who have
largely depended for their continuing national identity upon
exaggerated gestures, individual and communal. This desire for
the extravagant has never been self-conscious—the romantic who
becomes aware of the absurdity of his gestures collapses into
insignificance—but it has been a recurring symptom of Scottish
vitality from the War of Succession to the First World War. Since
then, it has steadily declined. The Scots have become more
reasonable, and Scotland the Nation has begun to assume the
dreary aspect of a kind of outsize northernmost English county.
Here and there, of course, outbursts of the old, flamboyant
activity still erupt. But they are becoming more and more
spasmodic, and when they do burst through the greyness of
conformity their pyrotechnics rarely last even the nine days
proverbially attributed to wonder.

Yet those Scots who remain most ardently Scottish are still at
heart romantics. Whenever the enthusiasts begin to talk about
self-government for Scotland some reference to the patriotism of
Wallace or Bruce sooner or later finds its way into even the
driest economic discussion. Perhaps that is one reason why the
control of his own country has slipped, and is still slipping,
through the Scot's hands. Obviously, the inspired and necessary
thuggery practised by Wallace and Bruce has nothing whatever
to do with the harsh economic realities of our competitive
twentieth-century way of life. Yet the true patriot Scot cannot
forget them; cannot live without keeping his past in his pocket.
He must therefore either de-Scoticize himself or go on always
being the loser.

That, at any rate, is how it seems to me. Many would no
doubt disagree. But, then, this book is a personal survey of some
aspects of Scotland from the point of view of a returned exile. In
Clyde Waters: Variations and Diversions on a Theme of Pleasure I was
mainly concerned with the impact the part of Scotland which I
knew best and greatly loved had made upon my awareness in
boyhood and adolescence. That stage in my development—and in
the development of thousands of others whose first stamping
ground was the 'thirties—was marked off by a spectacular thunder-
storm and the declaration of war in September 1939. It was the
spring of 1946 before I was able permanently to return to

Scotland. What follows in these pages I have called a galli-maufry, because it is very much a collection of personal impressions and reactions to places, people, ideas and events.

In the jargon of the post-Second World War generation 'committed' and being 'engaged' are terms used to signify the fact that a writer or other artist has thoroughly immersed himself in the problems of his day and age. The writer who allows himself to become wholly committed ultimately ceases to be a writer, and becomes instead a politician or an administrator. Some degree of personal withholding is therefore necessary if objectivity is to be preserved and impressions recorded. Although I have been passionately committed to Scotland, my manner of withholding has been to settle in the countryside from which my ancestors emigrated to Ireland during the seventeenth century. I take part in local affairs from time to time when the occasion demands, but from my cottage by Loch Lomond I can survey the wider world subject to fewer distractions and irrelevancies than I found it possible to do living in a city. Here I am free from the corroding tittle-tattle of travelling littérateurs hot-foot from London with the latest scandalous gossip. Here, I need not be distracted from the enjoyment of life by those 'shop'-talking sessions in which writers try to add a few straws to the pathetic edifice of their own egos by denigrating others, paring with knife-edged envy. Here, the talk is of the weather, stock, the state of the roads, or of a neighbour's marrying, prospering or dying. Here, it is still possible to feel that one can belong; that the past still gives validity to the present. But to conclude this brief presentation of credentials, I can do no better than set forth my own personal myth, put down in verse simply because one of my principal enjoyments happens to be the pursuit of poetry.

From out his island-conqueror's clinking armour,
a Norman soldier's hot invading lust
went swarming North for gain, and got by storming
some Pictish lass's lulled and gullible trust.

A painted arrow pierced his words of loving,
threading them to a necklace strung with death.
She bent and laid them back on his cold body,
then bore his child outwith the Pictish faith.

The boy grew up with something of his father's
huge randy, roaring urge to satisfy,
and something of his mother's Northern sadness
that made him mope and question every sigh.

He was a strange unnatural combination
of action and inaction, dreams, despairs.
The Normans never braved the North to claim him;
the Picts, too, sensed he wasn't one of theirs.

In time, the common flood of life aroused him;
he rose, and rode away into the West,
where after many a doubtful rough adventure,
he plucked a Gaelic girl to grace his breast.

Some say he filtched the land on which they settled
beneath the little shadow of Duncryne;
but there, upon her gentle Gaelic features
he stamped the angry quarrel of his line.

Let no man say his children shirked their duty.
For half-a-thousand years they lived, begot
and worked the arts of peace; in times of warring
around Dumbarton rock they ranged and fought.

But deep beneath their blind and baffled brilliance,
the Norman and the Gael fought private war;
twice-angry blood, with neither ever winner,
inflicted on itself a double scar.

The man of thought provoked the man of action
with sudden dreams of faery and fierce joy
that strained all passing sense from human action,
and wove a meaning deeds could not destroy.

The active man, still dusty with hot glory,
found that the thinking man had dreamed away
his hard-fought gains, the flavour of his triumph,
all purpose from each act that won his day.

And yet the man of thought knew well that dreaming
with gentleness so drugs the credulous heart
that but for all the Norman's measured scheming
he would have perished, beaten from the start.

Thus they remained apart from generations
of Lomond clansmen, Lennox and Colquhoun,
these Lindsays whom hard-rivalled chiefs respected,
whose blood yet clanged so loudly out of tune.

Till tyrant Cromwell's pious-swearing Roundheads
came sweating over Inveruglas isle
to trample loyalty beneath singed bracken
and spread God's ruin mile by bleeding mile.

One Lindsay, sick with fratricidal feuding
and forced God-bending, feared the bitter sway
of drooling, fleetching Monk, so reived a galley
and steered her towards a distant Irish bay.

He reeled her up the shores of green Loch Swilly,
where sea-birds screech against a mist-smoked sky,
and half the rains of Donegal come seeping
through peaty moors and fields alight with rye.

Beside a brattling burn he built his steading,
taming the feckless womb of virgin soil
to yield him yellow crops in such profusion
they fertilized his dreams upon his toil.

The shrew-land won, he wooed a farmer's daughter
and married her, a lilting brown colleen.
For twenty years, he reaped upon her body
as brave a brood of bairns as could be seen

in all God's holy Ireland. Such contentment
broadened his days, caressed his slow decline,
as made him think that he at last had quieted
the rearing blood that roared across his line.

Alas for his deluded, dying notion!
Before the sightless shade that we call Time
had smudged his worth from off the kirkyard tombstone,
or yet one crack had split the village chime,

his children's children saw the seasons shrinking,
their labour vain, the land turn thin and sour,
while Poverty and Want stalked through the nation
to strangle men with one last searing hour

that knotted up the veins of wasted bodies
to scraggy parcels, tight for busy Death
to lift at his convenience, and relieve them
of the sore, strengthless misery of breath.

Poor sense there seemed in twice-unequal struggle
when famine and the Catholic Irishry
were priming men to fight for what seemed freedom,
toppling the arrogant Ascendancy.

So back to Scotland came the ancient quarrel.
New generations bred old history:
romantic realists and cynic dreamers
entailed the blood now held in trust by me.

2

How I came to be here

THOSE seventeenth-century emigrating Lindsays settled at Rathmelton (pronounced locally Ra-mel-ton), and for more than a century and a half apparently lived full lives among the Scoto-Irish community. Like so many Scots settlers, they probably worked harder than most of the natives whose land they had appropriated. Today, the record of Lindsay achievement may be read on the tombstones in the village kirkyard, where schoolmasters, ministers and farmers take what the crumbling lettering of their memorials assures posterity is well-earned rest.

While I was a boy no one ever told me about my colonizing Irish ancestors, although I often heard about my mother's English forbears. Like most of the descendants of the colonizers, the Irish Lindsays remained Protestant, and had little sympathy with 'The Troubles'. My father at one time bore a slight resemblance to De Valera, a fact to which my attention was first drawn by a school friend. In the early 'twenties this great and gallant Irishman was regarded in Scottish middle-class circles as a rowdy anti-English nuisance. When I mentioned my father's resemblance to De Valera to my mother I was firmly reproved, as if I had said something rather shocking. However, the cumulative influence of long-ago generations can sometimes assert itself over later prejudices, and my present affection for Ireland, its people and its literature has thus, in all probability, deeply racial roots. A chance association first quickened it.

While I was still quite young I came under the influence of a gentle, impractical Irishman, Ted Verschoyle, who had married a distant family connection and settled in a bungaloid suburb on the Western fringe of Glasgow. I spent my Easter holidays there,

accompanying 'Uncle' Ted on long rambles through the surrounding Strathblane and Strathendrick countryside; rambles so
long, in fact, that my little legs were frequently exhausted long
before Courthill was sighted on our homeward way. While we
walked, Uncle Ted talked in his lilting Irish voice, giving me, a
dreamy town-bred boy, my first lessons in natural history and
arousing instincts and interests which have subsequently kept me
a confirmed countryman. In the world's eyes, though not in mine,
Ted Verschoyle was more or less a failure. He had a humdrum job
with the Post Office in Glasgow. His home life was dominated by
his wife. Yet he never complained as he went about the endless
household chores foisted upon him, accepting domestic unhappiness as the price to be paid for the solitary delights of wandering
through the fields and woods. But when he was out with me on a
ramble this quiet, tweedy man with the frizzled hair, whose face
wore a permanent look of surprise, revealed by his enthusiasms
that locked hopelessly away in his heart was the warmth and
vision of a poet. I was almost at boyhood's end when he died, as
patiently and pointlessly as he had lived. For me, he had made
Ireland seem a land of poetry and kindliness, thus unwittingly
leading me later to discover for myself the heady delights of the
poetry of Yeats, Joyce, Higgins, Padraic Colum, 'AE', Seumas
O'Sullivan and the other writers of the Irish Renaissance.

When some of the Lindsays came back to Scotland in late
Victorian days they returned to their native county, Dunbartonshire. During the 1920s one far-out branch of the family had a
jeweller's shop in Helensburgh. One Lindsay became a grain
merchant there. Another made paving-stones. I remember reading
the name *Lindsay* inside a brass oval on paving-stones in the streets
of Helensburgh when I was very small, and thinking that to
have one's name proclaimed abroad in this way was a very sure
and satisfactory immortality. Not a single named paving-stone
survives in Helensburgh today.

I myself was born and brought up—except for the long and
impressionable holiday months spent down the Clyde at Innellan
—in Glasgow. Glasgow has its distinctive qualities and a subtle
fascination, about which I shall have more to say. But the Second
World War loosened Glasgow's hold over me. In spite of the
discomforts of billeting in a succession of mansion houses stripped
and chipped, the charms of rural England gave me my first

experience of living in the country all the year round. Like most 'townies', I had never been out in the fields a whole night through, until the Army initiated me into the surprising pleasures of such an experience: the damp smell of the hedgerows and ditches across which we blundered on our night-long manœuvres; the excitement of watching the dawn rising steadily through the steaming mists hanging above the fields; and the reassuring stirring of familiar human sounds as farm doors creaked and implements clattered, in the new grey daylight, counterpointing the pathetic futility of the activity for which we so unskilfully rehearsed. Principally, however, I was astonished to discover that one could get one's clothes wet through, sleep under a hedge wrapped only in a ground-sheet and not catch even a cold.

The last three years of my war kept me behind a desk in London. In spite of V1's, V2's and the pressure of over-work, living in London was an exhilarating experience. So much so that when the prospect of settling there as a civilian came before me I was tempted to stay. It would certainly have been pleasant and, in some ways, so easy to relapse into the absorbing bustle of the megalopolis, and permanently to savour that pace and variety which Dr Johnson likened to life itself; so easy, yet in the end for me impossible. Fond as I am of London, I have never ceased to feel an alien in its streets. The leisured assurance of the Southern English upper classes; the easy superiority of a people who have never been conquered and who harbour the instinctive assumption that the Scots and the Welsh, who submitted, are unimportant and slightly comic, while the Irish, who did not, are odd and troublesome—these things, constantly implied in attitudes if rarely consciously formulated, made it impossible for one perhaps over-sensitive Scot ever to be unaware that in England he could never really enjoy the sense of belonging.

In any case, in Scotland itself exciting things were beginning to happen. Two decades before, the sense of nationhood had quickened, manifesting itself in a literary revival. Under the stimulus of the Labour Government's centralizing nationalization plans, Scottish Convention was beginning to prepare the way for its National Covenant, by which two million people pledged themselves through their signature to work for the achievement of self-government for home affairs. What Scotland at that time meant to me personally I could not easily have defined. All I knew was that I must return. I knew, too, that although, for economic reasons, I should probably have to live for a while in Glasgow again, I must ultimately settle in the country. I should have liked to live on the shores of the Firth of Clyde, at Innellan, that mild and pleasant place which looks out upon a gateway to the world through which ships of all shapes and sizes constantly pass. But a home which could be reached only by steamer, or by a seventy-five-mile-long mountain-climbing road from Glasgow, was out of the question. In the end it was chance that brought me back to the countryside of my ancestors, the land of Lennox. I bought a half-share in a caravan.

To the eye of the layman one caravan looks more or less like another: a box on wheels with windows and a door. No doubt most of the caravans on sale today are all that a good caravan ought to be. The half which I bought in 1948 was not.

I read about it in a newspaper. Full of that first-time enthusiasm which is so often the undoing of the otherwise canny purchaser, I tracked the caravan to a back-yard in an obscure suburb of Glasgow. As soon as I had finished introducing myself, the man who owned it assumed that off-hand of-course-I-don't-care-if-you-buy-it-or-not-for-another-man-is-coming-round-to-close-the-deal-at-half-past-six attitude usual on such occasions, and kept reiterating that it was an unrepeatable bargain.

It probably was. Of its three cross-bars beneath the floor, only one was intact, one had been broken and faked with flimsy metal plates, while the third had been broken and not fixed at all. Furthermore, the caravan was not lined, which meant that it warmed up in summer until it became a hot-box, and cooled to the condition of a refrigerator under the lightest fingering of October frost. Nevertheless, I bought a half-share in it without having found anywhere to put it.

The first thing the freshman caravan-owner discovers is that he cannot park his caravan even with the difficulty he may park his car. The moment of truth is the discovery that farmers are no more partial to itinerate vanners than the city police are to static ones.

Up and down the countryside around Glasgow the other half-owner and I towed our liability. One laird assured us he would have been delighted to have had us on his land, but he feared we might catch a contagion from the pollution which affected his river. Another would not have us because our coming and going might disturb his beasts. After listening to about a dozen such pseudo-sympathetic refusals we began to feel like lesser Flying Dutchmen, doomed to travel the roads for ever. Then someone suggested Gartocharn, a tiny village at the middle of the base of the mountain-folded triangle of water which is Loch Lomond. There we found a smallholder willing to allow us to rest our caravan on his land.

Our arrival was unpropitious. We were granted permission to put our caravan in a field near the lochside. But on the evening of our hesitant approach and eventual arrival the rain came down with an intensity it rarely musters, even in Scotland. Our caravan was being towed by a venerable Rolls-Royce; a proud, stiff-backed vehicle, which, in its hey-day during the 'twenties, might well have taken some patrician dowager once a week round two or three of the better shops. It was not at all the sort of vehicle to pull a caravan down a country lane rutted with grass-topped troughs of mud. The old car slid and juddered in ceaseless protest, until finally it won its own way. The caravan had to be squelched and churned into its permanent position by four pairs of wearily inexpert hands.

However, it was something to have secured half a caravan-hold in Lennox. At least I now enjoyed a position of some advantage in bidding for a more permanent home. During the next eighteen months my wife and I inspected, hopefully, something like thirty properties. These ranged from vast deserted mansions —'desirable, easily run family homes', for which only a modest price of three or four thousand was being asked in return for a quick sale—to tumble-down cottages harbouring various combinations of wood-worm, dry-rot and common or garden wet-rot.

The most unusual house in this collection of might-have-beens was a villa at Fintry, a hilly village in the foothills of the Campsie range, put up for sale by one of the better-known property agents in the West of Scotland. One Saturday afternoon we de-bused in the main street of Fintry, a rather bleak village straggled out mostly along a single street. Angry little mutterings of obviously discontented people clustered round the bus stop waiting for a bus back to Glasgow.

We soon discovered the reason for their discontent. Tempted by the enticing description of the villa, their natural suspicion of property agents lulled by the high reputation of the firm concerned, between thirty and forty would-be country-dwellers had come up to Fintry to look at a hovel that had been lived in by a hermit for a quarter of a century. Since the hermit's demise, the roof had collapsed, a beam had crashed through the first floor and the outer walls had started to crumble. In the middle of this dripping wreckage stood a new bath, unconnected and forlorn, which a relative of the deceased had ordered, apparently with the idea of modernizing the ruin.

Eventually, after long months of unrewarding search, a cottage fell, so to speak, into our laps. We were sitting round a local fireside when a contractor called to discuss the felling of some trees. 'I don't suppose you know anyone who wants to buy a cottage in Gartocharn, do you?' asked the contractor. 'I want rid of one, quickly.'

Fate does not do that sort of thing twice to the one person. The man got an answer with an alacrity which surprised him, and a few days later I had a home in the land of my ancestors.

3

Reconnaissance through History

IT USED to be a military axiom that the first task in any operation should always be to reconnoitre and secure your base. What, then, is Lennox, terrestrially and historically?

There is no lovelier or more varied part of Scotland than the countryside which makes up the old lands of Lennox. It is first and foremost a land of lochs and mountains. Loch Lomond is its show-piece, the most famous stretch of water in the English-speaking world. But glinting among its hills are lesser lochs no less lovely: Loch Arklet and Loch Katrine, Loch Achray and Loch Vennachar, Loch Ard and Loch Chon. Others reflect the chilly silence of the peaks which are their guardians, and are nameless except to the student of cartography or the mountaineer. On the Northern fringes of the Lennox country lies Loch Lubnaig; to the West, the sea lochs, Gareloch, Loch Goil and Loch Long; at its heart Scotland's only natural lake, the Lake of Mentieth. The Kilsyth Hills and the Campsie Fells stand sentinel to the South; Ben Ledi, Ben Venue, Ben Vorlich and Ben Vane and the foothills of the Argyll and Perthshire Highlands range to the North; in the East and South, more rounded and gentler in mien, stand the Luss and Kilpatrick Hills.

It is a countryside of cool summer greens, and brilliant autumn browns and yellows; a countryside which seems 'romantic' to the traveller, though its history goes back far beyond the cult of the picturesque which first led people to apply that vague and much overused term to scenery. Thanks in no small measure to Sir Walter Scott, whose poem 'The Lady of the Lake' and whose novel *Rob Roy* are set, for the most part, in Lennox and the fringes round it, the cult of the picturesque has

attracted almost as many devotees to Lennox as to the Hebrides
and the Western Highlands.

Lennox takes its name from *Leven-ach*, the field of the Leven.
(Loch Lomond was originally called Loch Leven. A similar
nominal association may be found in the Kinross district between
the Lomond Hills and Loch Leven.) But the erratic spelling of the
Middle Ages resulted in *Levenach* becoming *Levenax*, and so, by
an understandable process of elision, *Lennox*.

The earldom was created by William the Lyon about 1174,
who bestowed it on his brother David, Earl of Huntingdon. He,
however, seems only to have retained his territory for a decade
or so, thereafter resigning the earldom in favour of Aluin, the
first of the Celtic earls.

The land which these earls held in feudal sway was much
more extensive than the present county of Dunbartonshire, for it
included parts of Stirlingshire, those areas of Perthshire con-
tiguous to Loch Lomond, and a stretch of Renfrewshire on the
South bank of the Clyde. That is why a mid-twentieth-century
proposal to revert to the ancient title, in order to avoid the
confusion which is sometimes caused between the spelling of
Dunbartonshire (which makes use of the original 'n') and the
county town of Dumbarton (which perpetuates the 'm', a Middle
Scots corruption), was rejected.

They were doughty fellows, these Celtic earls. They had to be
if they wanted to stay alive. The third earl, Maldwin, got a
confirmatory charter from Alexander II. This, however, excluded
Dumbarton Castle from the territory, probably for strategic
reasons, and certain fishing rights, probably for selfish reasons.
One of the most remarkable of the Lennox earls was undoubtedly
Earl Malcolm. He swore his acknowledgment of Margaret of
Norway as heir-apparent to Alexander III, and agreed to her
marriage with Edward I of England. But when Margaret died,
and the English king decided to apply other means than diplo-
macy to gain control of Scotland, Malcolm supported Robert the
Bruce. In 1296, early in the Wars of Independence, Earl Malcolm
took part in the invasion of Cumberland and the storming of
Carlisle. Even when Sir John Mentieth, that 'faus Mentieth' who
betrayed Sir William Wallace to the English, was Edward's
Governor of Dumbarton Castle and Sheriff of Dunbartonshire,
Earl Malcolm indulged in what we would nowadays call com-

mando raids on behalf of the Bruce. The earl maintained his stand for the independence of Scotland after Bruce's death, and finally fell beneath the Scottish flag at Halidon Hill in 1337, a worthy and courageous old patriot.

Trouble came to the house of Lennox soon after James I returned from his long English exile. In an attempt to establish his authority, the young king executed the over-ambitious and unruly regent, Murdoch, Duke of Albany, and his two sons, at Stirling. Murdoch's father-in-law was a Lennox, Earl Duncan. For some crime, real or imaginary but no longer discoverable, he, too, shared Albany's fate. His daughter, Isabella, Countess of Lennox, who had her seat on the island of Inchmurrin, in Loch Lomond, succeeded him. When she died in 1459 a dispute arose between her sisters, Elizabeth and Margaret, the second and third daughters of Duncan. (Duncan's son, Donald of Lennox, must presumably have been mentally defective, since, though legitimate, he had been by-passed in favour of Isabella.) The lands of Lennox were divided between the warring ladies, but the title could not be divided, so it remained in the king's hands. James III bestowed it on his Chancellor, Lord Avondale, during that nobleman's lifetime. In 1493 it was awarded to the grandson of Elizabeth and her husband, Sir John Stuart of Darnley. The new earl thus became Lord Darnley and Earl of Lennox. Margaret married Sir Robert Mentieth of Ruskey. The estate of Ruskey, together with Margaret's minority share of Lennox, was eventually divided between their grand-daughters' husbands, Sir John Haldane of Gleneagles and Sir David Napier of Merchiston.

A Lennox fought at Flodden. Earl Matthew shared the command of the right wing of the Scottish army with the Earl of Argyll. John, the next earl, attacked Dumbarton Castle with the Earl of Glencairn in 1514, during James V's minority, but was overcome by the regent Albany and forced to surrender it. Nothing daunted, Earl John assembled an army of ten thousand men and marched to Edinburgh to rescue the young king, who was held in virtual captivity by the Douglases.

John's son, Matthew, a governor of Dumbarton Castle, entered into treacherous negotiations with the English king, Henry VIII, who made him a grant of lands in England. But when Earl Matthew sailed up the Clyde with an English army to offer an English pension to his deputy in Dumbarton Castle,

George Stirling of Glorat, the loyal deputy, promptly threw him out. The earl then ravaged Bute and Arran before returning to England and twenty years' exile.

His son, Lord Darnley, became the second husband of Mary, Queen of Scots, as a result of which union Earl Matthew became grandfather of the future James VI, and once again a power in his own land. He was killed during a raid on Stirling Castle in 1571.

The earldom now came back to the king, who gave it, first, to his uncle, Lord Darnley's younger brother, and, on that nobleman's death without issue, to the king's grand-uncle, Lord Robert Stewart, Bishop of Caithness. He, however, resigned it in 1579, in return for the earldom of March, and the king conferred it on Esmé Stewart, Lord D'Aubigny. When Charles, the sixth duke, died without issue, and the title and its honours once again came back to the Crown, Charles II settled the revenues of the lands of Lennox on the dowager duchess, and in 1680 granted to his own illegitimate son Charles (by Louise Renée de Perrencourt de Querouaille, Duchess of Portsmouth and D'Aubigny) the dukedom of Lennox, the earldom of Darnley, the English dukedom of Richmond and the earldom of March. In 1702 the long royal connection was finally severed, when, upon the death of the dowager duchess, the Duke of Richmond and Lennox sold all his lands in Scotland, mostly to the third Marquis of Montrose. Montrose, who became a duke five years later, bought not only the heritable jurisdictions but also the sheriff-dom of the county, which had been in Lennox hands since 1503.

It is amusing to read that when heritable jurisdictions were abolished in Scotland in 1748, and compensation was paid to the holders of these feudal powers, Montrose rated the Lennox jurisdiction at four thousand pounds, but was granted only five hundred and seventy-eight pounds, eighteen shillings and four-pence. The third marquis, however, had himself held his lands for only a short time. He had bought the lands of Buchanan from the heirs of the Buchanans of that ilk when the family became extinct in 1682, building for himself a mansion near the old Buchanan peel, the ruins of which still stand. The Montrose mansion survived until 1850, when it was burned down. Thomas Pennant, who visited it in June 1772, thought it built 'in a low and most disadvantageous situation, within a mile of the lake, without the least view of so delicious a water'. After the fire it was replaced by a large mock-baronial castle, which, in later years, did duty as a guest-house for wealthy Americans and as a military hospital in the Second World War, before having its roof dismantled soon after the death of the sixth duke. Only a small part of the original Montrose lands remain in the family.

Let us now return, for a moment, to the two grand-daughters of Lady Margaret Menteith, who shared the moiety of the lands of Lennox between them, for some of their descendants and kinsfolk achieved distinction. John Napier of Merchiston, a kinsman of Margaret's younger grand-daughter and the inventor of logarithms, is said to have been born within sound of the tumbling waters of the Pot of Gartness where, in July, the salmon leap through the air to surmount the falls and reach their spawning ground. The elder grand-daughter, who had married Haldane of Gleneagles, was widowed at a still personable age. In 1515, while living peaceably in her castle at Strathearn, enjoying the pleasant attentions of that 'noble and valliant Squire William Meldrum, umquhile laird of Cleish and Binns', whose adventures Sir David Lyndsay gloriously celebrated in racy and rumbustious verse, the lady heard that the Macfarlanes were harrying her lands around Boturich Castle, on Loch Lomondside. The gallant squire immediately set out for the West, besieged the castle, brought its Macfarlane commander to his knees, then characteristically spared his life. As Lyndsay puts it:

> 'And sa this Squire amorous
> Seizit and wan the lady's house,
> And left therein a Capitane,
> Syne to Strathearn returnit again:
> Where that he with his fair Lady
> Receivit was full pleasantly
> And to take rest did him convoy.
> Judge ye gif there was mirth and joy.
> Howbeit the chalmer dour was closit,
> They did but kiss as I supposit.
> Gif other thing was them between,
> Let them discover that luvers been:
> For I am not in luve expert,
> And never studyit in that art . . .'

Little study was really necessary, however, for a few lines later the poet tells us that in due course:

> '. . . this Lady fair
> Ane dochter to the Squire bare . . .'

There now only remains to be mentioned the family which owed its initial advancement to its superiors, and which replaced the Lennoxes when that powerful house came to an end. In the reign of Alexander II, Humphrey of Kilpatrick obtained from Maldwin, third earl of Lennox, a grant of the lands of Colquhoun. In accordance with the custom of the time, Humphrey's descendants called themselves after their most extensive territorial acquisition. Their first stronghold was the Castle of Dunglass, by Bowling. A later stronghold at Luss, on Loch Lomond, was replaced about 1774 by the mansion which is still the family seat.

The territory of the Colquhouns fringed the Highlands, and was therefore a temptation to the clansmen across the water, the McGregors and their friends the Macfarlanes and the Macaulays. Indeed, there was a good deal of feuding between these clans, culminating in 1603 in the rout of the Colquhouns in Glen Fruin, when, as the result of a Macfarlane ambush, the Colquhouns lost about a hundred men. The Macfarlanes were said also to have massacred some scholars from Dumbarton who had come up the glen to see some good clean sixteenth-century fun. After the massacre, the chief of the Colquhouns paraded the widows of his murdered men before James VI, who ordered the McGregors to be outlawed. Their very name was proscribed, and the clan was hunted by the Earl of Argyll, who, true to Campbell tradition, had previously been urging the McGregors to harry the Colquhouns, with whose chief he happened to have had a personal quarrel.

Several Colquhouns have achieved minor appearances in Scottish history. Sir John Colquhoun was made one of the Earl of Stirling's baronets of Nova Scotia by Charles I, and fought with the king throughout the Civil War, a loyal action which cost him a fine of two thousand pounds when Cromwell conquered. The seventeenth laird, Sir Humphrey Colquhoun, was a member of the last Scots Parliament, and strongly opposed incorporating union with England. He died without male issue and, so that his daughter's husband—a Grant—could inherit the estate and title, he resigned his baronetcy to the Crown, being given a new grant which made it possible for his son-in-law and his heirs to inherit the title provided they took the Colquhoun name, and that the Colquhoun and Grant lands should never be amalgamated.

The same Sir James Colquhoun who built the family seat of Rossdhu was inspired by the new town of Edinburgh to develop the Clydeside village of Milligs into an industrial town which was to attract 'bonnet-makers, stocking, linen and woollen weavers'. In 1777 he laid out the spacious streets of Helensburgh, naming the town in honour of his wife. Here, Henry Bell, its first provost, had his Baths Hotel—which still stands, without the baths but with the addition of a somewhat unsightly top storey and now called the Queens—and here his early steamboats plied, carrying some of the first tourists down the Clyde. There are plenty of industrial towns on Clydeside which have neither individual charm nor architectural distinction. It was therefore fortunate that Sir James's industrial dreams did not materialize, and that Helensburgh has remained a well-planned, spacious, tree-decorated residential town and holiday resort. The Colquhouns are still the superiors. Indeed, the Colquhouns today retain more of their ancestral lands than any of the other ancient families, anecdotes of whose dubious on-goings largely make up the history of the lands of Lennox.

So completely has our manner of living altered in the last half-century that, with every passing decade, their names and their doings are drained of a little more reality, while their deeds, in the re-telling, increasingly assume the cold rigidity of a tapestry or a classical frieze which, however it may interest us, has little power to move us. Already, only people with a strong sense of the past can re-create in their minds the draughty and dangerous conditions in which the lords of Lennox lived and loved and died; still, for the most part, middle-aged men by our standards. A sense of the past is one of the richest gifts the gods can bestow, but they do not bestow it widely. As the half-legendary power of the men and movements that made the Scottish nation retreats before the sharp impact of a never more-challenging modernity, can the old concept of nationhood survive? Or is the enduring stuff of nationalism to be looked for, not among the stories of the leaders of a country or a locality but among the casual records of the people themselves, and of those who moved as strangers in their midst?

4

Travellers' Tales

CERTAINLY the shape of history is filled in and given its depth by ordinary people, the nameless natives and the curious travellers whose industrious pens recorded the impact of clean first impressions. The gossipy private literature of the journalizers and diarists, observers of the little things, often tell us more of human interest about the past than all the official histories put together. The study of Scotland's private literature has for long been one of my minor enjoyments. What, then, have been the reactions of travellers to the lands of Lennox over the centuries?

Loch Lomond, the wedge driven into the hills that hold up the Highlands from the Lowlands, inspired wonder long before it lent itself to the development of the cult of the picturesque. The historian Nennius, or his interpolator, and the chronicler Geoffrey of Monmouth recorded that it had three hundred islands peopled with human beings, three hundred and fifty rocks peopled with eagles, and three hundred and fifty rivers flowing out of it, though only one flowed in. Obviously these early writers had never been near the place.

There is, however, corroborative later evidence to show that Loch Lomond was for long regarded as one of the wonders of Scotland. The Danish diplomat Peder Swave, who came to Scotland in 1535 to try to persuade James V to support Christian II in forcing the citizens of Lubeck to re-acknowledge the Danish king's authority, which they had just cast off, kept a Latin diary while he was in this country. Visiting Dryburgh, Swave met a man of high rank, John Scott, who had abandoned his wife and estates to become a hermit. Either Scott, or the canon who was trying to effect a reconciliation on behalf of Mrs Scott, treated Swave to an account of the wonders of Scotland which the Danish diplomat faithfully chronicled. One of these related to 'a certain floating island in Scotland, which deflects from one shore to the other with the ebb and flow of the tide'.

A hundred years later Sir William Brereton, a Cheshire gentleman who later won distinction as a general in the Parliamentary Army, set out on a tour of Scotland and Ireland. He was probably the first tourist to visit the country purely and simply for pleasure, though that pleasure was mainly the satisfaction of his curiosity. From notes which he made during his travels he afterwards constructed a journal. He recorded that his host at Falkirk regaled him with a list of Scotland's wonders, rather in the manner of those biggest-in-the-world boasting stories which used to be attributed to Americans in the days before Russia offered their country serious size-rivalry. One of the wonders which Brereton heard about was the 'meare or lake called Loemund . . . wherein are the flitting islands which move (my host, Mr. Fleemeing, affirmed he hath seen it): it is most rough in calm weather; the fish are without fins'.

Mr Fleemeing may not have been quite such a line-shooter as his story suggests. The proverbial wonders of Loch Lomond were: 'Waves without wind, fish without fins, and a floating island.' Unwary and inexpert boaters still encounter 'waves without wind', often at the cost of their lives, when they leave the calm waters of Balloch or Balmaha too far behind, and find themselves suddenly caught in deep water by treacherous gusts channelled by the surrounding mountains. The 'fish without fins' may possibly have been the freshwater herring, the powan, which are peculiar to Loch Lomond and have only very small fins; or they may simply have been eels. A writer in Blaeu's *Atlas* of 1653 suggests that 'the fish which they speak of as having no fins, and which they commonly call *Paones*, are a kind of snake and therefore no cause of wonder'.

The 'floating island' is less easy to explain. The story may have originated in the credulous mind of some early traveller who, weary after a long day's ride and unaware of the number of islands in the loch—thirty-six—and the similarity in appearance of those that are thickly wooded, imagined that one island had moved across the water which he had ridden so laboriously round.

On the other hand, legend avers that the floating island was

made of large oak beams mortised into one another by one Keith
Macindoil, a fourth-century contemporary of Finmacoul, or
Fingal.

It was largely curiosity about the nature of the physical world
that brought Thomas Pennant to Scotland in 1769 and again
in 1772. Pennant, to whom Gilbert White wrote some of the
Selborne letters, was an accurate observer, though there was little
poetry in his soul; only a supreme confidence in his country and
its achievements, and an imperturbable certainty that the social
order was well-founded and just.

On his first visit, he travelled on horseback from Inveraray, and
pronounced Loch Lomond 'the most beautiful of the *Caledonian*
lakes' (his italics were perhaps meant to suggest that the verdict
might not be valid farther afield!). He heard about the McGregors,
'a murderous clan infamous for excesses of all kinds; at length, for
a horrible massacre of the *Colquhouns* or *Cahouns* . . .' and noted
that 'as a result of the suppression of their very name by act of
council . . . the remnant, now, dispersed like *Jews*, dare not even
sign it to any deed. Their posterity are still said to be distinguished
among the clans in which they have incorporated themselves, not
only by redness of their hair, but by their still retaining the
mischievous dispositions of their ancestors.'

At Luss, which he saw in the riotous reds, yellows and browns
of mid-September, he had a meal in the 'tolerable inn on the
borders of the lake', and met some of the inhabitants of the
village. Among them he discovered 'most amazing instances of
contemporary longevity; and perhaps proofs of the uncommon
healthiness of the place'. These compose the venerable list:

'Rev. Mr James Robertson, Minister, aged	90
Mrs Robertson, his wife	86
Anne Sharp, their servant	94
Niel Macnaughton, Kirk-Officer	86
Christian Gray, his wife	94
Walter Maclellan	90.'

Pennant's visit took place, of course, long before there was
any form of compulsory registration of births. But confirmation
exists that the minister survived Pennant's first visit by three
years, and that Robertson died at the age of ninety-three.

Pennant's second visit took place in mid-June 1772, when he was on his way out to the Hebrides. He came across the Stockiemuir to Drymen (where he recorded that the name of the parish derived from 'Druim, a back, from the ridges that run along it'), approaching 'the charming Loch Lomond' above Balmaha, and was much taken by the view of the islands. He noted that the top of Ben Lomond 'is composed of a micaceous slate, mixed with quartz'; that *sibbaldia procumbens*, a plant unknown in England, grows on the upper parts; and that '*ptarmigan* inhabit its summit, and roes the woods near its base, the most southern resort of those animals in our island'.

Presumably he climbed the mountain, though he does not specifically say so, for he described the view from the top of its 3,192 feet. 'The prospect from the summit [is] of vast extent: the whole extent of *Loch Lomond* with its wooded isles appears just beneath. *Loch-loung*,[1] *Loch-Kettering*,[2] *Loch-earn* and the river *Clyde* form the principal waters. The mountains of *Arran* appear very distant, and to the North *Alps* upon *Alps* fill up the amazing view.'

Pennant attempts a scientific explanation of the floating island, relying as evidence for its existence upon Camden's *Atlas Britannica*:[3]

'The surface of Loch-Lomond has for several years been observed gradually to increase and invade the adjacent shore: and there is reason to suppose that churches, houses and other buildings have been lost in the water. Near Luss is a large heap of stones at a distance from the shore, known by the name of the old church; and about a mile to the South of that, in the middle of a large bay, between *Camstradden* and the *Isle Inch-laverack*, is another heap, said to have been the ruins of a house. To confirm this, it is evident by a passage in Camden's *Atlas Britannica*, that an island, existing at this time, is now lost, for he speaks of the isle of *Camstraddan*, placed between the lands of the same name

---

[1] Loch Long.   [2] Loch Katrine.
[3] In his *Atlas*, published in 1586, Camden writes: 'As for the floating island, I shall not call the truth of it in question, for what could hinder a body from swimming that is dry and hollow like a pinnace, and very light? And so Pliny tells us that certain green lands covered with rushes, float up and down on the lake of Vundimon.' He then leaves it to the neighbours who know the nature of this place to judge the truth of a distich by Neckham which Defoe paraphrased: 'With Rivers Scotland is enriched, And Lomond there a Lake, So cold of Nature is, that Sticks, It quickly stones doth make.'

and *Inch-Lavarack*, in which, adds he, *was an house and orchard.*
Besides this proof, large trees with their branches still adhering
are frequently found in the mud near the shore, overwhelmed in
former times by the increase of water. This is supposed to be
occasioned by the vast quantities of stone and gravel that are
continually brought down by the mountain rivers, and by the
falls of the banks of the Leven: the first filling the bed of the lake;
the last impeding its discharge through the bed of the river.'

There is no real evidence that the surface level of Loch
Lomond has altered as Pennant imagined, and some geological
evidence to suggest that such a change could not have been
possible. But an island may have been formed by sedimentation
which, for one reason or another, may have suddenly shifted,
bringing disaster to the 'house and orchard', and giving rise to
the floating-island legend. Eighteenth-century travellers usually
found Loch Lomond too wild and majestic for their well-ordered
ideas. Dr Samuel Johnson was much too practical a traveller to
cherish belief in the buoyancy of islands, the more so since the
main object of his Scottish tour was to sink the Ossianic claims
floated by James Macpherson. But when the doctor arrived at
Rossdhu, the home of Sir James Colquhoun, towards the close of
the famous tour of the Western Islands which he and Boswell
undertook together in 1773, the doctor described his host as
'owner of almost all the thirty islands of the Loch, which we went
in a boat the next morning to survey'.

It would seem to have been a not untypical day on which
Johnson, Boswell and the building laird of Luss, who was soon
to lay out the town of Helensburgh inspired, perhaps, by his
conversation with the learned doctor, sailed over the waters of the
loch. For Johnson recorded:

'The heaviness of the rain shortened our voyage, but we
landed on one island planted with yew[1] and stocked with deer,
and on another containing perhaps not more than half an acre,
remarkable for the ruins of an old castle,[2] on which the osprey
builds her annual nest. Had *Loch Lomond* been in a happier
climate, it would have been the boast of wealth and vanity to

[1] Inch Lonaig.
[2] Inchmurrin, with the ruins of Isabella's castle.

own one of the little spots which it incloses, and to have employed upon it all the arts of embellishment. But as it is, the islets, which court the gazer at a distance, disgust him at his approach, when he finds, instead of soft lawns and shady thickets, nothing more than uncultivated ruggedness.'

After dinner at Rossdhu, Boswell tells us that the doctor discoursed with Lady Helen Colquhoun, and that the conversation 'took a religious turn', allowing Johnson to set forth his arguments on the merits of 'a form of prayer for publick worship', his hostess apparently defending the Scots fashion of impromptu prayer.

Rain also greeted the French geologist B. Faujas de Saint Fond when he rode up Loch Lomondside *en route* for Staffa in 1784. Travelling in that spirit of eager inquiry characteristic of the period, Faujas and his party left Dumbarton at five o'clock in the evening, intending to sleep at Luss and spend the next day on the islands 'on which, we were told, there were charming habitations'.

He did not arrive at Luss until ten o'clock at night, and was disappointed to find that the village consisted of one 'single, sorry habitation by the side of the lake', which he took to be a fishing hut. The landlady of this establishment met the party at the door, making signs to them not to speak, and shepherding them into the stable.

' "The Lord Judge," said the hostess, "does me the honour to lodge here when on circuit. He is there; everybody must respect him. He is asleep. His horses are in the stable; so you see there is no room for yours; have the goodness then to go away."—"But mistress," said one of our postillions, for we durst not venture to speak, "look at our poor horses, look what a terrible rain."—"Very well, let us look," said she. We went out, and she added "No noise: don't disturb his lordship's sleep, respect for the law. May you be happy! and be off." And she shut the door and double-locked it after us.

'We could not help laughing at this laconic eloquence, which admitted of no reply; such respect for a judge is a fine thing.'

So the amiable French scholar and his party rode fifteen miles 'in a dark night, and frightful weather, always along the banks of the lake', until at three-thirty in the morning they arrived at Tarbet. There, awakened by the call of the postillions (who, not unnaturally, had 'wished all the judges in the world a hundred times to the devil, and poured forth a thousand insults on the landlady of Luss'), they found the hostelry full of jurymen on their way to Inveraray. However, the horses were sheltered and the landlady provided food and tea and offered two mattresses from her own bed for the weary travellers to rest upon.

An experience of this sort would have put off most travellers; but not Faujas. As so often happens, a perfect summer day succeeded the night's rain-storm.

'The sun was brilliant and warm; the sky a fine azure. We breathed pure air on the banks of the lake, and saluted the nymphs who presided over its beautiful waters.

'From this point of view, the appearance of the lake is superb, though only a part of it can be seen, on account of its great extent. It is interspersed with little islands, several of which are only barren rocks, but others show little cultivated plots, and hillocks picturesquely grouped.'

Faujas much regretted that his failure to get accommodation at Luss had left him with insufficient time to explore the islands. Indeed, he had to be content with a walk of an hour and a half before 'a breakfast of tea taken out of the landlady's china cups', a much-prized gift from the Duchess of Argyll. Even so, the impression made on him induced a final rhapsodic paragraph, and a wish which unfortunately does not seem to have been granted him:

'The superb Loch Lomond, the fine sunlight that gilded its waters, the silvery rocks that skirted its shores, the flowery and verdant mosses, the black oxen, the white sheep, the shepherds beneath the pines, the perfume of the tea poured into cups that had been given by kindness and received with gratitude, will never be effaced from my memory, and make me cherish the desire not to die before again seeing Tarbet. I shall often dream of Tarbet, even in the midst of lovely Italy with its oranges, its myrtles, its laurels, and its jessamines.'

Faujas de St Fond's main purpose in visiting Scotland was to examine the geological structure of the island of Staffa, and he was, in fact, the first geologist to do so. He was an enthusiastic volcanist. Like the best scientists of his day, his interest spilled over into many other fields of science, and he was zoologist, botanist, mineralogist, physicist and chemist as well as geologist. While the scientific aspects of his Scottish journey occupied much of his *Journal*, he had an eye for social conditions and for scenery, as his rhapsody on Loch Lomond shows. He was thus, in his way, ahead of his time.

A critical note is discernible in the more superficial account which the artist Charles Dibdin left of his sojourn by Loch Lomondside a few years later. He was not, however, unappreciative of the weather.

'It was a beautiful morning,' he recorded, 'and, taking a sudden turn upon a height, the lake in one moment opened like a mirror with Ben Lomond, though at the distance of nineteen miles, apparently reclining on its bosom. On the right a mossy hill with plantations, villas, and other rich and diversified objects at its foot and on its brow, served to make a bold approach to the foreground, to which in extensive grandeur the veriest tracks of land and clumps of trees in increasing continuity presented all the beautiful correctness of natural perspective.'

Dibdin was very much a child of the eighteenth century. It was 'beautiful correctness' which he valued most.

'I climbed a very high hill . . . on purpose to get the lake and its islands in a birds-eye view; but it would not do: the lakes were all spots and the mountains were all crouching, and how ludicrous it must be to see Ben Lomond crouch. I can easily conceive how those who pant after endless variety are soon satiated with nature in Scotland. The objects are never so tremendous as they are majestic, and this arises from their possessing such immense extent, that it is physically impossible to discern many of them at a time, all of which precludes any great diversity.'

The travellers who came to visit Loch Lomond at the close of the eighteenth century were neither men out to satisfy curiosity like Dibdin; nor to make scientific or quasi-scientific investigations like Pennant, Dr Johnson and St Fond; but men and women who came to look at scenery for its own sake. Sir Walter Scott is commonly credited with having first attracted the flow of tourists to Scotland, but the cult of the picturesque had really begun before Scott had established himself either as poet or novelist.

It was, in fact, the influence of Burns that first brought some of the Lakers to Scotland in 1803. They came not in search of scientific fact or to satisfy or disprove credulity where so-called 'wonders' were concerned, but to see and enjoy the countryside, to meet the people and to visit the scenes of Burns's life. Though the Wordsworths typify the tourists of their age, William Wordsworth and his sister Dorothy were no ordinary travellers. Both were self-trained observers who saw people and places with sympathy and clarity. Wordsworth himself reflected his Scottish impressions in a number of poems, and Dorothy set down her notes on the Scottish tour in vivid prose both honest and homely, since her book was never intended to be read beyond the family circle.

Travelling 'with one single horse and outlandish Hibernian vehicle' the Wordsworths, accompanied by Coleridge (who, moody and discontented, left them before their tour had taken them far into the Highlands), rode through Bonhill, where they criticized the Latin inscription on the memorial to Tobias Smollett,[1] down the Vale of Leven through Balloch and along the Western shores of Loch Lomond to Luss. Here, they encountered a Highland welcome, the landlady at the inn insisting that Wordsworth and Coleridge should sleep in a garret, although there were vacant rooms on the first floor, and grudging them a fire in the lounge in the evening.

Next day, Thursday, 25th August, 'a fine morning, the sky was bright blue, with quick-moving clouds, the hills cheerful, lights and shadows vivid and distinct', they hired a boatman to row them out to Inch Tavannach. There they landed, and climbed a little hill. The view that slowly rolled farther out beneath them as they climbed inspired Dorothy to describe it with enthusiastic lyricism, yet in terms of strictly accurate observation. Indeed, the new attitude to landscape for its own sake is nowhere more brilliantly illuminated.

[1] For which Dr Johnson was partly responsible.

'We had not climbed far before we were stopped by a sudden burst of prospect, so singular and beautiful that it was like a flash of images from another world. We stood with our backs to the hill of the island, which we were ascending, and which shut out Ben Lomond entirely, and all the upper part of the lake, and we looked towards the foot of the lake, scattered over with islands without beginning and without end. The sun shone, and the distant hills were visible, some through sunny mists, others in gloom with patches of sunshine; the lake was lost under the low and distant hills, and the islands lost in the lake, which was all in motion with travelling fields of light, or dark shadows under rainy clouds. There are many hills, but no commanding eminence at a distance to confine the prospect, so that the land seemed endless as the water. . . . Wherever we looked, it was a delightful feeling that there was something beyond. Meanwhile, the sense of quiet was never lost sight of; the little peaceful lakes among the islands might make you forget that the great water, Loch Lomond, was so near; and yet are more beautiful, because you know that it is so. . . .'

Wordsworth and Coleridge had a disturbed night because of a drunken intruder. Next day, the three travellers drove and walked up the loch to Tarbet where, after spending a night in the inn, the sitting-room of which was 'a square room, with windows on each side, looking one way, towards the mountains, across the Lake to Ben Lomond the other', they crossed the loch in the ferry-boat, visited Rob Roy's Caves (which, as Dorothy rightly observed, 'are in fact no caves, but some five rocks on the brink of the lake, in crevices of which a man might hide himself cunningly enough; the water is very deep below them, and the hills above steep and covered with wood'); and then 'pursued the road, a mountain horse track', which took them across to Loch Katrine.[1]

Sixteen years later the third member of the Lakers' poetic brotherhood, Robert Southey, came to Scotland, in company with his friend the great Scottish civil engineer, Thomas Telford. They also travelled during the late autumn, which, in the year 1819, seems to have been a fine one. Southey and Telford, with other members of their party, arrived in their coach and four on Loch

[1] Ketterine, as the Wordsworths wrote it.

Lomondside at the end of a tour that had taken them as far north
as Inverness.

On Sunday, 26th September, they drove across from Arrochar,
on Loch Long, to Tarbet, where Southey found 'a decent Inn
with a post office', and so down a 'very beautiful, but in great
part a very bad road' to Luss. Southey described his impressions
of that drive:

'The character of the Lake[1] where we came upon it is simple
and severe, Ben Lomond rising steeply, but not precipitously
from the opposite shore. The right bank which we coasted, is well
clothed with plantations of sufficient growth to be ornamental:
indeed on this side there is no waste ground. We were evidently
approaching an opulent country. . . . The Lake widened as we
advanced, expanding into a low country, where we had a wide
firmament and bright weather before us, while, behind, the
clouds were on the hills.'

At Luss he found the inn 'tolerable'. Proceeding South, he
drew a comparison between Ben Lomond and Skiddaw, entering
'a populous and richly cultivated country, with gentlemen's seats,
and ornamental grounds on either hand'. He, too, inspected the
Smollett memorial column, commenting: 'The family did well in
erecting it: it would become them to keep it in a proper state of
repair.'

Southey, partly under the influence of his travelling companion, and partly because of his own rather prosaic nature, was
concerned with practical matters like roads, bridges and canals at
least as much as with the splendour of the scenery.

The travelling Lakers pioneered the way. The tourists that
followed them dutifully admired, and claimed to have experienced
the appropriate Laker reactions. But from 1817 onwards tourists
no longer had to visit Loch Lomond on horseback. In that year
the steamer *Marion*, sixty feet long and weighing thirty-five tons,
began noisily to arrow the waters of the loch. She had been built
the previous year by David Napier, and named after his wife.
After a season on the Clyde she was taken up the River Leven to
become the first steamboat to ply on the loch. By 1820 she was

[1] The Lake Poets were curiously unwilling to call our Scottish waters by the
correct name of *loch*.

operating a tour, connecting with the Glasgow steamer *Post Boy*, the first steamer advertised to sail regardless of wind or tide. Lumsden's *Steamboat Companion* for the year 1820 sets out in enticing terms the details of the new way to explore Loch Lomond.

'The *Post Boy* steamboat leaves Glasgow every morning at 6 o'clock, with passengers for the *Marion*, plying on Loch Lomond, and lands them at Dumbarton, five miles from Balloch, from whence the *Marion* starts every day at 10 o'clock. The *Post Boy* again takes them up on their return to Dumbarton at 6 o'clock in the evening, so that by this conveyance a stranger can leave Glasgow in the morning, visit the beautiful scenery of Loch Lomond, and be again in Glasgow in fourteen hours. A coach runs from Dumbarton to Balloch for the convenience of passengers by the *Post Boy*, and again brings them back to meet the boat in the afternoon.'

One of the tourists who crossed the loch by steamboat was that strange character the Reverend Thomas Frognell Dibdin, elder brother of Charles Dibdin, the writer of rousing English sea-songs. Dibdin achieved the dignity of becoming Chaplain in Ordinary to Her Majesty. Most of his energies, however, were devoted to journalizing, and although his zestful verbiage upset his biographer, in the *Dictionary of National Biography*, it has ensured that his *Tour through Scotland*, published in 1838, retains an interest which more sober accounts might not still have possessed.

Dibdin made for Tarbet, 'the grand rally spot for Lakers', and stayed at the inn, then owned by the Laird of Stuckgowan, a Mr M'Murroch. So far as his accommodation was concerned, Dibdin was luckier than many of his predecessors. But he found other cause for complaint.

'We were fortunate in securing a good sitting-room, and two beds on the first floor: but, oh! what opportunities are lost—or what proper spirit is still wanting in these regions—to make inns, not so much comfortable in *themselves*, as attractive and delightful for *situation*! Here . . . an *hippopotamos* error has been committed —in the site of the house. It is close by the roadside, and commands the veriest smallest view of the lake.'

Dibdin was never slow to give advice.

'Build your inn, my good Laird of Stuckgoune, some three or four hundred paces to the left of a knoll—with twenty-five sleeping-rooms along a double corridor with stabling for half the number of horses (because travellers usually *post* it), and the largest barn in your lairdship's shall not contain the golden harvest to be annually gathered therein.'

Although Dibdin's advice was basically sound, and might yet be followed with profit by many modern hotel-keepers, he underestimated the rapidity of the impending expansion of the steamboat trade. Yet as he surveyed the view from his window on that late summer evening of 1838, the portent of the changed way of travelling swam into his ken.

'As we sat down to dinner, the steamer from Dumbarton . . . came in view, and put down, as it is daily in the habit of doing, a traveller or two for the inn. A band of music was on board and the lake and mountains re-echoed the Scotch airs that were played. The Fyne herring was doubly delicious: the sherry sparkled with a livelier tint in consequence.'

Next day Dibdin took the steamer from Tarbet to Rowardennan, rode up Ben Lomond to within five hundred yards of the summit and completed the ascent on foot.

'On reaching the very highest point, we stopped—to breathe as well as to look round. . . . Mountains here, planes there; towns in one place, lakes in another; islands, even to the distance of Arran and Bute, Ben Nevis on the far background on one side and the castles of Stirling and Edinburgh at equal distances on the other. Beneath our feet, the Loch, with the steamer reduced to a cockle shell, yet although at the height of 3,192 feet we heard the noise of the steam escaping from the valve! The woods and manor of Stuckgoune seemed the size of pasteboard toys, such as are shown to children in a raree show: Luss, a cluster of cottages: Rowardennan, a hut: the Tarbet Inn, a dog-kennel. *Ben Voirlich* and *Ben Venue*, which, in *The Lady of the Lake*, throw their mighty shadows upon the face of *Loch Catherine* [sic], and seem to be the mountain heroes of *that* scenery were, here, five hundred feet *below* us. One seemed to stand above everything earthly, in the immediate vicinity of the spot; although *Cruachan*, in the nearer distance, might teach even *Ben Lomond* a lesson of humility.'

Having thus provided us with a description of enthusiastic vividness, Dibdin goes on:

'I shall abstain from further particularity of detail; first, because the view from this lofty region has been so often and so well done; and, secondly, because I am not particularly attached to extensive views, unless chosen at favourable moments, and under a genial and transparent sky.'

Her Majesty's Chaplain in Ordinary had certainly a livelier pen than his employer. Queen Victoria's two journals, *Leaves from the Journal of a life in the Highlands* and its sequel *More Leaves*, may not rank high in the annals of British descriptive writing but they illustrate the change which came over nineteenth-century travellers as travel became comparatively easier.

Warmed by her completely genuine love of Scotland, and writing in the first instance with no thought of publication, Queen Victoria set down her honest reactions to what she saw. For her there was still a sort of mystical halo round the Scottish Highlands; but it was a less sentimental halo than that which shone for most later Victorian travellers, and she eschewed their *religioso* mood.

On Saturday, 4th September 1869, Queen Victoria set out on her pony Sultan from the house of Invertrossachs by Loch Vennachar, crossed the loch in a rowing-boat, drove in her carriage through the Trossachs to Loch Katrine and sailed on the steamer *Rob Roy* to Stronachlachar. From there she drove in a hired carriage past Loch Arklet along the road to Inversnaid, meeting on the way 'several large coaches, but with only outside seats, full of tourists'. The queen was reminded of the scenery in Switzerland, where she had once been happy with her late husband. Then:

'. . . we suddenly came upon *Loch Lomond*, and drove down a very steep hill to *Inversnaid*, where there is only one house (a small inn), and saw high mountains, looking shadowy in the mist (dry mist), rising abruptly from the loch. We went at once on board the fine steamer *Prince Consort* (a pleasant idea that that dear name should have carried his poor little wife, alas! a widow, and children, on their first sail on this beautiful lake which he went to see in 1847). She is a fine large vessel, a good deal larger than the *Winkelried* (in which we used to go on the *Lake of Lucerne*), with a fine large dining-cabin below, a very high upper deck, and a gallery underneath on which people can stand and smoke without incommoding the others above . . .

'We steamed southward, and for the first half nothing could be finer or more truly Alpine, reminding me much of the *Lake of Lucerne;* only it is longer—*Loch Lomond* being twenty-two miles long. We kept close to the east shore, passing under *Ben Lomond* with its variously called shoulders—*Cruachan, Craig a Bochan,* and *Ptarmigan*—to Rowardennan pier, where there is a pretty little house rented from the Duke of Montrose (to whom half *Loch Lomond* belongs) by a Mr Mair, a lovely spot from whence you can ascend *Ben Lomond,* which is 3,192 feet high, and well wooded part of the way, with cornfields below. After you pass this, where there are fine mountains on either side, though on the west shore not so high, the lake widens out, but the shores become much flatter and tamer (indeed to the east and south completely so); but here are all the beautifully wooded islands, to the number of twenty-four. Some of them are large; on *Inchlonaig Island* the firs are said to have been planted by Robert Bruce to encourage the people in the use of archery. Another, *Inch Cailliach*, is the ancient burial-place of the McGregors.

'On the mainland we passed *Cornick Hill*, and could just see *Buchanan House*, the Duke of Montrose's, and to the right the island of *Inch Murrin*, on which the Duke has his deer preserve. The sun had come out soon after we went on board, and it was blowing quite fresh as we went against the wind. At two o'clock we stopped off *Portnellan* for luncheon, which we had brought with us and took below in the handsome large cabin, where fifty or sixty people, if not more, could easily dine. Colonel Ponsonby also lunched with us . . . This over, we went to the end of the lake to *Balloch*, and here turned. It became very warm. To the left we passed some very pretty villas (castles they resembled) and places, amongst others *Cameron* (Mr Smollett's), *Arden* (Sir J. Lumsden's,

Lord Provost of Glasgow), *Ross-Dhu* (Sir J. Colquhoun's), the road to *Glen Fruin*, the islands of *Inch Connachan*, *Inch Tavanach*, the point of *Stob Gobhlach*, *Luss*, a very prettily situated village, the mountain of *Ben Dubh*, and the ferry of *Inveruglas*, opposite Rowardennan. Then *Tarbet*, a small town, where dearest Albert landed in 1847, and here began the highest and finest mountains, with splendid passes, richly wooded, and the highest mountains rising behind. A glen leads across from *Tarbet* to *Arrochar* on *Loch Long*, and here you see that most singularly shaped hill called the *Cobbler*, and a little farther on the splendid *Alps of Arrochar*. All this and the way in which the hills run into the lake reminded me so much of the *Nasen* on the *Lake of Lucerne*.

'The head of the lake with the very fine glen (*Glen Falloch*), along which you can drive to *Oban*, is magnificent. We (Louise and I) sketched as best we could, but it is most difficult to do so when the steamer keeps moving on; and we were afterwards much vexed we had not asked them to go more slowly, as we had to wait again for the Rob Roy steamer at *Stronachlachar*. From the head of *Loch Lomond* (where is the *Hotel of Inverarnan*) we turned; we were shown a hole in the rock, on the east side, which they called *Rob Roy's Cave* and landed at *Inversnaid*. The people (quite a small crowd) threw bunches of heather as we passed. Heather is everywhere the decoration, and there is indeed no lovelier, prettier ornament.'

The day, which had begun at half past seven in the morning, ended with a 'delightful drive' back through the Trossachs, but a stormy crossing of Loch Vennachar in the rowing-boat, which 'rolled and danced'. The queen records: 'Rode back and got up to the house by half past seven. This was the only *contretemps* to our most successful, enjoyable day. How dearest Albert would have enjoyed it!'

Few post-Queen Victorian descriptions of Loch Lomond have been uninfluenced by what earlier writers said. But the geologist Hugh Miller looked at Loch Lomond and the surrounding country with fresh eyes.

'In passing onwards from Luss, we first became aware that we were nearing the mica-schist formation by the peculiar contour of its hills, as seen at the distance of several miles, and now as we approached their grey rocks of silky lustre, we find that they are wrinkled and contorted, so as to remind us of pieces of ill-laid-by satin, that bear on their crushed surfaces the creases and crumplings of a thousand careless foldings; and, mark, further, that it is to these curves and contortions of the strata that the tuber clad outlines of the hills are owing, and, with these the bold, projecting knobs and sudden recesses which break up their surfaces into so many picturesque wildernesses of light and shade. Mica-schist rocks decompose into soils, which, though light and thin, are favourable to the production of grasses and the common dicotyledonous shrubs and trees of the Highlands, making the micaeous region picturesque in outline, rich in foliage, and soft in colour. A tangled profusion of vegetation forms quite as marked a feature in the landscape as the mural picturesqueness of the crags and precipices which the vegetation half consumes.'

It is not a far cry from the technical observation of Hugh Miller to the modern scientific method of observation reflected in the series of *Studies on Loch Lomond* produced by research workers at the University of Glasgow.

5

Lochside Diary

MOST of the people living around Loch Lomondside prior to the late eighteenth century would be unable to record their daily happenings for the simple reason that they could not write. The Lennox lairds might perhaps have kept account books; but few, if any, of these have come down to us. It is to the patient diligence of an obscure minister that we owe an authentic early glimpse of life in the parish of Kilmaronock, in which the village of Gartocharn now lies.

The Reverend Thomas Leckie was born in Glasgow in 1678, the son of William Leckie, merchant, and Jean Rae. At first young Leckie seems to have been intended for the family business, but he changed his mind, went to Glasgow University, was licensed to preach in 1702, and the following year came to the parish of Kilmaronock. For twenty years, until his death on 1st September 1723, he ministered to the people who lived in the district watered by the Endrick and encompassing much of the Southern shore of Loch Lomond, though bordering the still-turbulent Highlands. That he was conscientious in his ministry is highly probable, for six volumes of his sermons, written out in his clear, pointed hand, have come down to us.

Sermons, however, quickly date, since theology has to shift its positions in response to the latest discoveries of science as adroitly and blandly as women lower or raise their hemline in an effort to look like *now*. It takes the genius of a Donne to make the words of a sermon ring out over the ages with the enduring force and clarity of a good poem. The Reverend Thomas Leckie was no Donne, but he seems to have been a good pastor and a kindly family man. His first wife, Mary Park, died after bearing him two children: Broice, baptized in 1705, and Janet, baptized in 1707.

47

He took his second wife, Janet, from the district, for she was the daughter of a local laird, James Buchanan of Catter. By her he had three children: Anna, baptized in 1715, Robert and Ann. Janet survived her husband by only two years, though the Leckie children, brought up in the old thatched manse of Kilmaronock, made good marriages, and, in two instances at least, lived on into the closing decade of the century.

We meet Mr Leckie on 1st June 1718, on which day he made the first entry in a new volume of his diary: a leather-bound affair, shaped like a reporter's note-book, though measuring only about three inches by five. If we read from the front of the book, we find ourselves sharing the day-to-day comings and goings of his life up to 31st August 1719. Reading from the back of the book, we find a list of his expenses 'out laid' over the same period; an average of twenty-five Scots pounds a month. One-and-sixpence for 'five herrings'; six-and-eightpence 'to my wife to pay chickens'; one and eightpence 'to pay eggs'; eighteen shillings for a 'chopin of wine for my son'; innumerable shillings to the poor in various parts of the parish; one pound ten shillings 'to Geo. Mitchell, for thatching my house'; two pounds-thirteen 'for a hutch of coal'; and so on, down to the final entry, two shillings 'to my wife'.

Leckie ministered at Kilmaronock from a manse and in a church replaced almost a hundred years after this single surviving volume of his diary ends with the information: 'Went to bed after 11.' International events such as the serious illness of the King of Sweden, or war with France, reached him in his country isolation at far hand, by word of mouth. He could never be sure of the accuracy of such reports. Ripples of the troubles which had disrupted the country a generation earlier are perhaps reflected in his suspicious entries about the attitude of the Duke of Argyll to obscure matters of church government,[1] and to a difference of opinion with Lady Grizell[2] about the ruling to be followed for the running of the local school, then, of course, a church commitment.

More immediate troubles also fell to be recorded: the disappearance, for instance, on 30th January 1719, of ten cows

---

[1] Every landowner at that time was constantly concerned with parochial affairs, either as heritor or patron. Argyll would have such interests in Dunbartonshire.

[2] Youngest daughter of the second Marquis of Montrose, who married William Cochrane of Kilmaronock and died in 1726.

and a quantity of sheep, the result of a Sabbath-day swoop by Highland reivers; the rumour, false as it turned out, that the Old Pretender had been taken at sea by a British man-o'-war; the report in April, a few weeks later, that there had been a Jacobite landing in Ross-shire, and that there were armed men wandering about the Muir of Buchanan; the rumour, which reached Leckie's ever attentive ear on 25th May, that Rob Roy had been taken prisoner, news which so cheered the good preacher that he added to his account 'did bath myself in Endrick'; the disturbing information, recorded on 3rd June, that 'Rob Roy was come to his own house', and that the Earl of Mar had raised '3000 Highlanders'.

Clearly, Leckie did not himself harbour Jacobite sympathies. The entry for New Year's Day, 1719, reads:

'This morning I read . . . in bed; and after duty secret and private and breakfast with Mr Corbet, I began to discourse with him and exort him; and having given him some money, he began to tell that the Ministers of Scotland were not worth, and that he would be ane adversary to them if he could. Upon which I told him his friendship and favour was not much to be regarded, or all that he could do against them, or that he ought not to speak so, seeing he was so much obliged to them; the which he denied. I told him that I should rehearse to some of them his words and cariage, upon which he begged my malice over and over again, and having put up his cloaths, he went, at which I was glad.'

For the most part, however, Leckie recorded his journeys about the countryside and his calls at houses and farms which wear the names we know them by today: a quiet record of the kind of continuity which we accept without reflection; the stabilizing element in the traditions which make up our way of life, and yet of which we have so little written evidence. Thus the entry for 8th January 1719:

"This morning, I read. . . . After 10, went forth to examine in Aiber.[1] Before I began, I saw John McLean, Elder, and Eliz Ker, sick persons with whom I conversed and prayed, and then

---

[1] Aber. The site of the main village or township until 1850, when it was superceded by Gartocharn, half a mile farther up from the shore of the loch.

examined a great part of the town. After which I sent my horse
home, and went to Rosse with Dumakill's[1] daughter Margt and
son Jo: but there having fallen a great snow since yester night,
and being melted this day with a southerly wind, the Rosse burn
was over all its banks so that we could not pass it. Having walkt
to Mill of Ardoch, we designed to passe it there, but here we met
with Arch Govane, who wan over the burn and sent 2 lads and 2
horse, who took us over the burn and length of Rosse. When we
were at some meat, Craigievern, Elder, Glengyl, Wm Craig and
And Stewart came in on us, who with great difficulty had past
the burn. They did all together chat till supper, after which,
and worship, went to bed near 12. I lay alone in Mr Parlan's
bed.'

Varying this ordered routine with a little fishing in the
Endrick, Mr Leckie rarely rode far from home. An occasional
jaunt to Glasgow, usually on church business or to see his
relatives, was about the extent of his travelling. The record of one
such journey is a reminder of the uncertainty of human life,
particularly young life, in the early eighteenth century.

'Janry 13, Tues: This morning Jo McGovn did breakfast with
me, and gave me 2 bank notes 20 sh. ster. a peece, and then I made
ready to goe to Glasgow. I went about 11. I called at Balvie, but
mist the Lady. I gave to Mrs Burns a letter and some money
from Dunmakill[1] to give her. I came to Glasgow about 5. On the
way thither, I got a letter from Baylie Crawford, bearing that the
Duke of Argyll has kissd the king's hand, and was made Master
of Horse.

'After I had taken some meat in my quarters, I went and saw
my sister's child, Rebecca Maxwell, who seemed to be dying.
With her I prayed, and then I went and saw Mr Anderson. With
him I converst till after 9. Mr Jo Grant Muir of Affleck came in
upon us. After supper, and worship, went to bed about 12.'

Next day, Mr Leckie was early about his business.

'This morning Ja Maxwell and Pat Walker took their morning
drink with me. After shaving, went forth and bought shoes to my

[1] The Buchanans of Drumakil.

daughter Anne, and shoes to my horse, and saw Rebecca Maxwell, as also did tary some tyme in Rob Scots shop. I dined in my quarters, after which I met with Baylie Stirling, with whom I walkt to the Brimylaw, and then did rest in Rob Crawford's shop. About 5, met with Hugh Campbell, Mr Duncan Campbell's son, and drank and discourst a litle with him and then with Rob Crawford. I went and saw Rebecca Maxwell. Here I taryed till 9, at which tyme she dyed. I prayed this day with her 7 tymes. After I came home, I supt, and after worship went to bed about 12 a Clock.'

Next day, after discussing church politics at some length with 'Baylie Alexander' and being 'much refresht' from a sermon preached by 'Mr Jo Hamilton', he met his father-in-law after three, 'and brought him to the Magistrats'. They thereupon made Mr Buchanan 'burgesse and Gildbrother of Glasgow'.

Leckie goes on: 'We went with Provost Aird, Baylie Millar, Baylie Whithill, and Baylie Crawford to Geo Buchanan's, and drank wine and ale about 7. Baylie Crawford and I went to Ja Maxwell's to the light-wake, where I sat till about 8, and then went to one Will Inglis in Gallowgate and baptised a daughter to him called Kathrine.' After 'lecturing' to a 'great many' in Inglis's house, Leckie went back to the 'Magistrats', presumably to collect his father-in-law, for he records that the new guild brother 'got a share of my bed'.

Next day, Leckie attended the funeral of his niece, bought a cloak for his son and went 'to Pat Walker's, where we were very well entertained. There were several others with me; Baylie Crawford and my sister, Will Thomsone and wife and Mrs Buchanan. We came home near to 10.'

On Saturday, 17th January, Mr Leckie prepared himself for the return journey. He finished his shopping, called on a friend, Mr Anderson, and then went to a coffee house to read the news. There, he discovered that

'the K of Spain is recovered, the schism bill is read a 3rd tyme before the House of Commons, and voted repeal the same. It carryed by 58 . . . I mounted my horse after 12, and came to Balvie against 3. Here I mett with my father-in-law, and after I had dined and discourst together, he and I rode home against 8. I discourst with my wife and family till after 9, and then prepared for the following day. After supper, and worship, went to bed about 12.'

No doubt that hour's discourse was a pleasant one to Mrs Leckie, for the quality which comes alive to us out of her husband's neatly written but close-crammed pages, the ink turned light brown now with the passing of more than two centuries, is the sense of content.

Mr Leckie's world was a small one, troubled by the echoes of distant wars and royal deaths, by the incursions of marauders like Rob Roy and his kind, and by the uncertainty of human life and the effects of the weather. But, for all that, it was a well-ordered life, securely set within conventions generally believed in and accepted: a peaceful backwater in the never-quieted storm that is history.

6

Through the Poets' Eyes

VISITORS of an inquiring turn of mind sometimes wonder why so little Scots-Gaelic poetry of distinction has survived, even if only in translation. It is possible to turn to the fairly substantial quantity of Irish-Gaelic bardic verse and enjoy it in the English versions of Douglas Hyde, Kuno Meyer, George Sigerson, Robin Flower and other translators. How, then, does it come about that Scots-Gaelic poetry is so much more elusive? Have Loch Lomond, the largest inland water in Scotland, and Ben Lomond, the second-highest mountain, between them inspired not a single Gaelic poet?

It seems unlikely that the chiefs who controlled the lands of Lennox did not at one time maintain their own bards. Scottish bards, however, seem to have been less accomplished than their Irish counterparts. Edward Burt, an English administrator who came to Scotland in the service of Marshal Wade, described a bardic performance which he heard while dining with a Highland chief.

'After some little time the chief ordered one of them to sing me a Highland song. The bard readily obeyed; and with a hoarse voice, and in a tune of few various notes began, as I was told, one of his own lyrics; and when he had proceeded to the fourth or fifth stanzas, I perceived by the names of several persons, glens, and mountains, which I had known or heard of before, that it was an account of some clan battle. But in his going on, the chief (who piques himself upon his school-learning), at some particular passage bid him cease, and cried out to me, "There's nothing like that in Virgil or Homer!" I bowed, and told him I believed so.'

Dr Samuel Johnson, who traversed the Highlands almost half a century after Burt heard his bard, dismissed bardic poetry as of no consequence, because it could not be recorded.

'That the bards could not read more than the rest of their countrymen it is reasonable to suppose; because if they had read, they could probably have written; and how high their compositions may reasonably be rated, an inquirer may best judge by considering what stories, what imagery, what principles of ratiocination, and what comprehension of knowledge, and what delicacy of elocution, he has known any man attain who cannot read. The state of the bard was yet more hopeless. He that cannot read may now converse with those that can; but the bard was a barbarian among barbarians, who, knowing nothing himself, lived with others that knew no more.'

The surprising thing is that, under circumstances so handicapping, the eighteenth century should have produced Gaelic poets like Alexander Macdonald, whose 'Birlinn of Clanranald' is a bracing piece of work, and Duncan Ban MacIntyre, whose noble paean 'The Praise of Ben Dorain', like Macdonald's poem, has been breezily translated by Hugh MacDiarmid. Of course, the skills of sea and hill which these poets knew about lay far outwith Dr Johnson's range of experience. But neither these poets, nor their lesser colleagues, seem ever to have sung the praises of Loch Lomond.

The earliest poet to write of the loch, John Barbour, though a Lowlander, had similiar aims to the Highland bards, who sought mostly to extol the prowess in battle of their employers. Barbour sought to commemorate and extol the patriotism, strategy and courage of King Robert the Bruce a generation or so after Bruce's death, and at a time when the disturbed state of Scotland made the exaggeration of the king's heroic virtues a useful political tonic. In his long epic, *The Brus*, Barbour indulges frequently in that tedious cataloguing which was the Gaelic bard's stock-in-trade. But, whereas the bards rarely got beyond such recitals of flattery, Barbour could rise on occasion to considerable heights of literary achievement, as his famous passage on the nobility and priceless value of freedom testifies. He also possessed a superior narrative style.

In Book III of *The Brus* Barbour tells how Bruce, Douglas and their followers, retreating before the forces of John of Lorne, came down upon the North bank of Loch Lomond.

> 'The king, eftir that he was gane,
> To Loch Lomond the way has tane,
> And came thare on the third day.
> But thereat na boat fand they,
> That micht them ower the water bear;
> Then were they wae in great manner:
> For it was far aboot to ga,
> And they into doot alsa,
> To meet their faes that spread were wide,
> Therefore, endlang the lochïs side
> Sa busily they socht, and fast,
> Till James of Douglas, at the last,
> Fand a little sunken boat,
> And to the land it drew, fut hate.[1]
> But it sa little was, that it
> Micht owre the water but threescore flit.
> They send thereof word to the king,
> That was joyful of that finding;
> And first into the boat is gane,
> With them Douglas; the third was ane,
> That rowit them owre deliverly
> And set them on the land all dry.
> And rowit so often, to and fra,
> Fetchand aye owre twa and twa,
> That in ae nicht and in ae day,
> Comin oot owre the loch are they.
> For some of them could swim full weel,
> And on his back care a fardele[2]
> Swa with swimming and with rowing,
> They brocht them owre, and all their thing.'

While this laborious military operation was in progress, Barbour tells us that the king diverted his men who waited on the

[1] Rapidly
[2] Fellow

South side with stories, among them the tale of Fierabras the Saracen, son of Balan, Sultan of Babylon.

On 1st October 1788 Burns, who rode down Loch Lomond while on his shorter Highland tour, sat down in his farm at Mauchline to write to his bookseller friend Peter Hill in Edinburgh.

'I have been here in this country, about three days, and all that time, my chief reading has been the Address to Lochlomond you were so obliding as to send me. Were I impannelled, one of the author's jury to determine his criminality respecting the Sin of Poesy, my verdict should be "Guilty! A poet of nature's making!" It is an excellent method for improvement, and what I believe every poet does; to place some favorite classic author, in our own walks of study & composition, before us a model. Tho' your author has not mentioned the name, I could have, at half a glance, guessed his model to be Thomson. Will my brother author forgive me, if I venture to hint, that his imitation of that Immortal Bard is in two or three places more servile than such a genius as his required. e.g.

"They soothe the madding passions all to peace."
                                                            Address.

"To soothe the throbbing passions into peace."
                                                            Thomson.

'I have read Thomson at the same time, & I think the versification of the Address, in simplicity, harmony, & elegance, fully equal to the Seasons. Like Thomson too, he has looked into Nature for himself: you meet with no copied description. One particular criticism I made, at first reading; in no one instance has he said too much. He never flags in his progress, but like a true poet of Nature's making, kindles in his course. His beginning is simple, and modest, as if distrustful of the strength of his opinion; only, I do not altogether like

                            — "Truth,
The soul of every song that's nobly great"—

'Fiction is the soul of many a song that's nobly great. Perhaps I am wrong: this may be but a prose criticism. Is not the phrase, in line 7th, page 6th, "Great lake", too much vulgarised by everyday language, for so sublime a poem?

' "Great mass of waters, theme for nobler Song", is perhaps no emendation. His enumeration of, & comparison with other lakes, is at once harmonious & poetic. Every reader's ideas must sweep the

—"winding margin of an hundred miles".

'The following perspective of mountains blue—the imprisoned billows beating in vain—the wooded isles—the digression on the yew-tree—Benlomond's lofty, cloud-enveloped head, &c. are beautiful. A thunder-storm is a subject which has been often tried, yet our poet in his grand picture has interjected a circumstance, so far as I know, entirely original:

"the gloom
Deep seamed with frequent streaks of moving fire".

'In his preface to the storm, "The glens how dark between", is noble Highland landscape! The "rain plowing the red mould", too, is beautifully fancied. Benlomond's "Lofty, pathless top" is a good expression; & the surrounding view from it is truly great: the "Silver mist, Beneath the beaming sun" is well described; & here, he has contrived to enliven his poem with a little of that passion which bids fair, I think, to usurp the modern muses altogether. I know not how far this episode is a beauty upon the whole, but the swain's wish to carry "Some faint idea of the vision bright", to entertain her "partial listening ear", is a pretty thought. But in my opinion the most beautiful passages in the whole Poem, are the fowls crouding, in wintry frosts, to Lochlomond's "hospitable flood"—their wheeling round, their lighting, mixing, diving, &c.—and the glorious description of the sportsman. This last is equal to any thing in The Seasons: the idea of "the floating tribes, distant seen, far glistering to the moon", provoking his eye as he is oblidged to leave them, is a noble ray of poetic genius. "The howling winds"—the "hideous roar" of "the white cascades"—are all in the same style.

'I forget that while I am thus holding forth with the heedless warmth of an enthusiast, I am perhaps tiring you with nonsense . . .

'I must beg your pardon for this lengthened scrawl—I had no idea of it when I began. I should like to know who the author is; but whoever he be, please, present him with my grateful thanks for the entertainment he has afforded me.'

The author who afforded Burns so much entertainment was the Reverend Dr James Cririe, of Dalton, Dumfriesshire. In 1803 he brought out his *Scottish Scenery*, a descriptive poem dealing with many parts of Scotland. The 'Address to Lochlomond', which had been published separately in 1788, was included as one of the cantos. In the introduction to the collected volume, Dr Cririe wrote:

'The Author is aware that of late years, many have been employed in describing the same scenery; yet, as he attempts to treat the subject in a style somewhat different from any traveller who has preceded him, he hopes the design will obtain the approbation of those who have a taste for this species of composition, provided the execution shall be found, to any degree, to correspond with the beauty and grandeur of the subject.'

The reverend poet's ambition was perhaps hardly fulfilled; but his 'Address' is interesting because his approval of the wild scenery of loch and glen runs counter to the tenor of Augustan English feeling in the manner of expression in which his salute is couched. He reached the opposite conclusion from Wordsworth, who, a decade and a half later, compared Loch Lomond unfavourably with his English lakes because of the vastness of the Scottish loch. Wrote Cririe:

'Great Lake: fit theme for more exalted song,
What single view thy limits can explore?
Thy native beauties, wild and vast, awake,
With glad surprize, our intellectual powers.
They soothe the madding passions all to peace,
And fix the eye upon thy glassy plain,
Which holds to heav'n a mirror, blue and bright . . .

To thy stupendous size, what's Derwent Lake?
What all the Lakes of Cumberland to thee?

With those that grace her sister county join'd?
Those pretty ponds, let others flock to view:
But, here, let those whom Nature wild can charm,
With admiration gaze; nor e'er regret
The want of vain Regattas to enhance
What sober sense must relish and applaud.'

The poet seems to have climbed Ben Lomond by himself, and
to have been oppressed by the loneliness of the scene from the
top of the mountain, which he described with vivid detail:

'The setting sun, with parting ray uprear'd,
Ben-Lomond, last of all our mountains, gilds,
Day, as averse to leave the pleasing scene,
Slowly retires far North, nor quite forsakes,
But soon more bright and fair, returns to gild
With morning beams, his lofty pathless top:—
Oft thence, with eagle eye, th'advent'rous youth,
Whose daring soul danger and toil contemns,
Fir'd with the love of knowledge, and of fame,
A prospect wide, of vast extent, descries,
Of hills and dales, of firths, and winding shores.—
Northward, a wavy sea of mountains wild,
Interminable, bounds the striking view;—
Beneath, the lake itself, in part conceal'd,
The Clyde, with crowded sails and steamers, gay;—
Eastward, the mazy Forth, meand'ring slow,
For largest fleets a deep and safe retreat,
Rich with the treasures of remotest climes:
Edina's lofty tow'rs; the Eastern coast,
Far as the Cheviot fells:—the Western isles
Of Bute and Arran; Ailsa's conic rock;
Old Rothesay's royal tow'rs in ruins laid;
Hibernia's verdant hills and fertile plains.
The rival height of great Snowdonia, too,
In distant Wales:—the Skidda, Cumbria's boast,
Beyond the Solway Firth, unnotic'd stands;
While hills, o'er hills, still higher rise behind.
Perchance, a silver mist the vallies fills:
Beneath the beaming sun, a sea it seems,

A vast Pacific, spreading out immense
The mountain tops, like islands seen afar,
With joy and wonder fill the gazing swain.
Who stands amaz'd to view th' illusive scene,
But feels a deep regret, that all alone,
No friend is near to share th' enchanting joy.
Maria's absence chiefly he regrets:—
Tho' distant far her humble cottage stands,
Down in the wintery glen, deep-hid, secure
And shelter'd from the furious Northern blast.
Her, best and fairest of her sex, he deems,
From her unsully'd virgin bosom pure,
Pleasure reflected brings extatic bliss,
Instinctive, oft his wistful eye around
He anxious turns, to see if she be near;
But all in vain:— The long and steep ascent,
What tender female foot can bear to climb?
Fatigue, severe for shepherd swain robust!'

Possibly Cririe was somewhat out of training when he made the ascent. Certainly, twentieth-century Marias climb Ben Lomond every other day, and do not find the 'fatigue severe' too much for their tender female feet.

A less high-minded English rhymester also climbed the Ben towards the end of the eighteenth century, and inscribed some advice to his successors on a window of the inn at Rowardennan.

'Stranger! if o'er this pane of glass perchance
Thy roving eye should cast a casual glance,
If taste for grandeur and the dread sublime
Prompt thee Ben Lomond's fearful height to climb,
Here gaze attentive, nor with scorn refuse
The friendly rhymings of a tavern muse . . .
Trust not at first a quick advent'rous pace,
Six miles its top points gradual from the base;
Up the high rise with panting haste I passed,
And gained the long laborious steep at last.
More prudent you, when once you pass the deep,
With measured pace ascend the lengthened steep;

Oft stay thy steps, oft taste the cordial drop,
And rest, oh rest! long, long upon the top.
There hail the breezes; nor with toilsome haste
Down the rough slope thy precious vigour waste:
So shall thy wandering sight at once survey
Vales, lakes, woods, mountains, islands, rocks and
sea . . .

The scene tremendous shakes the startled sense
With all the pomp of dread magnificence.
All these, and more, shalt thou transported see,
And own a faithful monitor in me.'

The piece comes to a somewhat abrupt finish, possibly due to the limitations of the medium.

The most famous Loch Lomond poem is, of course, the Jacobite song which begins:

'By yon bonnie banks, and by yon bonnie braes,
    Where the sun shines bright on Loch Lomon',
Where me and my true love were ever wont to gae
    On the bonnie, bonnie banks o' Loch Lomon'.

O ye'll tak' the high road, and I'll tak' the low road,
    And I'll be in Scotland afore ye;
But me and my true love will never meet again
    On the bonnie, bonnie banks o' Loch Lomon'.'

As this song is as widely sung as any other associated with Scotland, it is tantalizing that so little should be known about it. Legend avers that the song refers to the last meeting of a Jacobite soldier, about to be executed at Carlisle, with his sweetheart who had journeyed down from the Lennox to take farewell of her beloved. Thus, the low road meant, for the condemned man, the grave; while the high road, for his girl, meant the road by which she would travel home.

There are obvious objections to this, the approved version, not the least of which is the fact that the Jacobite unfortunates at Carlisle were mostly executed without trial or delay of any kind, merely to have been found bearing arms being deemed a sufficient cause for their summary despatch. There is also a strangely related piece of ballad business between Ranald, who, on the morrow, 'marches to Edinburgh town, to fecht for the King and Prince Charlie', and his Moira. In a set of verses discovered by Lady John Scott, the veteran and doughty Border poetess who died in 1900 at the age of ninety, and whose work includes the version of 'Annie Laurie' most frequently sung today, Moira laments the probable death in battle of her gallant lover.

> 'Oh! weel may I weep—yestreen in my sleep
>   We stood bride and bridegroom thegither.
> But his lips and his breath were as chilly as death,
>   And his heart's bluid was red on the heather.
>
> Oh! dauntless in battle as tender in love,
>   He'll yield ne'er a foot to the foeman;
> And never again frae the field o' the slain
>   To Moira he'll come, and Loch Lomon'.
>
> Oh! he'll gang the hie road, and I'll gang the low,
>   But I'll be in Heaven afore him,
> For my bed is prepared in the mossy graveyard
>   'Mang the hazels o' green Inverarnan.'

In the case of Moira and Ranald, both were to die, he in battle, she of grief, but the future meeting place was not to be in Scotland.

> 'The thistle shall bloom, and the King hae his aim,
>   And fond lovers meet in the gloamin'.
> And I and my true love will yet meet again,
>   Far abune the bonnie banks of Loch Lomon'.'

When Robert Ford was writing his *Song Histories* at the turn of the nineteenth century he came upon some further variants of the idea of Loch Lomond as a meeting place for unlucky lovers. One such variant, given to him by a member of the family of Colquhoun of Luss, goes:

> 'We'll meet where we parted, in bonnie Luss Glen,
>   'Mang the heathery braes o' Ben Lomon',
> Starts the roe frae the pass, and the fox frae his den,
>   While abune gleams the moon thro' the rowan.'

Anyone who knows Loch Lomondside will realize just how impossible a lover's wish this arrangement is geographically, since 'bonnie Luss Glen' lies on the Southern side of Loch Lomond, while Ben Lomond stands on the Northern side.

Alfred Moffat has recorded that Lady John Scott once told him she and her husband had picked up the air and the verses from a poor boy in Edinburgh in the 1840s. It seems likely that Lady John worked over the Ranald and Moira verses in the way she worked over the rather feeble original version of 'Annie Laurie', producing out of traditional fragments the song as we know it today. Manuscript copies of 'Loch Lomond' were then circulated among the friends of Sir John and Lady Scott, and one of these copies came into the hands of the Edinburgh publishers, Messrs Paterson and Roy, who gave it to the musician Finlay Dun to arrange for them. 'Loch Lomond' was first published in 1845, the verses shown as being 'by a lady', the air attributed to tradition. From the structure and character of the air my own guess would be that it originated in the late eighteenth century.

All the early Loch Lomond poets were concerned mainly with description. Even the original anonymous author of 'Loch Lomond' set his human tragedy in a local scene for which he felt strong affection, and which he could not resist describing.

Sir Walter Scott's description of Loch Katrine in 'The Lady of the Lake' was said by Hugh Miller to be as full and as accurate a poetic account of the natural scene as could be devised. But Scott's best-known lines on Loch Lomond, written, perhaps, in the house of Ross Priory, are to be found in the boat song of the chieftain in 'The Lady of the Lake', in which the poet romanticizes vanished ghosts.

'Proudly our pibroch has thrilled in Glen Fruin,
  And Bannochar's groans to our slogan replied;
Glen Luss and Ross-dhu, they are smoking in ruins,
  And the best of Loch Lomond lie dead on her side.
     Widow and Saxon maid
     Long shall lament our raid,
Think of Clan Alpine with fear and with woe;
     Lennox and Leven-glen
     Shake when they hear again,
Roderigh Vich Alpine dhu, ho! ieroe!'

In similar warlike vein is Scott's 'McGregors' Gathering'. Hardly an evening-dressed, encored baritone appearing on a Scottish platform does not, at some time or other, solemnly gather his brows and thunder forth in stentorian tones the Victorian setting of Scott's rallying-call.

> 'Through the depths of Loch Katrine the steed
> shall career,
> O'er the peak of Ben Lomond the galley shall steer,
> And the rocks of Craig-Royston like icicles melt,
> Ere our wrongs be forgot, or our vengeance unfelt!
> Then gather, gather, gather, Grigalach!
> Gather, gather, gather.'

It is certainly pretty enough stuff; but Scott used Loch Lomond simply as a backcloth for the re-creation of the supposed heroic figures of a highly romanticized past.

The nineteenth-century poet who might have done better than most, Alexander Smith, only once directed his descriptive powers to Loch Lomond before the critics castigated his verse for its sensuousness and petrified his imagination.

> 'Whence come the waters, garner'd up
> So purely in that rocky cup?
> They come from regions high and far,
> Where blows the wind and shines the star.
> The silent dews that heaven distils
> At midnight on the lonely hills;
> The shower that plain and mountain dims,
> On which the dazzling rainbow swims;
> The torrents from the thunder gloom,
> Let loose as by a crack of doom;
> The whirling waterspout that cracks
> Into a scourge of cataracts,
> Are swallowed by the thirsty lake
> A lovely sheet their waters make.'

It might be argued, with some justification, that to describe Loch Lomond as a 'rocky cup', while geologically accurate, is making rather too much use of that licence which nineteenth-century poets assumed they possessed.

Loch Lomond

Drawn by C. Cordinar, engraved by P. Mazell, published 1794

Ben Lomond from Cameron Wood

Drawn by R. S. of the R. A., engraved by T. Medland, published 1782

Scotland was not rich in Victorian poets of talent. The rhymers, mostly amateur, who versified about Loch Lomond during the latter half of the nineteenth century are of interest because of their conspicuous failures rather than their small successes. It was no longer the scene itself which primarily interested them; not even those ghosts of the past that fascinated Scott. Loch and mountain became texts for religious moralizing, an abuse to which the Goddess of Poetry will not readily submit.

Philip Gilbert Hammerton, an artist and art critic of considerable reputation in his day, collected together his poetic effusions in 1855. He, too, had climbed Ben Lomond, and had been suitably impressed by the view from the summit. But he claimed to have seen more than a view:

'I had reached
The summit, and was standing to receive
The first bright glow of morning on my face,
When from his opening tent of crimson clouds
Came forth the risen sun! The stars have shrunk
Into the cold green sky—the moon is gone—
So pass the wandering lights that led my youth!
The lakes are blue and cold in the deep valleys,
And every isle attracts the rising mist.
But now the rugged peaks are flushing red
Before the orb that sternly looks on each,
Peering into the secrets of its face,
Across the lakes the spreading shadows flew,
And I beheld the outline of the peak
On which I stood, as clear as Arthur's side
As you may see the earth's circumference
On the eclipsed moon. Then brighter grew
The aspect of the scene, and those three lakes
That slept between me and the gorgeous east
Began to feel the presence of the sun.
Bright from a spring half down the precipice
Issued the tiny Forth, whose silver line
Followed a winding course; and in the South
That white horizon is the Firth of Clyde—
That hill, Dumbarton Rock—and that blue shape,
That almost seems to float among the clouds—

The Isle of Bute. Look down that dark ravine,
And watch the white and swiftly-climbing mist
Rolling in silence up the narrow fissure
Between these rugged, black, forbidding rocks,
Like troops of angels climbing fearlessly
Into a dark and rough and hardened soul,
Storming its blackened citadel with love.
The peaks around us have already plumed
Their crests with cloud, so let us look once more,
And then descend as quickly as we may,
Lest, blinded by the softly-creeping mist,
We overstep the precipice, or lose
The proper track and die in the morass.'

Mid-Victorian readers may have been able to picture in the mind's eye the image of a 'dark and rough and hardened soul' being fearlessly stormed with love; today the image seems technically incompetent, not to say slightly comic.

The morass into which 'the softly creeping mists' blinded Hammerton also trapped Sir James Colquhoun, the eleventh baronet, who was drowned in December 1873 while returning in an open boat from Inch Conachan, whither he had gone on an annual expedition to shoot deer for the poor on his estate. Among his papers was found a rhymed reflection upon the loch, much of which he himself owned.

'On Lomond's fair sequestered scene,
    Where broadly spreads its lake of blue,
My early days as blest have been
    As poet's fancy ever drew.

Blithe May is blooming fresh and young,
    And songsters chant their pleasing note.
Concealed the branches green among,
    For love hath tuned each warbler's throat.

Far surface of the lake serene,
    Unruffled by a passing sigh,
Reflected as from mirror's sheen
    The landscape's semblance meets the eye.

> Now seems a voice to whisper peace,
> So soothing in its vernal sway.
> And headstrong passion's rule must cease
> Before creation's fair away.
>
> Can e'er again the season bloom
> Those halcyon days when life was new—
> And dissipate the wintry gloom
> That saddens all that meets the view?'

He then proceeded to answer his own question by asserting that there are 'mansions lovelier far', and that 'the Resurrection shall but bring, the Dawn of an Unending Day'; by which time the Goddess, who has little concern with sectarian prophecy, had deserted the good baronet completely.

Lochlomondside and other Poems by John Young was published in 1872. His rhymed comment oddly combines religion and topography.

> 'A Poet-Preacher once, 'tis said,
> When Lomond and her isles lay spread
> Before his genius-flashing eye,
> Loaded the pinions of a sigh,
> Soul-born, with this impassioned cry—
> "O Joy! should it to man be given
> That a Loch Lomond be in Heaven." '

Pondering such a remarkable transformation, we may, with a clear conscience, let the library dust fall back once more upon the volumes of the Victorian rhymsters who hymned the queen of Scottish lochs, and turn to our own century.

For Iain Crichton Smith, Luss village is a symbol of a way of life that has gone for ever.

> 'Such walls like honey and the old are happy
> in morphean air, like goldfish in a bowl.
> Ripe roses trail their margins down a sleepy
> mediaeval treatise on the slumbering soul.

And even the water, fabulously silent,
has no salt tales to tell us, nor make jokes
about the yokel mountains, huge and patient,
that will not court her but read shadowy books.

A world so long departed! In the churchyard
the tilted tombs still gossip, and the leaves
of stony testaments are read by Richard,
Jean and Carol, pert among the sheaves

of unscythed shadows, while the noon day hums
with bees and water and the ghosts of psalms.'

The poet's sense of the transcience of things is expressed
without false sentimentality.

The poets of the cult of the picturesque saw in mountain
scenery grandeur for its own sake. The Victorians were unable to
look on grandeur without investing it with religious significance.
Today grandeur has lost its power to impress romantically; the
use of religion as an artistic response is discredited, and certainty
has been uncertained. So poets now try to see things as things in
themselves. Such was my aim in my own poem, 'A View of Loch
Lomond'.

'Mountains open their hinged reflections on the loch,
and these reflections, pummelled by the wind,
shape and reshape themselves, grow squat or tall,
are bent by shakes of light. We never find
the same place twice. Which is why coloured postcards
that claim to lay the constant on the table
(the camera cannot lie) are popular—
from me to you, a reassuring fable;
what trotting tourists purchase with their wealth;
the image they'd retain if they were able.

But landscape's an evasion of itself.'

7

The Poet and Society

OWEVER does one pass one's time in the country? That sounds the sort of thing a character in a *fin de siècle* post-Wildeian comedy of manners might say. But it is a question I am frequently asked, and I find it difficult to answer, because the mere idea of having to 'pass' one's time appals me.

When I was small time seemed a tedious commodity. There was such a mass of it, and it shifted so slowly. Adults like to sentimentalize about the joys of childhood long after their power of remembering has lost its innocence. Yet before adolescence awakens the senses, life's little gratifications seem so very few and far between—a party the eternity of three whole weeks away, or a visit to the circus after two more Fridays have laboriously crept nearer and nearer—and the long intervening voids are often boring and dreary.

Then suddenly life becomes at once both a prospect of infinite possibility and a lingering sadness. There is the discovery of shadows; music and poetry assume delight; other people cease to be simply convenient or inconvenient filled-in symbols, and sex presents its edgy challenge.

Nowadays, unfortunately, teenagers of the beat generation, newly made aware of life's potentialities at sixteen, seem to have rejected most of them before they achieve their twentieth year. With this rejection, at whatever age it occurs, death begins to set in; much earlier, I think, with the young angries than with my generation of the late 'thirties, many of whom at least carried their idealism and their lust for living through the Second World War. Sex channelled into marriage too often deteriorates to a deadly routine; the seasons no longer ring wild echoes in the blood; the arts, rejected, are powerless to console with their enrichment;

69

leisure means little more than tending vegetables in a garden plot,
or gaping at third-rate variety turns on the 'telly'. It is these
bored people, engulfed by 'the deadly, deadly middle years', who
ask those who refuse to give up the struggle, how one 'passes
one's time' in the country. Bunyan knew about them, and so did
Dante.

> 'Midway the journey of this life I was aware
> That I had strayed into a dark forest,
> And the right path appeared not anywhere.'[1]

Yet there is a way out: the realization that time is not for
passing but for laying hold of and squeezing till only the dry
pith is left. Like Marie Leneru:

'I am haunted by the need to *perfectionner l'instant*, to free each
particle of existence from the heavy weight which causes laziness
to dominate all our actions. Human indifference—that is what
astonishes me most on earth. No one seems to mind that he must
leave, at his death, so many unexplored possibilities that touched
us with their wings, but can now never become us, the best part
of ourselves . . . Wit and goodness and laughter and malice, *la
toilette* and change and noise, one must love all this *because there is
nothing else.*'

Nevertheless, these things are poetry. Poetry is a kind of love;
even satirical poetry in its protecting way. It is, therefore, love that
is lost when indifference kills the poetic response that comes with
adolescence, or else is driven out by organized superstition.

Calvinistic religion has deprived more Scots people of the
power of passionately savouring life than any other single force,
simply by inculcating the belief that the absolute enjoyment
of life militates against the enjoyment of the after-life which
Christian teachings promise. Their imaginative capacity has been
absorbed by dreams of an after-life, and very little imaginative
force has been left over for the life that certainly exists. The small
but intense pleasures which moving, sounding, smelling objects
all around us can constantly give are rejected, until the antennae
registering their changing presences decay from lack of use.

[1] *The Inferno*, translated by Laurence Binyon.

The almost inevitable lack of public interest in the art of poetry today is a kind of inverse reflection of the loss of sensitivity which the chromium-plated plastic-covered everything-cooked-and-ready nature of our civilization has brought about. No poet—not even a very minor one like myself—recognizing the charge put upon him by what Robert Graves calls 'the Goddess', can possibly allow this mass negation of response to pass unchallenged. For it paralyses the receptivity of those who, though not themselves poets, would normally be the poet's audience. Furthermore, it can overwhelm the poet himself.

A contemporary French poet, Patrice de la Tour du Pin, in *The Dedicated Life in Poetry*, has written:

'All things have a living utterance, but many have degraded their song; if one could recapitulate all the movements since birth of those who have degraded their song, one would see how they have dispersed their expressive movements into all the senses and sought self-affirmation, as it were, at the outer surface of the skin; they have manifested themselves in a wrong way, they have not clung to their power of expression as one of their limbs.'

The preservation of that song, and of necessary wholeness, is what du Pin means by 'dedication'. Today the idea of 'dedication' is suspect. Business tycoons talk of being 'dedicated' to their businesses, which means to the task of making money by buying cheap and selling dear. Trade Union leaders think themselves 'dedicated' to the cause of their members, which means to the business of securing higher wages, regardless of the social consequences.

For writers, a too self-conscious 'dedication' has its dangers, the most obvious of which is that too self-consciously dedicated people are apt to become pompous or precious inside their own closed circuit.

Even the major poets spent only a relatively short part of their time writing poetry. In the romantic past, when poetry, with or without the assistance of a private income procured by a family predecessor, was more of a paying business than it is now, poets commonly adopted the Poetic Pose. The nineteenth-century public expected it, and their poets happily provided it.

Wordsworth and Tennyson occasionally shagged their muses

down to exhausted shadows, so that these ladies were reduced to
producing for Wordsworth:

> 'Oh! what's the matter? what's the matter?
> What is't that ails young Harry Gill?
> That evermore his teeth they chatter,
> Chatter, chatter, chatter still?'

and for Lord Tennyson:

> 'The tall masts quiver'd as they lay afloat,
>   The temples and the people and the shore;
> One drew a sharp knife thro' my tender throat
>   Slowly—and nothing more.'

Southey, according to Byron, wrote 'much blank verse and
blanker prose, And more of both than anybody knows'—an
unfair judgment so far as the prose was concerned on the author
of that splendid classic, the *Life of Lord Nelson*. Browning took
tea with the adulating ladies of the Browning Society in the
chaste confines of whose members' drawing-rooms he sought to
explain his deliciously inexplicable obscurities.

In the previous century Burns found a happier way out of
the dilemma by song-repairing, and, in spite of all his trials and
tribulations, probably enjoyed better mental health than either
his idol Shenstone, trivially engaged in erecting grottoes and
follies in the grounds of his estate The Leasowes, or James
Thomson, poet of *The Seasons*, dividing his time between indolent
attention on the Great in their Stately Homes around London
and indolent inattention to the generalities of living alone in his
cottage by the Thames.

Earlier still, divinity kept Donne and Herrick resourcefully
occupied at a time when the basic assumptions of the Christian
religion were more or less universally acceptable. On the other
hand, Milton, who believed wholeheartedly in poetic dedication,
lived a private life of remarkable selfishness and cruelty. Not even
the most sanguine Victorian hymnist could find the image left by
Milton's footprints on the sands of time very encouraging.

The fact of the matter seems to be that a deliberate and
sustained striving after 'sublimity'—of itself a romantic concept

—has often led to posturing, and thus to at least a partial loss of integrity. The man who achieved 'sublimity' most easily and most often in his poetry spent his working life in the Elizabethan theatre, dashing off his masterpieces as and when the practical demands of theatrical life made them seem necessary. The prosiest poets may not always have failed to achieve great poetry from time to time, but they certainly sank to a far lower level of literary degradation than many lesser poets, who lived a full and normal life, allowing their poems to be set down when the overwhelming urge came upon them and for the rest of the time permitting vicarious experience to wash across their sensibilities as chance and circumstance directed.

It is, however, my belief that the posings and posturings, which have been practised since poetry was first recognized as an art, have to some extent represented poets' attempts to equate themselves with the sense of normality of which the attitude of society towards poetry has from time to time deprived them. There have been few poets, at any rate in these islands, whose day-to-day behaviour has not been affected by the degree of normality society has allowed them to assume.

Today the position of the poet in society has no parallel with his position in any previous age.

While the idea of the existence of a society the majority of whose members took a major interest in the literature of their time is, of course, as absurd as the notion that pre-television England was a nest of singing birds now rendered gapingly dumb by the illuminated box which occupies the rallying corner of the living-room, the fact remains that these passionate minorities who supported the arts in previous centuries were numerous enough to enable the poet at least to maintain his material position. Today, that minority is so small and economically weak that the poet must have another job, not in order to be able to occupy himself fully, but to enable him to preserve his integrity.

Poetry has become a pastime rather than a vocation. Yet the poet must somehow come to terms with the conditions which have reduced the expression of poetry to this ancillary level, and at the same time preserve that absolute personal honesty the loss of which renders him unfit to perform the poet's function as a reporter upon experience.

It is difficult to achieve this balance living or working in a

Scottish city; at least, I found it so. Scotland has produced little
memorable urban poetry. One reason for this is that a young
person who may have poetic temperament goes into industry and
almost inevitably becomes involved in what, so far as genuine
dedicated living is concerned, are basically irrelevancies. Some of
these irrelevancies, like the boredom which accompanies the jobs
about eighty per cent of the population has to perform in order
to earn a living, very quickly result in irreparable damage to the
whole apparatus of sensibility. Other irrelevancies, like political
squabbling, are a dispersal of the energy of poetic feeling at what
du Pin calls 'skin level', and the outcome is usually at best
polemical versification, at worst pamphleteering.

Obviously it is essential that a poet today should not only
have experienced urban life, but also that he should be fully
conversant with the personal problems of industrial man. But the
poet must always be able to withdraw. In achieving such a
withdrawal the practical advantages of living in the country are
many. For one thing, it is much easier to construct a working
rationale. The country community retains a far greater sense of
wholeness than do most districts in cities and towns. There is also
a much sharper impingement of the ebb and flow of nature upon
the countryman's consciousness; and, however urbanized the
world may become, ultimately it must always depend on the skills
of the country if it is not to starve.

In the country, of course, one is also faced with the question
of earning a living as well as of making the fullest possible use of
time. The artist needs leisure, and plenty of it. Ideally, as Yeats
suggested, a poet should take his chances with life during the
formative years of late adolescence and early manhood, and then
settle into the life of a country gentleman: walking alone, riding
in company and perhaps swimming and boating. Country pursuits would healthfully utilize his non-creative energies, yet he
would be freed from the urban tangle of irrelevancies to pursue
his calling. Such a life, however, could no longer give a poet
complete satisfaction under existing circumstances, since society
puts little value on the end-product, his poems. No matter how
strongly some may protest that poets should not be privileged in
this or any other way, the fact remains that leisure is indispensable for artistic creation of any kind; a fact which has long been
realized by the Russians, whose creative artists enjoy privileges

far greater than their opposite numbers in Britain or America. Russian artists do not, of course, enjoy the ultimate privilege of allowing their muses to roam untrammelled; but that is another matter.

My own imperfect compromise has been to try to adapt those powers of observation which the pursuit of poetry naturally fosters, to the uses of radio and television, the media of entertainment and communication that the public at large at present find most acceptable. This constantly brings me into contact with people, and ultimately people are all that matter. Furthermore, it does not often involve the use of the written word, and so makes unnecessary the dreary grind of day-to-day journalism. But it does call for constant and severe self-discipline, the maintenance of a well-oiled mental shutter that can at will exclude the fallacious and the phoney from the creative side of consciousness.

The hardest task of all is to keep poetic perception keen and sharp, and to retain the ability to become wholly absorbed, however briefly or infrequently, in the business of creation, despite the foreknowledge that communication—the essential completion of the creative act—is likely to be difficult. In the Victorian hey-day of poetry, Tennyson earned a four-figure income from his work. Today a young poet is lucky if he sells between three or four hundred copies of his 'slim volumes', thereby perhaps earning about twenty pounds. Nevertheless, somehow or other he must resolutely go on writing so long as he has even a single reader, so that the ultimate essential value of creativity may be re-asserted and indifference be baulked of total triumph.

A poem that is a perfect poem, or even just a good poem, creates its own continuing existence and becomes virtually indestructible. It is to me inconceivable that the worst aspects of the purely material values which hold sway today can endure. Sooner or later, at however expensive a level, satiation point must be reached. The ensuing reaction should result in a renewal of interest in the arts, since they alone can provide an extra dimension to living.

8

Our Village

GARTOCHARN, where I have made my home, has almost
no recorded history. The name, which is Gaelic, means
'field of the cairn'. The cairn, which has long since disappeared, probably commemorated nothing more terrible than a
skirmish between two feuding groups of clansmen.

The village grew up in the middle of the parish of Kilmaronock, where Marnock, the holy man after whom the Ayrshire
town of Kilmarnock is also named, must once have had a cell. It
is a village which evolved out of those rhythms of the countryside
that persisted more or less unchanged for more than a thousand
years. Men were born here, learned their fathers' trades, strove
against the seasons to make the fields articulate, mated and
married (often in that order), had children whom they trained in
the age-old routines, and, when at last age crept up on them,
reminisced by smoky fire and draughty candlelight until time
carried them off to join their forefathers beneath the lichened
tombstones in the quiet kirkyard. Life was lived out in semi-
feudal simplicity, with the Big House at the apex of the social
organization.

Though the village as such is only just over a century old, the
way of life which it represents is much older; indeed, the village
was merely a coming together for convenience of the three focal
places: the church, the school and the inn. The Big House stands
in its own park several miles from the village, and in any case
the local laird's titular claim to respect and authority did not
stretch back further than about the middle of the eighteenth
century.

The church, which was put up for the 'Wee Frees', is a low

red sandstone building entirely lacking the airy dignity which characterizes the Georgian parish church a mile along the road, the second on the site and almost within hailing distance of the ruined peel tower of the medieval Catholic bishop's residence. The school stands by a burn. Though it replaced the school beside the parish kirk a century ago, it, too, has outgrown its usefulness and can no longer hold all the young children of the parish. Soon, it will be replaced by a bright and airy school; but the sense of continuity is not likely to be broken.

It is the inn, or hotel as it now calls itself, round which the most obvious signs of past ways are still grouped. For it was originally a coaching inn. Behind the house the stables still stand, dusty and deserted, except when the ponies of local children fill some of the stalls for an occasional weekend hour or two. The windows of the harness-room are broken, and stopped up with damp cardboard. The steps which once led to the hayloft have rotted completely away, and sometimes an owl hoots from the rafters of the coach-house. The tack-room is a coal-shed, the coachman's room a store for empty bottles from the hotel bar.

It was to the rhythm of the horse and the horse-drawn vehicle that the pace of life in this place was long ago adjusted. The motor car speeded up that rhythm, and so helped to shatter a social pattern that in any case had started to disintegrate. The first bus to run from the village was housed in the shed attached to my house, and where I now keep my car. It linked up the village with the urbanized Vale of Leven before the end of the 'twenties. Yet somehow the old pattern persisted up to the end of the Second World War.

Piped water came to the village. The ancient moss-green iron pump in which I acquired an eighth share when I bought my cottage still worked but was no longer in use when I arrived, and soon afterwards suddenly degenerated into a piece of broken, rusty machinery. Bathrooms were built on to agricultural cottages from which the occupants had been moved into gaunt blocks of concrete houses newly put up at one end of the village. The people who replaced them in the old cottages modernized them, joined up the drainage to the new public scheme and threw out dormer windows to make rooms of empty attic spaces, were folk like myself who had found town life intolerable; commuters who depended on cars to carry them everywhere, and whose arrival brought about the introduction of amenities the town-dweller accepts without question.

There was, for instance, the coming of electricity. It was the establishment of the North of Scotland Hydro-Electric Board that made it possible for water-generated electricity to be brought to Gartocharn, and to hundreds of other Scottish villages. There were, of course, delays and difficulties. Some people refused to have poles on their property, and the negotiating officials did not always display understanding for a point of view different from their own; materials were still in short supply; poles stood unlaced by the vital veins of wire for what seemed to us, going through the Victorian labour of filling oil lamps and stoves and trimming wicks, like a long age. Worst of all were those final weeks when, with our own houses wired and waiting, we looked out upon the linked-up poles in the village street, uncertain when the power would come to us. Eventually it did come, and the boon and the wonder of electricity, which we had grown up in Glasgow unthinkingly to accept, was experienced with all the re-discovered freshness of its first invention.

At first it was apt to be a little erratic. The supply had to be carried over Highland mountains on overhead wires, and until our local distributing system was duplicated a high wind or a heavy fall of snow could plunge us into sudden darkness. Groping for candles and the discarded paraffin lamps, we felt a strange grudge against the benefactor, science, which, for all its cleverness, could yet be so disconcertingly unreliable.

Then came street lights. The cars drove silence from country days; the electric street lamps drove the enveloping thickness from country nights.

The laird sold up, and died a few months later. Part of his estate was bought by a timber contractor, who immediately put up an aggressive fence across the main carriageway; part of it by a city property dealer who kept the Big House empty except for a caretaker, for almost a decade, hoping to get a much higher price than he paid for it. Farmers bought the farms which their families had formerly tenanted, and began to improve their property themselves. Little corners with hedgerows and lanes and thickets that had been only the laird's concern and were now nobody's property fell into overgrown neglect.

It was all part of an inevitable process of which I myself was necessarily an agent. Death duties undermined the long security of Big House rule. The failure of members of local authorities in Scotland to realize that it could be cheaper to modernize old cottages than to build new barracks threatened the very survival of the little houses. Had not enthusiastic townsmen taken over these little houses, modernized them and reared families in them, the wrench with the past would have been worse than it has been.

But many of the changes were inescapable. The horse has almost disappeared from the fields, and the tractor has taken its place. Every year more cars are parked round the hotel in which their touring occupants are eating. The four white miles of road on either side of the village that had for centuries buffered its unhurried ways with isolation have been reduced to insignificance. The railhead at Balloch, the link with Glasgow, has been electrified. The future of our village, and others like it, seems to hold alarming possibilities. Yet, like most human activities, change can, and sometimes should be, controlled in the interests of the majority.

In the first flush of idealism which animated many people weary of destruction towards the close of the Second World War, there was devised a plan whereby the Government should protect by law a number of areas whose natural loveliness could not be despoiled without loss to the nation. One of these proposed National Park areas was Loch Lomond, and the area of one mile around its shores. Several of the National Parks have come into existence, but so far all of them have been in England. Nearly twenty years after this admirable plan was first mooted the most famous loch in the world is still unprotected, and, subject only to the consent of the Secretary of State for Scotland, the area round about it may at any moment be built upon either for private profit or to gratify the whim of some dominating representative of local bumbledom.

So far as Gartocharn is concerned, the damage has not been as bad as might have been expected. Other Scottish villages have had to endure much worse. In our village three featureless double-storeyed blocks of houses have been put up without regard to the fact that they are quite out of keeping with their surroundings, and in defiance of the not unreasonable supposition that buildings of no architectural distinction should not be put up in proposed National Park areas.

But there have been worse threats. Some of our bumblers

have actually toyed with the idea of making Gartocharn an overspill area for Glasgow. More absurd still, a band of business men have proposed that they should be allowed to build, for their private profit, a new town on the Stockiemuir, which overlooks Loch Lomond. In Sir Patrick Abercrombie's long-term plan for the district this area is shown as one which should at all costs be kept free of 'development', and preserved as a recreational area for the nation.

To me it seems another sign of the decline of Scotland that Loch Lomondside should still be legally unprotected. To some, however, my attitude may seem reactionary. The fact of the matter is that the average Scot cares little or nothing about the land that is his heritage. For this state of affairs—worse than ever before— the planners must take some share of the blame. Their favourite word, 'development', bemuses many people. In my dictionary it is defined as 'a gradual unfolding or growth: evolution'. But as used in some planning circles—and the average planner is as average as the generality making up the rank and file of any other pro- fession or trade—it has come to carry with it the automatic suggestion of improvement. If a block of town slum property is demolished, and a block of modern flats put up in its place, that is development the worthiness of which no one would dispute. In such a case the definition is properly realized. But the concept of the so-called inevitability of development is being resorted to increasingly to justify such acts of official bumbling as the knock- ing down of an historic peel tower in the middle of a Glasgow housing scheme (instead of making it into a linking feature with the past, of which the residents would have been proud), or the destruction of the mansion house of David Dale, the distinguished Glaswegian (to make way for an urgently essential children's playground, which, five years after the demolition, was still not in being). In cases like these clearly planning is being used as a cover-word for stupid political prejudice.

In other quarters of Scottish bumbledom the idea has found currency that to 'develop', even if the resulting growth be can- cerous, is to move with the times. Moving with the times all too often means jettisoning irreplaceable buildings, or sacrificing much-admired beauty spots, for the sake of shoving up a few more ill-sited, mediocre-looking houses which could and should have been put up somewhere else.

Edinburgh: Princes Street from Calton Hill

Drawn by J. Ewbank, engraved by W. H. Lizars, published 1825

Edinburgh: the Old Town from Princes Street

It is doubly unfortunate in this connection that the average architectural standard of Scottish post-Second World War housing is about the lowest in Western Europe. In Scotland we have built first and foremost for cheapness, and have got only what we paid for. Were more economic rents charged by local councils for their houses, our new housing estates would not need to be so drably mediocre in appearance.

Needless to say, I am not suggesting that we do not need new houses. Scotland, particularly Glasgow, has an appallingly low standard of housing, and no energy should be spared in pulling down the city slums and building new and worthier homes. The Gorbals redevelopment scheme is an example of the imaginative approach, and there are similar examples of merit in other parts of Scotland which show up the inferiority of the general architectural level of the majority of new housing schemes. Buildings last, or should last, for a long time, and can become a reproach against the judgment of their builders and promoters. Conditions of expediency should never be allowed to overrule considerations which relate, not to the life-span of one or two generations, but to the generations of Scotland's boundless future. We criticize severely, and properly so, the unhygienic sprawl of hideous and inadequately designed building which accompanied the rapid industrial development of Central Scotland during the nineteenth century. Our ancestors worked in well-meaning haste. If we are not careful we may fall into the far more heinous error of repeating their misguided proliferations in our modern way, this time deliberately, under the sacred banner of planning.

PART TWO

. . . and Abroad

9

Glasgow—capital de facto

ONE of the pleasant aspects of the life I lead is the amount of travelling I am able to do at the expense of other people. In the decade during which I have been living in Gartocharn I have travelled the length and breadth of Scotland, interviewing people, exploring the present, or striving to unravel the past. There is no better way to get to know intimately a country or the force and foibles of its inhabitants.

'Up there,' said a faded Dickensian colleague, waving his hand in the direction of Edinburgh Castle, 'our own kings and queens once lived. They can't take that away from us'.

'They', of course, were the English, and the remark harmlessly illustrates both our Scots sense of inferiority, and the tenacity of Scots pride. Edinburgh has plenty of tenacity, and, in the eyes of some Glaswegians at any rate, more than its share of pride. But in spite of Edinburgh's capital status let us first take a look at Glasgow and the countryside around it, for Glasgow has played a bigger part in the shaping of modern Scotland than Edinburgh, and is, besides, the city where I was born.

Many writers have recorded their memories of a Glasgow childhood. For some, it was dancing in the streets and hectic games round chalk-marked sour-smelling close-mouths; for others, it was junior gang fights and the stale odour of poverty that hangs about so many tenement back-yards. The best accounts of this kind of Glasgow upbringing—those which glow with the lustre of enthusiasm—are admirably done; the worst—those which labour a class grudge—have the depressing influence of the cold-mutton-and-kitchen-sink school of Scottish short-story writers. There are other aspects of Glasgow's life than slums and razor-slashing, and I confess to harbouring some resentment against those who would have us believe that the only genuine ingredients of a Glasgow portrait must be shit and seduction.

I was born in a terrace-house nursing home among Charles Wilson's patrician mansions, built in 1854 on the heights of the Woodlands district. Plenty of people still move about its stately terraces and circuses; in all probability more people than were ever there before. But the purposes for which these dignified town mansions were put up have altered, and houses that were once gracious homes have now been reduced to providing accommodation for consulates, doctors' consulting-rooms, nursing homes, private hotels and business offices. The outward shells still stand; but, inside, elaborately ornamented plaster-ceilings bisected by partitions, and carved mantelpieces mutilated or smoothed over with hardboard façades, survive only as the stranded flotsam of an age of opulence that has for ever receded.

Nineteenth-century Glasgow—and most of Glasgow as it is today went up in the latter part of the nineteenth century—is a dirty, decrepit city full of dreary tenements that look as if they might at any moment crumble where they stand—as some of them do!—and fantastically ornate public buildings. Yet for all that it seems to me to possess more indigenous character than any other British city of comparable size. A claim of this sort may seem too facile a generalization.

How can any city really be said to possess character? How much of what is called a city's character is really a projection from the minds of writers who have lived their formative years in it? And what, in any case, does one mean by character?

When I was living in London I used to think a lot about Glasgow's character, always with a feeling of nostalgia. One nervously cold night in 1943 I climbed out of the London cellar where I had been sheltering during an air-raid. Back in my top-flat bed-sitting-room, I tried to analyse the not uncritical affection which I felt for the place, as a gesture of thanksgiving for still being alive.

Earlier in the day, on a cold blue afternoon, I had watched the pigeons nid-nodding and strutting to and fro across Trafalgar Square. Suddenly, for no obvious reason, they rustled into mass flight, almost as if they had been prompted by my silent longing for the North.

'Two purple pigeons circle a London square
as darkness blurs and smudges the shadowless light
of a winter evening. I pause on the pavement and stare
at the restless flutter of wings as they gather flight,
like rustling silk, and move out to meet the night.

And my restless thoughts migrate to a Northern city—
fat pigeons stalking the dirty, cobbled quays,
where a sluggish river carries the cold self-pity
of those for whom life has never flowed with ease,
from a granite bridge to the green Atlantic seas;

the bristling, rough-haired texture of Scottish manners;
the jostling clatter of crowded shopping streets
where lumbering tramcars squeal as they take sharp corners;
the boosy smell from lounging pubs that cheats
the penniless drunkard's thirst with its stale deceits:

where my heart first jigged to the harsh and steady sorrow
of those for whom mostly the world is seldom glad,
who are dogged by the flat-heeled, footpad steps of
        tomorrow;
for whom hope is a dangerous drug, an expensive fad
of the distant rich, or the young and lovesick mad:

where chattering women in tearooms, swaddled with furs,
pass knife-edged gossip like cakes, and another's skirt
is unstitched with sharp words, and delicate, ladylike slurs
are slashed on the not-quite-nice or the over-smart,
and smoke to the eyes is a hazy Turkish hurt.

I remember Glasgow, where sordid and trivial breed
from the same indifferent father: his children side
with the mother whose sour breasts taught them first to feed
on her hot, caressing hates that sear and divide,
or swell the itching, distended bladder of pride.

Yet my guilty sneers are the tossed-down, beggar's penny
which the goaded heart throws out, in vain, to procure
the comfortable forgetfulness of the many
who lie in content's soft arms, and are safe and sure
in the fabled Grecian wanderers' lotus-lure;

who forget the sullen glare of the wet, grey skies,
and the lashing Northern wind that flicks the skin
like a whip, where poverty's dull and listless eyes
are pressed to the window, hearing the friendly din
of the party, watching the lights and laughter within.

But oh, I cannot forget, so I wait and wonder,
how long will the thinly dividing window hold,
how long will the dancing drown the terrible anger
of those, the unwanted, who peddle their grief in the cold,
wrapped in their own despair's thick and unkindly fold?

Yet evil is no pattern of places
varied, like terraces, from town to town,
A city's charms and individual graces
are but the sculptor's bleak and basic stone,
the photographic face without a frown.

The wound is in this bewildered generation,
tossed on the swollen, analytic mood,
its compass-point no longer veneration
of that lost God who rewarded the simple and good,
vivid and real, now, only in childhood.

For we, the children of this uncertain age,
breathing its huge disasters and sad airs,
have seen that our warm, humanitarian rage
is impotent to soothe war's animal fears,
can never quell the lonely exile's tears.

So the heart, like a wounded seabird, hungers home
to muffled memories on faintly-beating wings
which once soared over history's surge and foam,
to that calm shore where each new hero flings
the careful stone that fades in slow, concentric rings.'

There are those who maintain that places are of themselves of
little importance, and that only states of mind should provide a
poet with his raw material. With that view I entirely disagree.
Places are the mirrors of people, and as such very much the

proper study of mankind. Furthermore, savouring and contrasting the atmospheres of places can of itself be a delicious minor pleasure. The atmosphere of Glasgow is as distinctive as the atmosphere of Paris, Amsterdam or Copenhagen. It is, of course, a far less civilized atmosphere; indeed, there are many who find it almost barbaric in its crude intensity. But the intensity is, or was, unmistakably there, and it is not necessary to have been brought up a Gorbals dead-end kid to be able to savour its quality.

Glasgow's intensity reflects neither glory in learning nor the hedonistic enjoyment of life, but the dour, determined making of money. Even today, when it is more or less impossible to make any, the habit persists, almost savagely. Unlike their Continental peers, however, Glasgow's nineteenth-century merchant princes did not know what to do with their money. They spent, but often eccentrically rather than wisely.

Her public buildings proudly proclaim this curious 'lost' aspect of Glasgow's intensity. Most of them may be architecturally indefensible according to modern taste, but at least they have the flamboyance and the assurance of men conscious of their own solid worth and determined to assert their belief in themselves in what they conceived to be a fitting manner. To them, the styles of ancient Greece and Rome—sunny styles that demand the sweeping light of the Mediterranean to illuminate their dignity and caress their detail—were the harvest of a primitive past that could fittingly be copied to adorn a sooty sandstone warehouse, or, mixed with a touch of borrowed Gothic, used to grace a block of offices or a railway station, all of which, in the space of one short winter, would inevitably be encased in a more or less permanent coating of grime.

Where else in the Western world can one find so gloriously and whole-hearted a piece of inappropriate idea-pinching as in William Young's Municipal Buildings, put up between 1883 and 1889 at a cost of £520,000? So incredible is this achievement that I sometimes wonder if Young was really a man with a gargantuan sense of humour, who, by surrounding Glasgow's douce Victorian City Fathers with a replica of the sensuous trappings of an Italian Renaissance nobleman, was not, in fact, perpetrating a monstrous joke, the echoes of which still continue to sound? I hope this was so, for it is the kindest view one can take.

On Glasgow's tenements, so marked a feature of the city, no

such niceties were wasted. Much praise has been lavished on those who built Glasgow of grey sandstone. The fact is, however, that sandstone has withstood the corrosive atmosphere of an industrial town much less satisfactorily than brick would probably have done. If Glasgow's Victorian captains of industry ever experienced occasional qualms about the insanitary housing conditions of their workers—a doubtful proposition, since their social sense was as undeveloped as their architectural taste—these qualms could quickly have been allayed by the provision of charitable institutions and of churches built in a style mainly borrowed from medieval Germany.

The zeal and intensity with which their architects magpied other people's creativeness never ceases to astonish me. Is there anywhere a more intensely absurd building than Glasgow's Kelvingrove Art Gallery? So firmly did the passion for ornamentation burn in the bosom of its architect, that scarcely a surface large enough to carry a decorative device was left unadorned.

Strictures upon Glasgow's Victorian rebuilders can easily become unrealistic, since we are necessarily judging their achievements with senses which cannot easily be attuned to their code of values. It is, however, frequently perturbing to hear prominent mid-twentieth-century Glaswegians speaking of their city as if it were Rome, or Copenhagen, or Vienna, instead of, in the words of Douglas Percy Bliss, 'a relic of the carboniferous age'.

On the few Glasgow occasions when intensity and good taste did manage to combine, the results were reasonably happy. The architects who united these qualities, however, were rarely native Glaswegians. Certainly, Sir William Bruce, who built the Merchants' House in 1665, only the steeple of which now survives; William Adam, who built Pollok House in 1752; and his son Robert, who put up the Trades House in 1791; had, none of them, any natal connection with the city. One of those who had, David Hamilton, was responsible for the Royal Exchange (now the Stirling Library) in 1830, and for the Western Club. Alexander (Greek) Thomson celebrated his Hellenic convictions with striking effect in a number of Glasgow churches, of which St Vincent Street U.P. Church (1857–9) is the best of those that survive, though altered in use, and in Great Western Terrace (1870). More recently, Charles Rennie Mackintosh raised his finest monument, the Glasgow School of Art, on the top of Garnethill. When it was opened in 1909 it was a splendid and exciting achievement, the first Scottish breakaway from the Victorian tradition of borrowing. It is now seen to be a European corner- stone of the new school of architectural functionalism which subsequently developed in Scandinavia and America.

Mackintosh's intensity is reflected in the way he forgot about the limitations of those who might come to study in his school, and in his contemptuous disregard for the disorderly assortment of buildings which surrounded his site. Wide, light studios, such as no art school of the time in Britain possessed, take up the main floor, though for half the year the light that pours through them is diffuse and grey.

Today Mackintosh's triumphant assertion of his principles stands on its hill-top, surrounded at the bottom of steep slopes by shops, many of which are filled with articles of poor design. Though painters and sculptors still learn the technique of their arts on Garnethill, the Glasgow School of Art has now become principally a design centre.

I, for one, welcome this long overdue insistence on the importance of good design. For far too long Scotland has relied almost solely upon her heavy industries; but the old heavy- industry criterion of 'Does it work well?' cannot be the sole criterion where the products of the new light industries are concerned. For the Danes, the Italians, and many other European manufacturers, also ask themselves, 'Does it look good?' and insist on being able to provide an affirmative answer.

It is not only through its buildings, however, that Glasgow proclaims its intensity. Throughout its history it has put itself passionately on the side of the forces of common sense. It was, for instance, strong for the Reformation, a movement which may have had many deplorable consequences for Scotland but which at the time must have seemed to uphold common sense against a more corrupt illogicality. Glasgow also stood firmly behind the Covenant. It was in the cathedral of Glasgow that the Reverend Alexander Henderson uttered those words of defiance that forced the issue between King Charles, with his illogical belief in the divine right of kings, and the leaders of the Church of Scotland, with their singularly down-to-earth attitude, to conflict and climax.

It might be argued that in opposing the Union of the Parliaments in 1707 Glasgow for once deserted the cause of common sense; but there are many who would maintain that Incorporating Union, such as was forced upon Scotland, rather than Federal Union, as proposed by Andrew Fletcher of Saltoun, was a defeat for common sense. In spite of the strong Celtic strain present, even in the character of the eighteenth-century Glaswegian, Glasgow remained loyal to common sense and the stolid house of Hanover in the final test-by-arms of 1745.

Professor R. H. Tawney has demonstrated that the revolt against the Catholic Church in Europe was not unconnected with the creation of trading conditions more favourable to the merchants of the expanding Hanseatic ports. A Scottish parallel can be drawn, for Glasgow's concentration on commerce has been intensely single-minded. First, there was the trade in tobacco, pioneered in the seventeenth century and developed to its height of prosperity in the eighteenth. The American War of Independence brought many of the wealthy tobacco lords down in ruin. In a remarkably short space of time the cotton trade, again dependent on America, had built up new and greater Glasgow fortunes. The American Civil War rocked Glasgow's prosperity even more violently than the War of Independence had done; but, by the 1870s, heavy industry had already laid the foundations of Glasgow's third era of prosperity. Steel, shipbuilding, the making of locomotives; these and other similar industries made Glasgow the sixth city of Europe, and built up fortunes which lasted until the world of the nineteenth century was shattered by the First World War.

All three eras brought forth men who went about the business of producing material wealth and amassing personal fortunes with a passionate intensity which it is difficult not to respect. Many of the tobacco lords had streets in nineteenth-century Glasgow named after them as a tribute of admiration by their successors.

The personal intensity that made Glasgow's expansion possible in the eighteenth and nineteenth centuries was, so to speak, a product of internal combustion. The leaders and developers often struggled through the limited schooling which was all that was considered generally necessary, and from poor and humble beginnings raised up large businesses and substantial fortunes. They were Scotsmen, these men who laid the economic foundations of their country's fortunes, and brusquely proud of being so. Nor was there any shortage of recruits to maintain their ranks.

A man who conceives the wish to build a large business today is likely to be considered a sad case of anti-social behaviourism. Certainly it is almost impossible to amass even a small fortune by trading. No doubt both these factors have helped to account for the fact that much of the dour intensity has gone out of Scotland's industrialists. The average Scots industrialist of the mid-twentieth century is often a pale replica of his grandfather, obstinately clinging to ideas that in his grandfather's day were new and adventurous. But the climate of political opinion is no longer kind to initiative. Crippling taxation and the wearisome strain of striving to maintain labour relations which preserve some measure of economic sense are apt to dishearten passionate individualists. So more and more Scottish firms that have been run by families for generations are every year swallowed up by much larger English or American commercial whales foraging the same competitive seas.

With the fire gone out of his belly, and world demand for the products of heavy industry sadly shrunk, the Scots industrialist now finds himself constantly being lambasted for failing to provide more jobs. With his traditional addiction to common sense he could reasonably argue that he fails to see why he should be attacked for not doing what his ancestors were able to do but he himself may not, and at the same time be attacked for failing to create new opportunities for employment. Whatever the reason, it is to big English firms, anxious to expand and large enough to be able to absorb the extra transport costs often involved bringing in raw materials and carrying out Scottish-made goods to the main markets of Britain, and to American firms seeking a European foothold, that Scotland has now to look for some improvements in the pattern of its economy. Unfortunately, branch factories, whether British or American, are obviously vulnerable whenever the winds of world trade take a chilling turn. Permanent vulnerability is perhaps the price that has to be paid for the suppression of the old Scots individualism.

Individuality allied to cautious conservatism is to be found in the make-up of the ordinary Glaswegian. Much of his thinking is decidedly old-fashioned. For instance, he still takes the view that not only is the motor car a plaything of the idle rich but that it is a worthy object for scowling defiance. Thus, Glaswegians have the reputation of being the worst jay-walkers in Europe. Citizens who plunge recklessly into a thick stream of flowing traffic, exuberantly zigzagging their way from bumper to bumper and daring drivers with hostile glares to knock them down, would, in most Continental towns, be booked as dangerous nuisances, and in most English cities be seriously injured or killed. Yet in Glasgow a surprisingly high proportion of jay-walkers escape unscathed from their foolhardy exploits. To Glaswegians jay-walking does not apparently seem a dangerous pastime. Their forefathers crossed the roads at will before them, and they themselves see no reason why they should make concessions merely because traffic conditions have changed.

Glaswegians have also retained their individuality and their intensity in the matter of drinking. The workers' traditional drink is still a pint of beer followed by a chaser, or small whisky. This combination, in Glasgow almost as inevitable as ham-and-eggs, is, when repeated, a good deal more dangerous. So much so that Glasgow drinking is still largely a business for men only, a state of affairs which not even the teenage co-ed teds have materially altered.

Statistics for drunkenness in Glasgow show a marked decrease over the last century. First and foremost this reflects improved social conditions, though possibly also the decline in personal intensity (in this respect at least not unwelcome). Though Glaswegians no longer rot themselves with over-drinking to drown the miseries of poverty, affluent drinking has produced a new and more serious social menace, since it involves innocent people. The number of drunken drivers of cars has increased startlingly in recent years. In most European countries the police have power to charge any driver whose blood is found to contain a percentage of alcohol higher than that which would be present after the consumption of a single glass of sherry. Drunken drivers are very properly treated as irresponsible criminals, and discouraged from repeating their anti-social behaviour by imprisonment, a heavy fine and suspension of their driving licence. In some countries second offenders are banned from driving for life. But in Glasgow, as in most parts of Scotland, the menace of the drinking car-driver is not taken seriously. It cannot be taken seriously, because the police have insufficient powers to deal with it, and the law of the land treats the small percentage of major offenders who alone can be caught under its inadequate provisions with misplaced leniency. Any night, outside any public house, rows of parked cars advertise the fact that their drivers are happily lowering their responsiveness, secure in the knowledge that, unless they reduce themselves to obvious incapacity, the law cannot touch them.

In most other respects, however, the Glasgow man is self-conscious about making an exhibition of himself. He will allow himself to be outrageously put upon in shop or restaurant rather than create a scene. He loathes carrying flowers, and, as an anonymous shrewd observer once remarked, hates to have to blow his child's nose in a bus. He is undemonstrative, and, according to the cartoon humorists, a singularly off-hand lover. If taxed with the comparatively poor standard of cooking practised in his city, his reply would probably be that he eats to live and does not live to eat, a naïve evasion of the fact that there is never any justification for doing anything badly, and that good eating is elsewhere widely regarded as a highly civilized minor pleasure. His diet is more starchy than that of his English counterpart, and his consumption of biscuits is the highest in these islands. In spite of the rise in his standards of living since the Second World War, his traditional high tea has not been displaced. It is particularly noticeable that although Glasgow has had its share of espresso coffee-bars and new teak-fronted restaurants in the 'fifties, many of their owners have found that the conservative and limited tastes of the customers soon forced them to abandon their Continental notions and come down to the tea-and-bun or fish-and-chip level.

The Glaswegian's hobby is football, which he follows with the devotional fervour his ancestors reserved for religious controversy. So intense is this fervour, indeed, that warfare does not seem to lie far below the surface of feeling. On certain lamentable occasions it has, in fact, broken out.

The Glasgow man is not, on the whole, interested in culture. His favourite theatrical fare is pantomime, but pantomime far removed from the ancient Roman entertainment which was a gruelling test of a single actor's skill in diverse characterization. Nor has Glasgow pantomime anything to do with the troubles of Harlequin and the other related characters who featured in popular Renaissance pantomime entertainment. Glasgow pantomime is an illogical locally flavoured mixter-maxter of slapstick comedy, catchy tunes and leg-kicking, held together by a few slender threads extracted from a foreign fairy-tale. The Principal Boy (paradoxically a leggy girl) always gets the Principal Girl in the end, while the 'baddy' goes down to his inevitable tragicomic end. Pantomime is the Glaswegian's *Everyman*, in which the belief that right will always triumph over wrong is annually reasserted in different pretty trappings. Many other cities stage pantomime for children during the Christmas season. In Glasgow a spectacular pantomime is the principal theatrical event of the year, and adults as well as children keep it running for about five months.

The overt religious significance of Glasgow's 'morality' pantomimes is the more curious, since Glasgow is not predominantly a Christian city. About a quarter of its adult population maintain regular church connections, though half as many again make use of the Church to celebrate life's terminal events, or for marriages in between. Nevertheless, a front of total belief is solemnly preserved, and the stranger who finds himself alone in Glasgow on the Sabbath had better be equipped to amuse himself and be prepared to eat in an expensive hotel or go hungry.

Glasgow's atavistic Calvinism does not keep the shop windows in darkness, and one rewarding Sabbath pleasure is to watch Glaswegians walking up and down the main streets of their city, dressed a little awkwardly in their Sunday best and shop-peering like creatures in an aquarium.

The individuality of the Scot is still reflected in his features, and it is usually possible to tell a Scot's face, whether its owner be Lowlander or Highlander. Glasgow is, *de facto*, the capital of Scotland's Gaelic community. Today, more than twenty thousand Gaels have their homes in the city. Anciently, Glasgow owed its foundation to Lady Lochow, an ancestor of the present family of Argyll, and the Celtic influence (linguistically as well as sportatively) has always been strong. It is, indeed, to the strong mixture of Gaelic blood in the Glaswegian's veins that his dogged intensity has usually been attributed.

I do not think that the average Glasgow man-in-the-street—

if such a drearily uniform creature exists!—could be described as handsome. Two basic main types of male face are to be found in Glasgow's streets; the long, mournful-looking introspective Highland face, and the rounder more extrovert face of the competent Lowlander. Most faces are not, of course, straight-forward basic types. The face of many a Clydeside shipyard worker is often basically Highland in structure, but later Lowland generations have etched in dourness and determination, reflecting the Clydesider's traditional (but now fast-waning) pride in good craftsmanship, which was probably originally a transplanted Highland quality.

What of the average Glasgow woman? She could perhaps best be described as homely. Highland girls share to some extent that bird-like beauty of feature which characterizes the Irish colleen. But Lowland girls are more often notable for what Stevenson called 'plain country faces'. Generations of urbanization have not made the Glasgow female face any less plain.

But faces behind glass windows do not reveal all there is to know about variations in regional character. Speech plays as important a part as the face itself. The Scots tongue is fighting its last-ditch battle for survival in the slums of Glasgow. It has long since shed its court finery, and worn out even its wholesome eighteenth-century homespun. Now, happed in shawls and tatters, its vowel sounds flattened, its consonants elided, it skulks around school playgrounds in the more overcrowded districts of Glasgow, doggedly resisting extermination either by school-master's belt or by legislation from St Andrew's House. Yet, for all its toughness, the Scots that does survive in Glasgow is a poor, bloodless thing; a clinging-together of vowel and accent now, its distinctive words almost totally abandoned in favour of mis-pronounced English or American slang. The English that is replacing it is still an uneasy usurper, though among middle-class Glaswegians it has held undisputed, if mispronounced, sway for more than a century.

More rude things have been said and written about Glasgow than about any other European city. Many of these harsh judgments are probably at least partially true; but Glaswegians obstinately refuse to believe them. They regard 'knocking' Glasgow as a popular journalistic pastime, given encouragement by McArthur's novel *No Mean City*, McLeish's play *The Gorbals'*

Story and Bliss's ballet *Miracle in the Gorbals*. Before very long the Gorbals will be of no further use as the most appropriate European setting for novels or plays about sordid overcrowding, for Glasgow's scheme to redevelop the area will include work by some of Scotland's most distinguished architects; work which will make the new Gorbals one of the city's show-piece districts.

Nowadays no one is likely seriously to give the toast: 'Here's tae us. Wha's like us,' though many Glaswegians still privately hold the belief that they have few equals. Among professional people there still persists a strain of anti-semitism, which manifests itself, for instance, in the exclusion of Jews from Glasgow's oldest golf club and from the Trades' House. Some older people still harbour a strong antipathy to Roman Catholicism. Allied to this is a marked distrust of foreigners, particularly 'thae trashy, bleezin' French-like folk'. The younger generation, being less concerned with sectarian religion and more widely travelled, seems unlikely to perpetuate these prejudices.

But Glasgow's parochialism does allow it to perpetuate the myth of its alleged superiority over Edinburgh, and one much-admired Glasgow journalist devotes a considerable amount of his professional energy to keeping this myth alive.

The intensity of Glasgow does, however, reflect itself in some ways which deserve whole-hearted praise. The old Highland traditional hospitality has been adapted to suit Glasgow's individuality, and the warmth of the welcome given to strangers has an honest straightforward quality quite its own. Glaswegians have no 'side' and are impatient with people who stand upon social pretension. The intensity of their directness and their traditional addiction to the common-sense view may not have allowed very many of them to become distinguished diplomats, but at a more ordinary level these qualities have endeared them to the people of other countries, particularly once-subject countries where any suggestion of patronage is bitterly resented.

Glasgow is one of the most fortunate of European cities in that round rather more than half its circumference lies some of the loveliest countryside in these islands. As the guide-books have it, twenty minutes by car from the centre of the city will take the traveller West to Loch Lomond and the Firth of Clyde, North towards Stirling and the Highlands and South-West into Ayrshire.

The Firth of Clyde was developed soon after Henry Bell's *Comet* had opened up the possibility of making the journey to and from the coast in a single day. Earlier travellers had to depend on hired wherries, and, once afloat, were more or less at the mercy of wind and tide. But the rapid development of the steamboat during the 1820s and 1830s began a rush for sites on which to build those villas which still ribbon the Cowal shores, a rush which reached its height in the 1870s. Hitherto, places like Dunoon and Rothesay had been little more than Gaelic-speaking clachans, the church and the manse the only buildings which did not have thatched roofs. The pre-steamboat-age travellers had difficulty in talking to the natives because of the language barrier, and difficulty in getting provisions, most of which they had to bring with them in hampers. But by the middle of the nineteenth century shops had been built for residential holiday-makers, and the Highland clachans had become prosperous semi-Lowland towns and villages.

The towns and villages on the Firth of Clyde were thus very much the product of the same social circumstances which produced the stately homes of Glasgow. Since the end of the First World War places like Hunters Quay and Innellan have altered no less startlingly in character than the city whose successful men of business brought them into being.

In the between-the-wars period houses from which an Edwardian owner had daily departed throughout the summer season in his carriage and pair to catch the city steamer, and been met again in the evening, his day's work done, had changed hands, and were being rented by the month as a means of livelihood. It was mainly middle-class Glasgow families who took these holiday houses. But since the Second World War a further change has occurred. The Glasgow families who would once have gone contentedly 'doon the watter' (that delightfully laconic description of the journey down the Clyde devised by the Victorian working man) now go farther afield, and the Clyde holiday resorts have become increasingly dependent upon visitors from other parts, mainly the North of England. These new-style Clyde-coast holiday-makers come, not for a month, but by car for a few days or by coach for a week or fortnight. Many of them are accustomed to the bright lights and rackety bustle of the large English seaside resorts, and are becoming increasingly insistent that the resorts on the Clyde shall cater for their tastes. This, in many cases, the Clyde places are unable, or unwilling, to do.

Most of the Clyde-coast resorts depend solely on tourism for their livelihood, yet they do not attract enough visitors for the provision of entertainments and amenities on the scale of the English resorts to be an economic possibility. Dunoon, whose Town Council recently built an exciting-looking contemporary hall containing a theatre, several assembly rooms and a licensed restaurant, soon found that the returns from the letting of the hall outside the short summer season, and the off-season profits from the restaurant, were not sufficient to prevent their enterprise turning into something of a burden. On the other hand, many of the Clyde resorts have resolutely refused even to consider providing the sort of amenities to be found at Blackpool, Southend or Clacton, on the grounds that those who come to Scotland should not want sophisticated entertainment but ought to be content to enjoy what nature has obligingly provided. I have every sympathy with this point of view; but unfortunately it can too easily be turned into an excuse for justifying the resurrection of the latent Scots hostility towards tourism, and could become merely proof that the customer who stays away refuses to recognize that he is wrong.

The holiday resorts along the Ayrshire coast do not have to make so much effort to attract tourists, for Burns has done much of their advertising for them. It is, indeed, Burns rather than Scott who should be regarded as the founder of the tourist industry in Scotland. Within five years of his death, the Words-worths had visited the scenes of Burns's later life, and at his grave Wordsworth had written:

'I mourned with thousands, but as one
More deeply grieved, for He was gone
Whose light I hailed when first it shone,
And showed my youth
How Verse may build a princely throne
On humble truth.'

Since 1881 the cottage at Alloway in which Burns was born has been preserved as a memorial, and alongside it a museum has been built. Like nearly everything else connected with the Burns cult, a visit to this combined memorial is likely to embarrass the sensitive visitor who has a sincere interest in literature. The cottage, with its tiny rooms and byre leading off the living-room, breathes that over-varnished, antiseptic air of artificial preservation which is probably inevitable if old buildings of this humble sort are to be kept standing. It is an aroma that can be found in the cottage birthplaces of many great men, and if sometimes it seems difficult to sense their presence in surroundings from which the smell of reality has so obviously receded, we may console ourselves by remembering that their achievement tells us far more about their personalities than the mere furniture of their early lives.

Nevertheless, relics, letters and manuscripts can be so arranged and catalogued that an inquiring visitor who moves systematically through a museum of this sort is made to feel that he has, so to say, experienced a well-illustrated biography of the person commemorated. The cottage birthplace most like that of Burns is the little white house at Odense, in Denmark, where Hans Christian Andersen was born. Like Burns, Andersen is regarded in his own country as being its greatest literary figure; like Burns, too, Andersen has achieved a world-wide reputation, and his works have been translated into many languages.

There is a further similarity in that behind the birthplace at Odense a museum has been built. But there the similarity ends. The visitor to Hans Andersen's birthplace moves round rooms in which the mementoes of the writer's life are chronologically arranged. In the official guide-book these objects are skilfully used as the threads round which is woven a clear and concise account of Andersen's life. In the museum the collection of Andersen's works in many languages and the books and articles about Andersen and his achievement is comprehensive, occupying the best part of a large room.

By comparison, the Burns museum leaves much to be desired. There is in it a fine collection of Burns manuscripts. But within its bleak walls truth and legend are inextricably mixed; the genuine and the spurious lie side by side; the catalogue is a mere aid to identification; the collection of books is not up to date; the books are housed by bequest, in separate cases, as if the names of their donors, prominently displayed, were more important than the books themselves. The impression which the place creates is one of sentimental, old-fashioned muddle. Rarely can so many trivial and worthless objects have had to carry the weight of so much enthusiastic irrelevance.

A visit to Burns's birthplace and museum at Alloway may tell us disappointingly little about the poet whose works the Scots still revere, though rarely read; but the surrounding countryside speaks more plainly. In some ways Ayrshire and the South-West have altered considerably since Burns's day. The house of his friend John Samson of Orangefield is finishing its existence as part of the terminal buildings of Scotland's only international airport. An atomic-power station is in operation near Annan. The Ayrshire coastal resorts are seasonally thronged with summer holiday-makers, and most of the towns and villages have more than doubled in size. Though Ayrshire and Galloway are still primarily agricultural areas, the horse has almost completely disappeared from the fields. Yet, in spite of change and the speeding up of the pace of living, Burns's imprint still rests upon the countryside, providing a curious continuity between the past that was his and the present that is ours; a continuity which would probably have been broken if the South-West had ever become heavily industrialized. It is impossible to pass the places, the castles, the bridges and the rivers of which Burns wrote without being aware that he has given them an articulate identity, which, perhaps subconsciously, those who live in the South-West still strive to preserve.

However phoney the Burns cult may be, the forceful genuineness of Burns's achievement cannot be sullied by the antics of the cult-worshippers. More than anything else it keeps modern Scotland clasped to the best that is in her past.

IO

Edinburgh—capital de jure

MY EARLIEST recollections of Edinburgh are of a cold place which I visited occasionally with my parents to see my brother, who was at a boarding-school. In Edinburgh the people spoke differently, and there was a zoo.

Each of these childish recollections has some basis in fact. The zoo, climbing the slopes of the hill of Corstorphine, from the top of which the breathless visitor is rewarded with a sweeping view of the Pentland Hills and a tantalizing glimpse of the Firth of Forth, is undoubtedly one of the most spectacular in Europe. The speech of the people in and around the Old Town is still a kind of Scots. Though few indigenous words survive, Edinburgh Scots is a fuller, rounder speech than Glasgow Scots. This is partly due to the fact that until comparatively recently the countryside came right up to Edinburgh's doorstep.

The speech of the inhabitants of Edinburgh's New Town, and of those who live in its Victorian and later suburbs, is English with, however, a characteristic distortion of vowel pronunciation. I do not suggest for a moment that all the citizens of Edinburgh whose speech is not Scots mouth the English *patois* of Morningside; but enough of them do so to make it easily recognizable and, indeed, seem almost characteristic. The origins of this linguistic peculiarity were severely practical, and may be traced to the Union of the Crowns in 1603 when King James VI of Scotland made his lavish way towards London to mount the throne of England in succession to Queen Elizabeth. On that expensive journey he took with him a large retinue of Scots courtiers. Understandably, the king's Scots followers were not particularly popular with the English courtiers. It is presumably to the English courtiers' expressions of resentment, which would naturally take the form of mimicking the rougher speech of the Scots, that the image of the Scot as an uncouth figure of fun—an image which has persisted in various guises down the centuries—goes back. It soon became obvious to the Scots themselves that the surest way to get on in their new surroundings was to try to modify their speech. Many of them were able to write English indistinguishable from that written by Englishmen to the manner born. Poets in the royal circle, like Sir Robert Aytoun and Sir David Murray, turned out polished English sonnets which certainly could not be faulted on linguistic grounds. But the tongue proved a tougher patriot than the mind, and towards the end of the eighteenth century men of letters like Beattie, Hume and Boswell were still worrying about their idiomatic Scotticisms.

One effect of this urgent desire of the Scottish upper classes to rid themselves of all traces of their native speech was to make them strain after verbal correctness. To this day the rougher sounds of the old Scots tongue are still reflected in the English spoken by the majority of Scots. But among a minority, perhaps the descendants of those whose ancestors strove out of self-interest to purge their speech of every trace of Scottishness, the original effort to achieve English correctness is perpetuated as a kind of verbal strain. What is sometimes referred to as the Morningside accent, though a caricature of Oxford English, might thus be described as a consequence of history.

History is also largely to blame for Edinburgh's physical coldness, for the city developed around the Castle on the Rock, and the earliest fortifications on that site were put there for strategic reasons alone. The mud-and-wattle town which grew up around the Rock housed the humble folk whose services were necessary to the great ones in the castle. When the first stone-built lands, or tenements as they are called in Glasgow, went up at the end of the sixteenth century, the limitations enforced by the defensive need to confine building to the spine-like ridge running down from the castle to the Abbey of Holyrood kept Edinburgh warmly huddled upon itself. In the middle of the eighteenth century, before the overcrowded Old Town began to spill off the rocky spine, Edinburgh was a cosy, friendly place. Social distinctions were less isolated than in other parts of Scotland, since noblemen, judges, professors and philosophers occupied the lower floors of lands which also housed dancing-masters and tradesmen.

When George Square and Brown Square first began to drain away the social cream of the city's population, and David Hume reluctantly moved to his New Town house in the street on the other side of the Nor Loch, ironically named St David's Street in his honour, Edinburgh had started to create the conditions which bred that aloofness which strangers to the capital have so often experienced, and still comment upon to this day. The spacious classical streets, the squares and the noble crescents, with which imaginative architects from Robert Adam to William Playfair glorified for almost sixty years the slopes leading down towards the Forth, form as splendid an architectural heritage as any town in Europe possesses. But the finely pro-portioned rooms of the New Town houses must always have been difficult to heat, and inevitably fostered a sense of withdrawnness which the cramped conditions of the Old Town could never have bred. Furthermore, the New Town was so constructed that its broad streets, which Stevenson thought 'draughty parallel-ograms', mercilessly channelled the winds from the East.

While eighteenth-century town planning and the prevailing climatic conditions no doubt account for much of that restraint which is so marked a characteristic of the Edinburgh tem-perament, there is also the occupational factor. Apart from the brewing of beer and the printing of books, Edinburgh has never had any major traditional industries. Because of this, she was spared the hectic industrial expansion which, throughout the early-middle years of the nineteenth century, completely trans-formed Glasgow. But the Law, the Church and the delegated Governmental functions remained firmly centred in the Scottish capital, so that her professional classes occupied a position of decisive influence. Restraint is, or should be, a desirable charac-teristic among judges, lawyers, ministers and those who operate impartially the Civil Service.

Even today, although the influence of Edinburgh's 'Establish-ment' has contracted, Edinburgh somehow lacks the quality of enthusiasm. By common consent, she is deemed to be one of the loveliest cities in Europe. Yet the welcome she gives to those who visit her, though sincere, is always encased by a dignified restraint; almost as if, conscious of the fact that her standing as

Scotland's capital now rests almost entirely upon a courtesy title,
she felt that too great a show of enthusiasm might betray the
falseness of her position.

When in 1947 the then Lord Provost of Edinburgh, Sir John
Falconer, inaugurated the first Edinburgh International Festival
of Music and Drama, he declared it his hope that by bringing
together the noblest products of the arts Edinburgh would be
making a major contribution to the rebuilding of the values of
civilization temporarily laid aside by the Second World War, and
so fostering better understanding between men of goodwill
everywhere. At that time Europe was still broken and dis-
organized. Foreign travel was difficult, and the pre-war European
festivals were only beginning to pick up the traditions that had
been torn down and trampled upon in 1939. The scale on which
the Edinburgh Festival was originally conceived by the im-
presario Rudolph Bing was immense. We who for so long had
been starved of lavishly produced opera, and the music-making of
great foreign orchestras, found brought to our doorstep a glut
of riches the private savouring of which would have involved
weeks of weary European travel.

Unfortunately, however, there was a hidden flaw in Sir
John Falconer's lofty conception, a flaw that has now begun to
show an ominous surface track. No Festival of the Arts can put
down permanent roots in soil which is none too favourable for
the maintenance and growth of strong native artistic traditions.

Salzburg has Mozart; Bayreuth has Wagner; and Munich
has Richard Strauss; Venice specializes in contemporary music
appropriately enough, since at least one of the most distinguished
pioneers probing music's frontiers, Luigi Dallapicolla, is an
Italian; and Vienna is the spiritual heart of the great golden era
begun by Haydn and rounded off by Mahler.

Edinburgh, on the other hand, has almost nothing on to
which the imported arts of her festival can be grafted. To go to
Edinburgh in late summer, to savour the smell of Scotland's
history lingering still in the narrow wynds of the Old Town, to
hear and see music and opera in the evening, and to enjoy the
spacious Northern light which fills out the streets and built-upon
valleys of the beautiful city, is a wholly delightful experience. But,
because much of what is performed in Edinburgh is imported
from native centres which can now be easily reached by the

average holiday-maker, the Edinburgh Festival is beginning to look rather like a gorgeously dressed shop window full of exotic goods from many parts, but behind which there is only an empty store.

When the Festival was first founded there seemed a danger that it would develop into something totally un-Scottish, and even quite moderate people found themselves aligned with the haggis-and-bagpipe brigade, whose conception of a Scottish festival seemed to be a series of recitals of bagpipe-music varied by tirades of left-wing political versifyings. Then, in 1949, Robert Kemp had the idea of preparing a shortened acting version of *The Three Estates*, Sir David Lyndsay's four-hundred-year-old morality play which had done much to hurry forward the Reformation.

Lyndsay, who had dandled James V on his knee and became that monarch's Lord Lyon King of Arms, was no dour Calvinist, but an energetic, liberal-minded, scholarly diplomat, who apparently wrote several other plays, all of which are lost, and about double the number of his surviving poems. Possibly because of the pressure of his official duties, or possibly because of his temperament, he was a careless metreist. Many of his poems betray signs of insufficient revision, the adoption of the easiest solution when some technical difficulty brought his muse to a halt. In spite of this, Lyndsay was interested in people, and it was out of his racy colloquial style, with its frequent summings-up in the form of potted proverbial wisdom, that the eighteenth-century Scots Revival movement, which culminated in the achievement of Burns, derived its literary direction and much of its verbal energy.

The vices which Sir David Lyndsay satirized in *The Three Estates* happened to be particularly associated in the middle of the sixteenth century with Roman Catholicism, which in Scotland still held dominant sway. But they are, in fact, human vices constantly with us in different guises. Sir Robert Romeraker, who in one of the funniest scenes in Lyndsay's play sells pardons and ridiculous relics to the poor, is first cousin to Burns's Holy Willie.

The success of the Festival adaptation, in which Kemp had as collaborators Cedric Thorpe Davie, who composed the music, and Tyrone Guthrie, whose lavishly spectacular production was of itself thrilling, thus triumphantly asserted the basic Scottish values upon which much of our later Scottish literature was created.

Unfortunately, the aspect of the Reformation which Lyndsay could not foresee—the emergence of a new religious tyranny whose high priests were far more joyless and bigoted than their predecessors of the old faith—produced a climate of hostility to the theatre, the fogs of which were not finally dispelled until the present century. In such a climate, it is hardly surprising that no Scottish plays of distinction or even consequence were written from Lyndsay's day until Sir James Barrie began successfully to project his skilful but limited view of the Scots Kailyard upon the London stage.

The Three Estates, which has been revived on several later festival occasions, could not give the Festival roots; but at least it provided it with a Scottish background. Regrettably, we have little else with which to reinforce that background. Allan Ramsay's pastoral opera *The Gentle Shepherd*, its china figures carefully dusted, was revived to provide a charming late-night diversion. The staging of the only other actable older play in the Scottish repertoire, John Home's *Douglas*, merely justified the suspicion that 'Wullie' Shakespeare's position was always completely unaffected by this fustian piece of rhetoric, which, for long unstaged, has somehow carried with it the overtones of much of the enthusiasm it aroused in the Edinburgh of the 1760s; an enthusiasm due as much to the fact that it was the play which circumstances ordained was to loosen the Church of Scotland's blighting grip on the theatre in Scotland, as to intrinsic merit.

The plays of James Bridie, Eric Linklater, Robert McLellan, Robert Kemp and Alexander Reid do not offer unlimited festival possibilities, though works by all of them have been staged in Edinburgh, as has also an historical drama in Scots about Sir William Wallace by the poet Sydney Goodsir Smith. The only Scots play so far fully to measure up to the international standards of drama which the Festival very properly sets itself has been *The Three Estates*, though many of the other Scots plays presented have provided the kind of cultural local colour which visitors to Edinburgh expect to be able to enjoy.

If it has proved difficult for Scotland to be generously represented by native drama at the Edinburgh Festival, it has proved almost impossible to find much Scottish music worthy of performance. The Reformation, which withered the Scots dramatic impulse, also blighted the prospects of her polyphonic school of composers; men like Carver and Johnson, who, understandably, fled to England. Apart from such charming pre-Reformation music as is contained in the Scottish volume of *Musica Britannica* (*Music of Scotland*, a selection from which has been performed at the Festival), Scotland has produced no art music of distinction from the sixteenth century to the twentieth. One or two pieces by Hamish MacCunn might perhaps be allowed in under the local-colour clause. More use could be made of the songs of Francis George Scott, whose music has so far been presented only in programmes of such patriotic mediocrity that many festival visitors were scared away. More should certainly be heard of the music of Iain Hamilton and Thea Musgrave, the most gifted of Scotland's younger composers, some of whose music has already been heard at the Edinburgh Festival. But even after making every possible allowance for the Scottish music that has already been performed, and the works which might reasonably be included in future programmes, the native musical resources which the Festival authorities may draw upon are pitifully small.

It is true that Scotland is rich in folk-music. A number of attempts have been made to present concerts of folk-music. But folk-music is too delicate to be able to withstand transportation from its native hearth or heath to the formalized atmosphere of marbled concert hall. As well catch a butterfly and pin it by the wings to a piece of cardboard as present folksong deprived of the movement of its immediacy.

Early critics of the Festival used to be told by Persons In Authority that such a display of imported products should inspire Scottish artists to go away quietly and try harder, so that they, too, with diligent application, might eventually turn out a play or a symphony worthy to be included with the lave in the cultural jamboree. Advice of this kind shows so woeful an ignorance of the processes of artistic creation that, had it not come from people responsible for mounting a Festival of the Arts, it would have been instantly dismissed, along with all the other laborious platitudes that daily drop from the ever-voluble lips of Persons In Authority.

Until a climate exists more favourable to artists than that

which Scotland can at present offer, not all the festivals of
Europe mounted simultaneously in Edinburgh could influence
the Scottish arts to any appreciable extent.

In the arts, as in most other spheres of activity, it is not the
short spurt that matters most, but the long pull. For three weeks
every year Edinburgh enjoys a glut of operas, plays and concerts.
I, for one, enthusiastically and unashamedly wallow in this
delicious excess. But, for the remaining forty-nine weeks,
Edinburgh is more or less a cultural desert, more barren even than
Glasgow, since she has a smaller population. Edinburgh's commercial theatres each winter offer a season of professional opera
which usually runs for one week. There may also be two separate
weeks of ballet. The serious plays professionally presented in
these theatres could be counted on the fingers of one hand. While
the resident repertory company does gallant work, it is inhibited
in its choice of plays by the fact that its theatre is owned by the
Church of Scotland, an inhibition which, unfortunately, results
in the exclusion from consideration of many of the most exciting
and controversial plays of the day. Most Scottish writers of
consequence have to go to London to have their work published.

Meanwhile, the Festival finds itself hampered by financial
troubles. Although the Scottish Tourist Board has estimated
that during the three weeks of the Festival about one and a quarter
million pounds come rattling into the city's tills, it is only too
apparent that the Festival is of no interest whatever to the
average citizen of the capital of Scotland. Vociferous objections
have been raised to the proposal that a penny or so might be
put on to Edinburgh's remarkably low rates to make what has
become Britain's biggest single tourist draw financially secure. It
has been said that the yearly cost of this solution to every citizen
of Edinburgh would work out at the price of one packet of
cigarettes.

In the light of these unencouraging facts, how can any
Edinburghan seriously advance the claim that his city should be
regarded as a centre of European culture? In a country the size of
Scotland, plain speaking is frequently unwelcome. We like to
cherish our illusions, passionately to defend the third-rate if it
happens to be a home product, be entirely free to ignore what is
happening in the world around us, and be able to bury our heads
in the peat bog as often and for as long as we please. However,

'facts are chiels that winna ding', as even the most elastic-necked
ostrich sooner or later discovers.

It is probably to our commercialized brand of Calvinism that
we owe the persistence of our belief that the arts must be a paying
proposition if they are even to be tolerated in our midst. Speaking
of the Edinburgh Festival's financial difficulties, Sir Arthur Bliss
once remarked to me that if the Festival ever paid its way there
would be something wrong with it. Music has never paid. In the
Middle Ages it was mainly supported by the Church, and from
the sixteenth to the eighteenth centuries by cultured kings and
princelings. Even in the nineteenth century, when popular
concerts developed, the tradition of patronage still buttressed
music-making in the changing social conditions.

There is no earthly reason why music should pay for itself.
We do not expect education to finance its own continuance; nor
do we expect libraries or art galleries to yield monetary dividends.
The arts exist for the enrichment of the human spirit. If there be
some spirits too mean to benefit from such enrichment, the fault
and the loss are theirs alone. Until a more enlightened attitude to
the Scottish arts replaces the present mood of mass indifference,
there can be neither revival nor development of artistic creativity,
and the Edinburgh Festival will remain a glorious, precariously
balanced, imported show-piece. It would be a sad day for
Edinburgh if her festival ever had to be abandoned because of lack
of money; a day, too, the dolorous effects of which would reflect
adversely on the city's fair name and fame, even in cities where
an allegro means no more than an altazimuth, and a quaver is
thought of solely in association with a surfeit of whisky.

Not least among the pleasures which those who come to the
Edinburgh Festival may enjoy is the ease with which it is possible
to get down into the Border country. The Eastern coastline of
the Border country is to Edinburgh more or less what the Firth
of Clyde is to Glasgow: a holiday playground, which does not,
however, offer the scenic magnificence of the Cowal coast. But
the real Borderland is no playground. From Berwick-on-Tweed,
which by tradition and in feeling is indisputably Scottish and
should long ago have been restored to the Scottish county from
which it was detached in 1482, along the course of the Tweed, by
Teviotdale and Annandale, by the Till and the Gala, the past
cries out to the blood with a loud voice. Here, castles like

Neidpath and Hermitage are gaunt monuments to the violent way of life which the Borderers had to endure for centuries. Raids and reivings, burnings and sackings went on almost endlessly, not only as a natural consequence of the long quarrel between the English and the Scots but also because of the struggle to maintain political and social balance between the Border families on the Scots side. Life expectation was not high, and a man's longevity prospects depended almost entirely upon his ability to keep himself alive by the skill and strength of his own arms.

This uncomfortable, desperate way of life, in which no man dared ever allow himself to be separated from his sword and no woman could ever feel quite certain that she and her children were safe when the man of the place was away, has been preserved for us with astonishing vividness in the Border ballads. Originally passed from mouth to mouth, these ballads had been worn smooth by usage long before collectors began to note them down at the beginning of the eighteenth century. One of the differences between the genuine ballad, which deals with an event that actually happened, and the imitation ballad of the nineteenth century, which deals with purely fanciful events, is the manner of approach. The genuine ballad, having story-telling or news-giving as its primary purpose, wastes no time in descriptive or scene-setting preamble, but gets down at once to the business on hand, as a good newspaper reporter should. Thus, 'Jamie Telfer o' the Fair Dodhead' begins:

> 'It fell about the Martinmastide,
>   When our Border steeds get corn and hay,
> The Captain of Bewcastle hath bound him to ride,
>   And he's owre to Tividale to drive a prey.'

Or again, take the opening stanza of 'Gil Morrice', wherein all that we need to know about the *dramatis personae* is told us in six terse lines:

> 'Gil Morrice was an earl's son,
>   His name it waxed wide;
> It was na for his great riches,
>   Nor yet his meikle pride,
> But it was for a lady gay
>   That lived on Carron side.'

From this single stanza, we are made aware that Morrice was a rich, swaggering dandy, far from popular, whose indiscretion over his affair with someone else's lady (else why should there have been gossip?) provided a welcome opportunity for the ballad-maker's friends to get their own back. A less salubrious Sunday newspaper would probably have taken a whole column to cover the situation, and by giving every available detail would have diffused the impact which the balladist makes by presenting only the structural facts.

Because of the economy of their telling, the ballads re-create for us the personal tragedies of long-past Border times with the impact of perpetual newness. Having once become familiar with the ballads, it is thereafter impossible to move about the Border country without being aware of the continuance of a kind of atmosphere; an atmosphere of association, perhaps. Nor is this admission mere facile romanticizing. The dourness and hard-headed determination which made the Borderers reliant individualists and formidable opponents in feuding days, is still reflected in the features of many of their descendants. Few Scots faces can equal those of the Borderer for sheer force of character. Moving about the Border counties, it is easy to understand why Border men retain a more passionate affection for their native airt than men from most other parts of Scotland. Nor is it difficult to appreciate the inevitability of the nature of Sir Walter Scott's achievement.

Abbotsford, his mock-Gothic home by the banks of the Tweed, may seem a comic piece of architectural grotesquerie; but it is the visual amalgam of many of those aspects of the Scottish past which Scott held in high esteem. As such, it demands, if not our veneration, at least our gratitude. For the national personality of Scotland was already becoming schizophrenic, and in danger of breaking down altogether, when Scott began his literary career. It was because he shored up our past against our ruin that Scotland was able to carry a viable image of herself throughout the nineteenth century. It may have been in some respects a false image, but it resulted in the spread of European interest in Scotland, and gave back to us at least a measure of our self-respect.

From our modern standpoint, it is easy to condemn Scott, the poet, because he had so little sense of 'otherness'; easy to sneer at Scott, the novelist, because he set his face so resolutely against drawing upon the life of his own times as the raw material for his writing. It is also obvious to us now that he saw the past in a kindly glow of romanticizing light, which coloured even the behaviour of his villains in their horridest moments. Because he was interested primarily in action, and the course of action depended upon men rather than upon women in the times with which he dealt, Scott's heroines lack the confident lineaments of his heroes. But had Scott's gifts and virtues been other than they were, it is extremely doubtful if his influence on Scotland would have been as beneficial as in fact it was. For, by reminding Scotland of her past at a time when she was in danger of forgetting it altogether, he gave her a future, and made her scenery and her story known throughout the then civilized world.

The theorists of the Scots Renaissance movement have attacked Scott for deserting the Scots cause and providing a powerful impulse towards the development of the Anglo-Scottish tradition, which some of them deplore. This line of thought seems to me a perversion of historical fact. There was one major novelist writing for the most part in Scots, and using small-town Ayrshire life as his raw material, while Scott was alive: John Galt. Yet what influence has Galt had on the course of Scottish literature? The circumstances of the moment forced Galt to write his pot-boilers in English. They served their bread-and-butter-earning turn, and are now quite forgotten. But are the masterpieces, the tales which so gloriously preserve the tang not only of the old Scots tongue but of the Scots way of thinking, much more widely read? The answer, alas, is no!

Scott was a product of historical and social circumstances the direction of which he could not possibly have altered. Dialogue apart, had Scott chosen to write in Scots, and in the Scots manner of Galt (for Galt's intrinsic Scottishness is as much a matter of texture as of language), it is likely that Scott's influence would have been little greater than that of the Ayrshire novelist. Scott's upbringing, his background and his occupation, all militated against the adoption of the nationalist attitude from which the twentieth-century movement draws its strength. Nevertheless, what he did, at the time he did it, was of inestimable value to Scotland. You have only to read his letters and his journals, and you are instantly in contact with a great and a good man; a man whose very wholeness makes the neurotic instabilities of many of his modern denigrators seem pathetically futile.

In the second half of the twentieth century Scott's star has fallen low in our sky. Romanticism is out of fashion, and, characteristically, Scotland's self-confidence has never been more shaky. Scott's most considerable ability was, of course, his gift of story-telling. However ponderous and tedious the descriptive preludes to his moments of action may seem to us, now that time has grown shorter, the moments of action themselves retain their sweeping excitement. For that reason alone, it seems unlikely that the Waverley Novels will remain in the limbo of well-spoken-of but, for the most part, unread classics, where they are presently languishing. Future generations will once again read and enjoy them. But their effectiveness as a talisman against our weakening sense of nationhood is almost certainly finally spent.

Many of the Border towns salute their past with an annual Common Riding ceremony. Most of these ceremonies, originally intended to be a civic inspection of the defences, lapsed in the eighteenth century. By then they had long ceased to have any practical significance. Their revival, within the last half-century, suggests an awareness of a sense of emptiness, of a need to hold on to the past.

All pageantry nowadays is apt to seem ridiculous. Yet, as Burns cryptically noted in his diary, after contemplating the ruins of Linlithgow Palace: 'Ceremony and show, if judiciously thrown in [are] absolutely necessary for the bulk of mankind, both in religious and civil matters.' The Border ceremonies have *virr* and energy, call for considerable prowess on the part of those who take part on horseback, and are enthusiastically supported by the local populations. So long as no false significance is attached to them, they probably achieve some good, and certainly do no harm.

But paying homage to the trappings of the past is no longer a solution to the problems of the present. There is undoubtedly a sense of emptiness in the Border counties, not dissimilar to that which pervades the Highlands. Both areas share one central problem: the unwillingness of young people to live in country places or even small towns, often for the perfectly valid reason that there is no longer work to which they may turn. The centralizing processes of industrialization have removed economic reason from the practice of many country crafts and concerns. Most of the everyday things a local community requires, and which were once made locally, are now made more cheaply and effectively (though not necessarily better) by workers in factories in the central belt. True, the old skills of mill and hillside are preserved in the Borders; and although the weaving of tweed, which has been the economic mainstay of urban Border life for at least two centuries, has been affected by the invention of man-made fabrics, and by the restrictive import quotas of the United States, Border cloths and Border knitwear in the high-quality ranges remain unsurpassed.

Nor is there to be found anything comparable to the Highland attitude of resigned despair in the Borders. A sturdy self-reliance makes itself felt; and, indeed, not without cause. Agriculture, the main Border industry, thrives, and the Borders already enjoy a prosperous tourist trade, with Abbotsford and the four great medieval abbeys of Dryburgh, Kelso, Melrose and Jedburgh as the principal attractions. Border tourism should certainly develop and extend in the years ahead; not only because the rolling Border-land countryside is restful to the eye, as well as full of varied interest for the curious imagination, but because the Borderer himself is not affected by unctuous pride, and has no inhibitions about setting out to make visitors to his countryside both comfortable and welcome.

II

Dundee—jute, jam and journalism

UNDEE is Scotland's monument to lost opportunity.
What a superb city it could have been, nobly built about
the Law and commanding the approaches of the Firth
of Tay! Once, a long time ago, Dundee did impress an observant
traveller with its charm. When Thomas Morer visited Dundee in
1689 he found it 'a very pretty town'. No one could call it that now.

It is usual to blame Dundonians for the characterless sprawl
which their city became during the jute boom of the nineteenth
century, and to condemn them for destroying their few distinguished buildings, like the Adam Town House, which were
of lasting value. But history has taught the Dundonians to value
property lightly. Their city has been sacked more frequently and
systematically than any other Scottish city.

Halfway through the twentieth century Dundee is certainly
the ugliest city in Scotland. Were it not for the presence of
the sea along its fringes, it might even qualify for the ugliest
in Britain. But the presence of the sea ensures that, even in the
depths of Dundee's most crowded and dilapidated districts,
there is never that feeling of airlessness, that physical smell of
squalor, which often characterizes the slum districts of Glasgow.
Yet Dundee has none of Glasgow's modest redeeming features
of layout; no dignified Blytheswood Square; no spacious tree-
lined Great Western Road; not even a vaguely classical-looking
Buchanan Street.

There has been comparatively little change in the outward
appearance of the core of either Glasgow or Dundee for a
century. In the 1860s Victorian expansion, which led to the
destruction of much that could well have been saved, was in full
flood-tide. It was this steady rise in industrial prosperity which

brought about the rebuilding of the centre of Dundee. There was no overall plan. In the 1960s another wave of reconstruction is about to sweep away the centre of Victorian Dundee, and the drab grey stone of the last century will give place to the gayer-coloured building materials of the present. This time there will be an overall plan. The whole of the Overgate is to come down. There can be fewer places where it is possible to assert quite confidently that, so far as the architectural aspect of a city's centre is concerned, nothing is worth saving.

Because modern Dundee grew up on the chance success of the jute boom, the city still seems to cling to an attitude of jute-mindedness which world political changes, notably in India, have made hopeless. The development of the plastics industry has cut down the uses of jute at home, and the introduction of automation into the jute factories has reduced the demand for labour. With the inevitability of the shrinking of the jute industry in mind, a writer of the 1930s once went so far as to describe Dundee as 'Scotland's superfluous city'. George Blake's argument was that Scotland was over-citied in relation to her population, and that Dundee should gradually be allowed to contract its size. Thirty years later it has become clear that it is Glasgow, not Dundee, which will have to shed some of its population and its industries; indeed, the Glasgow overspill plan has already come into operation. Meanwhile, Dundee is able to offer facilities for the introduction of light industries, facilities which will become more attractive when the road bridges over the Forth and the Tay have been completed. The new Dundee may be a worthy city. The old Dundee is the only European city I have visited in which I have found myself wholly unable to experience that sense of place which is one of the chief delights of travelling.

It is a curious fact that Dundee's contribution to Scottish literature has been mainly distinguished for its badness. Dundee provided Scotland's worst poet, William McGonegal, with a home. C. M. Grieve has pointed out that 'the Great McGonegal' was not really a poet at all, but merely a forceful example of the kind of doggerel versifiers that exist by their thousands in every community. McGonegal differed from the others only in so far as his incredible insensitivity preserved him from the realization of how appallingly incompetent his work really was. The Scottish public found, and still do find, the incongruity between

McGonegal's aspiration and achievement so absurd that they read his verses to laugh at his tragic innocence. Most Scots are in any case quite unable to distinguish the difference between poetry and verse; therefore, among the work of writers who make words rhyme, or seem to rhyme, the 'poems' of McGonegal still sell second only to those of Burns.

It is perhaps not without significance that Dundee is the centre of the 'soft magazine' trade in Scotland. The presses of Dundee turn constantly and profitably, providing children with comics and adolescents and adults with a pabulum of sentimental fiction which, however varied in title, remains in substance the same. Many of the weeklies which come from Dundee are not only redolent of the nineteenth century in typography and layout but are obviously catering for a nineteenth-century Kailyard taste. Yet they sell in considerable quantity.

Angus, the county on whose coast Dundee stands, was, of course, the spiritual home of the Kailyard movement, whose high priest, Sir James Matthew Barrie, was born at Kirriemuir in 1860. Barrie, the Reverend John Watson, who wrote under the pseudonym 'Ian MacLaren', and who, though born in Essex, ministered in the Perthshire parish of Logiealmond before occupying the prosperous charge of Sefton Park, Liverpool, and the Gallovidian, Samuel R. Crockett, made up the Kailyard triumverate. Their foster father and chief publicist, Sir William Robertson Nicoll, was the son of a Free Kirk minister at Lumsden, in Aberdeenshire. Because the Kailyard movement which these men created, or at least formalized, attracted so much support during the autumnal Victorian years, and because Kailyard influence obstinately persists a century after the decade in which its principal prose practitioners were born, it must still be taken into account in any serious examination of the state of the Scottish *psyche*.

The name, which seems to have been first applied to the movement by the literary historian J. H. Millar, derives from an anonymous song which Burns included in his *Scots Musical Museum*. 'Ian MacLaren' used a couplet from that song as a motto for his most popular novel, *Beside the Bonnie Brier Bush*.

'There grows a bonnie brier bush in our kail-yard
And white are the blossoms on't in our kail-yard.'

The song itself is harmless enough. It reflects the singer's sentimental pleasure in a much-loved plot of earth. There may be a Jacobite overtone in the fact that the roses were white. Today, however, whiteness suggests bloodlessness.

A kail-yard is a patch in which cabbages are grown. An interest in the health of one's cabbages is a blameless peccadillo. Regarded as an arbitrary frame in which to examine a detail of the world of nature, and observed with scientific accuracy and detachment, a cabbage-patch might well prove a rewarding subject for an interesting piece of writing. But for 'Ian MacLaren' and his fellows the cabbage-patch was no microcosm; merely a sentimental symbol of parochial life. For the Kailyard writers the local scene was world enough in itself. They did not even report honestly upon their chosen world of rural Scotland, but falsified its outlines and relationships. The world of the Kailyarders is altogether too goody-good to be even half true, and contact with it soon fills one with nausea. Yet Barrie, 'MacLaren' and Crockett became best-sellers; Barrie is still highly regarded in some quarters for qualities other than his considerable stage craftsmanship; and the narrow, sentimental view of Scottish life which all three writers purveyed is still dished out weekly (though perhaps nowadays saccharine is used for the over-sweetening rather than sugar) by the publishing houses of Dundee. Clearly, Kailyardism must satisfy some continuing Scottish need.

Fundamentally, Kailyardism is a form of romantic distortion. Scott glorified the heroic past. Because his love of Scotland ran deep and strong, and the heroic qualities round which he wove his fanciful trappings embodied enduring fundamentals, his influence braced Scotland for more than half a century. The Kailyard writers, however, had no such anchoring fundamentals. They tried to give validity to a domestic present the outlines of which were already sixty years out of date when they began to write, distorting their picture to cater for the mid-Victorian taste for literary religiosity. 'Duchesses and hymns!' exclaimed Sir William Robertson Nicoll when his daughter questioned the saleability of the works of a Mrs Florence Barclay. 'Of course the books will sell.'

Ministers and members of ministerial circles occupied a considerable portion of the lists of *dramatis personae* in the original Kailyard writings. Courtship was coy and sexless as a toffee-paper.

Virtue invariably triumphed, and the range of mentionable vices was kept discreetly limited. For petty sins and omissions, forgiveness oozed generously. The big sins were never committed. It is, indeed, a far cry from the racy, randy folk who make up the backcloth of the Burns story to those dear good people living in Kailyard-land's rose-clustered cottages, where the discovery of a pregnant serving lass would be too terrible a nastiness to do anything but simply ignore.

To escape having to face up to the Present—a Present which, as George Blake pointed out, included the festering urban life of the overcrowded Clyde Valley, where industry was expanding so rapidly that Glasgow was outgrowing its capacity for decently housing the extra workers who came flooding in penniless from the countryside and from Ireland—the Kailyarders tried to perpetuate a false conception of the Past. The supporters of their Scotland wanted to avoid having to take account of the social implications of the changes that had befallen the nation. The cult of Kailyardism was simply the worshipping of Burns and the harking back to Mary, Queen of Scots, and Bonnie Prince Charlie manifesting itself in an even more fatuous form.

In an article in the *Saltire Review*, J. M. Reid recently asked who were 'the secret people', the readers of newspapers like *The Sunday Post* and magazines like *The People's Friend*, who still seem to want a diet of old-world Scots couthiness and decent piety, containing no suggestion of violence or the problems that vex the political leaders of the world? Who are they, indeed? Do they include those people who enjoy the McFlannels and the White Heather Club on radio or television? Wherever they are to be found they constitute the modern Kailyarders, for whom current international standards mean nothing at all and who only want to escape into a fanciful past. Yet in the present somewhat sorry state of Scotland, they are at least a buttress of her nationhood, even if the actual position they are engaged so staunchly in supporting is not intrinsically worth their loyalty.

Dundee is one of the four places in Scotland which have a permanent repertory company playing in its own theatre. The Dundee company has adventured in the wide oceans of international drama, but has spent little time in the firth of Scottish drama.

Twenty miles up the Tay, Perth, a former capital of Scotland

and the birthplace of the poet William Soutar, supports the oldest of the four repertory companies. The Perth Repertory Theatre was founded in 1935. It has premièred ten plays by Scots dramatists, and on several occasions taken to the road to perform in towns where live drama is rarely to be seen. The coming of television to Scotland has possibly hit it harder than the other repertory companies, since it draws a higher proportion of its audience from country districts than the companies in Dundee, Edinburgh and Glasgow. Like Dundee, it gives the healthy impression of being primarily interested in the drama, rather than with Scottishness for its own sake.

In Edinburgh the Gateway Theatre Company looks inward and plays safe, and so has established the reputation of being the theatrical counterpart of contemporary Kailyardism. I do not mean this observation unkindly. A company whose premises are owned by a Church can hardly be expected to present plays reflecting a society no longer Christian in orientation.

Most of the native adventurousness in the Scottish theatre comes from the Glasgow Citizens' Company, which is scandalously poorly supported in view of the size of the community it serves. Like three out of the four Scottish repertory companies, it operates in out-of-date Victorian premises in a scruffy district of the city. If the theatre in Scotland is to succeed in attracting and holding the younger generation it will have to persuade local authorities to build new and up-to-date premises in salubrious parts of the four cities: live theatres run without religious or political interference of any kind, dedicated solely to presenting international drama and new Scottish plays, not because they are Scottish but because they are good.

Scots plays of international standard hardly exist. In spite of the pioneer work put in by the Scottish National Players in the 'twenties, neither the four repertory companies nor Pitlochry's summer theatre in the hills have been able to midwife into lusty infanthood a native twentieth-century Scottish drama. Individual dramatists have produced occasional good plays. The whimsically didactic plays of James Bridie form the centre-piece of the modern Scottish theatre. His best plays can be numbered on the fingers of one hand: *Mr Bolfry*, *The Sleeping Clergyman*, *Tobias and the Angel* and possibly *The Baikie Charivari*. Many of the others have their merits, and will often be revived; but these four form the Bridie cannon. The output of Robert McLellan is even slighter. *Jamie the Saxt*, a brilliant character piece which was written for the great Scots character actor Duncan Macrae, and which depends upon the ability of the actor playing the title role for its success, *Toom Byres* and *The Flowers o' Edinburgh* are the most frequently staged. McLellan writes entirely in Scots. So usually does Alexander Reid, whose play *The Warld's Wonder*, dealing with the disagreements of two rival wizards, is generally judged to be his best. But the limitations of the language force Scots-writing authors to deal only with the past. *The Other Dear Charmer*, a dramatization of Burns's affair with 'Clarinda' Maclehose, stands out among Robert Kemp's plays, along with his Scots adaptation of Molière's *L'Ecole des Femmes*. Add Alexander Scott's witty romp *Right Royal*, also created for Duncan Macrae, and a handful of London West End comedies by Eric Linklater, Alan Melville, Roger MacDougal, N. Hunter and others, and, apart from the kitchen-sink or sea-coast-Kailyard pieces of Joe Corrie, Naomi Mitchison, Tim Watson and others, you have the Scottish theatre.

At least eight out of the twelve best twentieth-century Scottish plays look back in anguish. Apart from McMillan's *All in Good Faith*, McLeish's *The Gorbals' Story* and George Munro's *Gold in his Boots*, I cannot call to mind a single play of distinction which deals with contemporary Scottish problems and people.

Have we no problems of major importance? Do the clashes in relationships and the moral issues which impel contemporary French and American dramatists to write with vital urgency not involve Scots people? Or have we sunk so deeply into the torpor of impending dissolution that nobody cares enough any more?

I am occasionally invited to attend meetings of enthusiasts to debate 'What is wrong with the Scottish theatre?' I never go. No debate is necessary. Scotland is apparently unable to produce playwrights capable of realizing that a man and a woman sitting with a passion over a café table anywhere make up the stuff of drama, or able to interpret universal issues through local symbols. Our dramatists hark back to Border reivings; to Burns; to Knox's battle with Mary, Queen of Scots; to Burke and Hare, the body-snatchers; to Bonnie Prince Charlie; back, back, back in permanent reverse. And when occasionally they do venture a timorous glimpse at the present, they concern themselves with purely local issues, which they fail to universalize, just as they fail to evoke any modern overtones from their treatment of the past.

England's treatment of the Irish over three centuries sharpened in Ireland a concern for human values which resulted in the outburst of powerful, racy drama which forms a considerable part of the harvest of the Irish literary Renaissance.

Had Scotland been persecuted in a similar way, social tensions might have risen near enough the surface of events to have stimulated our embryo dramatists. The tensions of modern civilization are as much with us as with the Americans or the French; but they lie further beneath the surface, and are much more subtle than, for instance, the futile old-fashioned religious squabbling which still animates much post-Renaissance Irish drama. But most Scots would simply rather not talk about them. When an outsider, like John Osborne, did talk about them in *The Entertainer*, and the play was staged in Glasgow, some Scots made silly interjections from the auditorium, while others fluttered noisily out of the theatre, like ruffled hens.

Scotland's failure to produce a major or even a relevant post-Bridiean dramatist cannot wholly be attributed to lack of talent. Talent needs an inquiring atmosphere in which to develop. Alas! the atmosphere of Scotland, far from exhaling any quality of exciting inquiry, reeks of rotting complacency to the heights of John Knox's sanctimonious heaven.

12

Aberdeen—the Silver City

ABERDEEN, the third city of Scotland, where almost two hundred thousand people live, proclaims its personality before the traveller is properly within its boundaries. As the road from the South dips towards the Dee, a tang compounded of brine and smoke and fish-curing twitches the nostrils, and the grey granite buildings glint and glisten austerely in even the thinnest sunshine. Opinions differ as to whether or not granite is a sympathetic building material. It is certainly an enduring one, but it has become too expensive to be a practical proposition for the modern builder.

Aberdeen has its own sounds, too: sea-sounds, hooting sirens and growling foghorns; city sounds, whirring traffic and hissing railway-engines. But there is also the sound of the speech of the people themselves; a rich lilting Scots with a fuller indigenous vocabulary than is to be found anywhere else except perhaps in Buchan.

The Aberdonian is reputed to be mean. Shrewd might be a fairer description. He certainly has a keen business sense and a remarkable confidence in his own flair and acumen, and for many Aberdonians Aberdeen is virtually the world.

How does the third city of Scotland earn its living? In medieval times Aberdeen thrived as a market town and a port. The salmon fisheries of the Don and the Dee were developed to increase prosperity. In the eighteenth century fishing, shipbuilding, the woollen and textile trade, paper-making and the ancillary crafts and industries associated with the life of the neighbouring farming community were established or further developed.

Granite stone from the Rubislaw and Kemnay quarries came into demand for paving in places as far away as London as well as for durable headstones, bringing work in plenty for masons. The Industrial Revolution did not seriously ravage Aberdeen for the fortunate reason that the surrounding countryside possesses no quickly reapable minerals. Aberdeen's wealth was, and still is, in the land and the sea and the ingenuity of her people. The railway boom brought increasing internal prosperity, in spite of a temporary set-back caused by a financial crisis in 1848. In 1882 a converted Irish tug, the *Toiler*, made her first successful trawl, netting a profit of two hundred pounds in the first month. She toiled to some purpose, too, for soon trawling for white fish opened up a huge new source of possibility for Aberdeen, and one which she developed energetically over the next half-century. The fish trade set up a demand for related trades like coopering and curing. Nearness to the North Sea fishing grounds and cheap transport helped to give the Aberdeen fishing industry its prosperity. Some say the profits came too quickly, and that not enough of them were ploughed back. Now, cheap transport has become a remembrance of things past, the home fishing grounds have been overfished to exhaustion and the Aberdeen trawler fleet has not been adequately modernized to keep pace with its rivals out of Grimsby and Hull. There are signs that a few owners are adopting a modern outlook, but it may be too late in the day. The industry as a whole is in serious difficulties, and it may not be long before the centralizing tendency of the age cripples out of existence fishing ports like Aberdeen which are remote from the main British consumer markets.

But Aberdeen's other industries continue to thrive, with the manufacture of agricultural machinery and the tourist trade as lusty relative newcomers upon the commercial scene.

The city has the distinction, shared only with London, of having won the praises of that gloomy self-centred genius, William Dunbar. He seems to have been among the courtly company when James IV's queen came to Aberdeen in 1511, to be entertained by the magistrates of the city at a cost of two hundred pounds. The opening flourish of the poet's rhymed 'Thank You' letter has a conventional ring, which suggests that at first he regarded his task simply as a routine royal duty.

> 'Blyth Aberdeane, thow beriall of all touns,
>   The lamp of bewtie, bountie and blythnes,
> Unto the heaven ascendit thy renoun is
>   Of virtew, wisdome, and of worthiness. . . .'

However, by the time Dunbar reached his concluding stanza, a much more heartfelt note is discernible.

> 'O potent princes, pleasant and preclair,
>   Great cause thow has to thank this nobill toun,
> That, for to do thee honour, did not spair
>   Their geir, riches, substance, and persoun,
>   Thee to ressave on maist fair fasoun;
>   Thee for to please they socht all way and mien;
>   Theirfoir, sa lang as Quein thow beiris croun,
> Be thankfull to this burcht of Aberdein.'

The face of the worthy provost who first tore open and read this curiously two-way rhymed expression of thanks must have been well worth seeing!

Sir Thomas Urquhart of Cromarty was an alumnus of Aberdeen University. In 1650 Richard Franck, a trooper in Cromwell's army, was so impressed with Aberdeen that six or seven years later, when conditions in the Commonwealth seemed to him to have become intolerable, he came back to have a second look at it.

Franck's *Memoirs*, the account of this tour, were edited and published by Sir Walter Scott in 1821. They are couched in the form of a dialogue between two characters, Theophilus and Arnoldus. Franck was probably acquainted with the works of the entertainingly garrulous Urquhart, for there are points of resemblance between the styles of the two men.

When Theophilus and Arnoldus came to Aberdeen, then principally a market town and a port, they felt that they were arriving at a place famed for its tolerance, because of the opposition of the 'Aberdeen Doctors'—liberal Episcopalians like Robert Barron, William Leslie, James Sibbald and William and John Forbes—earlier in the seventeenth century to the principles of the Solemn League and Covenant. So Theophilus asks:

'Is this that Aberdeen so generally discours'd by the Scots for civility?'

and Arnoldus answers:

'Yes, and humanity too; for it's the paragon of Scotland.'

Thereafter, Arnoldus, in his role of guide, goes on to elaborate the merits of the city.

'It stands in a cultivated country, that never knew the face of sterility; whose banks are bathed with the glittering streams of Dee, and her walls shaded with fertile corn fields, promulgates plenty. . . . Here, the sun so moderates the cold in winter, that it seldom or rarely freezes her sands; whose increase is multiplied from the generous breasts of the ocean. And from whence both the mariner and merchant accumulate treasure, because to drag it forth from the solid deeps of the sea; when at other times they import their goods into the Highlands, as they export commodities into remote countries.'

With rather greater a regard for syntax, Arnoldus describes Old Aberdeen as 'the mother city of New Aberdeen, and a university to boot, wherein stands an old weather-beaten cathedral, that looks like the times, somewhat irregular'.

Old Aberdeen, or Aulton, up from the mouth of the Don, was, in fact, badly placed for commercial convenience, and did not develop much, except perhaps in grace and learning. Eventually it was swallowed by the new town, which had the advantage of a good harbour.

Aberdeen, in spite of its sustained passion for higher education, has not been particularly productive of poets who have expressed the *ethos* of the North-East, although John Barbour, John 'Tullochgorum' Skinner, Alexander Ross (author of 'Helenore, or The Fortunate Sheperdess'), John McEwan (who wrote 'O weel may the boatie row', one of Aberdeen's theme-songs, and whose jeweller's shop stood on the site of the present Athanaeum Restaurant), and, of course, George Gordon, Lord Byron, all had Aberdeen connections.

In prose John R. Allan has provided us with a delightful record of the warmer side of North-East farm life in *A Farmer's Boy*. The three novels which make up *A Scots Quair*, and which J. Leslie Mitchell wrote under the pseudonym of Lewis Grassic Gibbon, in spite of an obsession with the imagined virtues of ancient Druidism and modern Communism, have more of the 'speak' of the soil in them than anything else that has been written about the North-East. *A Scots Quair* derives in approach, if little else, from *The House with the Green Shutters*, the single masterpiece of the short-lived George Douglas Brown and the work which dealt a death-blow to the pretensions of the Kailyard School, swinging to the opposite extreme in the doing. There is also a good deal of raw extremism in *A Scots Quair*, and the raised speech of its characters is a device borrowed from Gaelic literature. But Gibbon, who was an Aberdeenshire man, knew and loved his native airt with a love that was wide enough to encompass a fierce and critical hatred.

The most obvious aspect of the city of Aberdeen itself is its almost clinical cleanliness. Dirt cannot adhere to granite. Small wonder that the natives of such a city are hard; so hard, indeed, that they used to allow jokes about their own meanness to be manufactured on the premises and widely circulated,[1] thus establishing for themselves a reputation for comicality. Though the outskirts of Aberdeen are made of less durable materials than the city's heart, and differ little in standardized dreariness from the modern suburbs of any Scottish town, the main part of the city has a special character because of the preponderance of granite used in its building, mostly taken from the local Rubbislaw Quarry.

Can the stone-and-mortar character of a place affect the character of its inhabitants? Gibbon thought that it could, and did. In *Scottish Scene*, that acidulous, virile survey of Scotland which he and 'Hugh MacDiarmid' produced together in 1934, Gibbon wrote:

'Bleakness, not meanness or jollity is the keynote to Aberdonian character, not so much lack of the graces or graciousness of existence as lack of colour in either of these. And this is almost inevitable for anyone passing his nights and days in The Silver City by the Sea. It is comparable to passing one's existence in a refrigerator. Aberdeen is built, largely and incredibly, of one of the most enduring and indestructible and appalling building-materials in use on our planet—grey granite.

'It has a flinty shine when new—a grey glimmer like a morning North Sea, a cold steeliness that chills the heart. Even with weathering it acquires no gracious softness, it is merely starkly grim and uncompromising. The architect may plan and build as he will with this material—with its variant, white granite, he may rear the curvetting spires and swooping curlecues and

[1] I have the impression that this industry is now in decline.

looping whirlimagigs of Marischal College—and not escape that sense of one calamitously in jail. Not only are there no furbelows possible in this architecture, there is amid it, continually, the uneasy sense that you may not rest here, you may not lounge, you cannot stand still and watch the world go by . . . Else presently the warders will come and move you on.'

Gibbon's is perhaps an extreme view, and it could be argued that the coldness of granite is at least a quality which aids preservation, whereas the softness of the grey sandstone favoured in most other Scottish cities and towns is the cause of some buildings only about a century old crumbling disastrously, the process of disintegration hastened by the chemicals lodged in our modern smoke-filled atmosphere.

My own earliest memories of Aberdeen are of one of its specialities: high tea. When a schoolboy I sailed several times from Leith to Orkney, where I spent a long part of my summer holidays with a friend on the island of Stronsay. On both the outward and the inward voyages the steamer put in at Aberdeen. After the rocking of the Pentland Firth and the smell of sick animals—the only really disagreeable aspect of sailing in coastal steamers not large enough for insulation to be effective—it was a pleasurable moment when the ship tied up in Aberdeen harbour and I could walk up the bustling quayside, overflowing with barrels and the smell of fish and tarry ropes, and climb the hill to a restaurant in Union Street, there to linger over the delights of a two-course high tea, one of which courses was a kipper or a finnan haddie.

Although these long-digested comestibles tasted as never before or since, I have never felt impelled to write a poem about Aberdeen's high teas. However, several contemporary poets have provided us with portraits of the city which in some measure offset Gibbon's harsh view of it. In 'Home Town Elegy', G. S. Fraser, the son of a former Town Clerk of Aberdeen, remembered the city in spring from a foreign land:

'Glitter of mica at the windy corners,
    Tar in the nostrils, under blue lamps budding
Like bubbles of glass the blue buds of a tree,
    Night-shining shop-fronts, or the sleek sun flooding
The broad abundant dying sprawl of the Dee:

For these and for their like my thoughts are mourners
That yet shall stand, though I come home no more,
Gas-works, white ball-room, and the red brick baths
And salmon nets along a mile of shore,
Or beyond the municipal golf-course, the moorland
     paths
And the country lying quiet and full of farms.
This is the shape of a land that outlasts strategy
And is not to be taken with the rhetoric or arms . . .'

The English poet John Holloway was for a time a lecturer at
Aberdeen University. Although he does not specifically mention
Aberdeen in his 'Poem for Deep Winter', the North-East flavour
of the opening lines is apparent:

'This is the grave season of the sun's transit.
The coast is mislost under frost. All day
A squab red foghorn, lonely by the bay
Tromps out rough music; and is never answered
Except in echo whined from the wide seaboard
Where bobbing gulls miraculously sleep.

Thin down the cliffedge combes, grey huddled sheep
Dumbly await their numb blue-fingered shepherd,
We walk by the two rivers at this season
Or down the cliffs; the land, the sea recur
At every rise, changeless . . .'

Both these poets were mainly interested in the texture of
living in Aberdeen. George Bruce, on the other hand, was more
concerned with the accumulated self-reliant character of the place
itself, a character which gives a double meaning to the familiar
descriptive epithet of Granite City:

'The brown land behind, south and north
Dee and Don and east the doubtful sea,
The town secured by folk that warsled
With water, earth and stone; quarrying,
Shaping, smoothing their unforgiving stone,
Engineering to make this sufficient city

That takes the salt air for its own.
The pale blue winter sky, the spring green trees,
The castigating thunder rain, the wind
Beating about the midnight streets,
The hard morning sun make their change
By the white unaltered granite—
Streets of it, broad roadways, granite pavemented
To the tall tenements, rectangular wide-walled stores,
To the kirks and pillared Assembly Rooms;[1]
Streets with drinking troughs for the animals,
And at the port quays crowded,
Overfed with horses, lorries, men and boys,
And always and at every point
Clatter on the causies.
Business is good, will be good here
At the dead end of time. Record then
This people who purposive and with strategy
Established a northern city, a coast town
That stands and stares by the waters,
Dee and Don and the sea.'

Though there is little to choose in nobleness of sweep and
flow between the broad and fertile estuaries of Aberdeen's two
rivers, chance has elevated the Highland upper reaches of
Deeside to a wider fame than the gentler pastoral Lowland hill
country of Strathdon has ever achieved. The British sovereign
who built a holiday home in the North-East unwittingly established the cult of 'Balmorality'. The love which Queen Victoria
had for Scotland was carefree and genuine. The influence that her
almost extravagant love of things Scottish had when it spread
abroad and inspired emulation was less happy. It was primarily
the scenery and the opportunities for riding the hills and for
hunting which made Deeside seem attractive to Queen Victoria
and Prince Albert.

Deeside has for centuries been a favourite place for the
practice of field pursuits. As long ago as 1616 John Taylor, the
Water Poet, then on a walking tour of Scotland, was received at

[1] The Music Hall in Union Street, built by Archibald Simpson (1790–1847), one
of the city's most distinguished public buildings. He was also responsible for Bon-
Accord Square and Crescent, Marine Terrace, the older part of Marischal College
and other public buildings and private dwellings.

Kindrochit Castle by the Earl of Mar. Although Taylor was a brash Thames bargee whose pretensions to learning and culture were of the slightest, he undoubtedly had a lively wit and was probably a vigorous talker. At any rate, his Cockney manners must have seemed so very different from those to which Mar and the Scottish noblemen were accustomed that they welcomed him to their midst as an honoured guest. Taylor, who kept a diary and was highly observant, recorded that:

'Once in the yeere, which is the whole moneth of August and sometimes part of September, many of the nobility and gentry of the kingdome (for their pleasure) doe come into these high-land countries to hunt, where they doe conforme themselves to the habit of the Highlanders. . . . Their habit is shoes with but one sole apiece; stockings (which they call short hose) made of a warm stuffe of divers colours, which they call Tartane: as for breeches, many of them, nor their forefathers, never wore any, but a jerkin of the same stuffe that their hose is of, their garters being bands or wreaths of hay or straw, with a plaid about their shoulders, which is a mantle of divers colours, much finer and lighter stuffe than their hose, with blue flat caps on their heads, a handkerchief knit with two knots about their neck; and thus are they attired.

'Now their weapons are long bowes and forked arrows, swords and targets, harquebusses, muskets, durks and Loquhaberaxes. [Taylor's spelling suggests that even in 1618 the Scots "ch" sound in Lochaber defeated the English tongue!] With these arms I found many of them armed for hunting. As for their attire, any man of what degree soever that comes amongst them, must not disdain to wear it: for if they doe, then they will disdain to hunt, or willingly bring in their dogs: but if men be kind to them, and be in their habit, then are they conquered with kindness, and the sport will be plentiful. This was the season that I found so many noblemen and gentlemen in these shapes.'

It is interesting to find Taylor observing both aspects of the Highland dichotomy of character: on the one hand, the touchy pride in dress and custom; on the other, the readiness to be 'conquered with kindness' which developed into the ghillie attitude of feudal subservience in Victorian times, and is still occasionally to be met with in the servants' quarters of decaying Highland mansions. The custom of dressing as the Highlanders do survives, and has been carried on by Queen Victoria's descendants.

There have been at least two previous homes on the site of the present Balmoral Castle. The first Balmoral was the property of the powerful Aberdeenshire family of Gordon, and, later, of the Farquharsons, who still own much of Upper Deeside including Invercauld, the neighbouring estate to Balmoral. As supporters of the Jacobite cause, the Farquharsons suffered heavy fines, and in 1798 sold Balmoral to the Earl of Fife. Thereafter it was leased to various owners, but finally to the brother of that Earl of Aberdeen who became a British Prime Minister, Sir Robert Gordon. In 1834 he demolished, or partly demolished, Old Balmoral, and began to build Balmoral Two, which was completed in 1839.

Nine years later Queen Victoria and Prince Albert became the lessees, and in 1852 the owners of the property. They paid thirty-one thousand five hundred pounds for it, demolished the castle and started to build Balmoral Three in the autumn of the following year. The prince himself had a hand in the design of the royal Highland home, but the architect was William Smith, whose father, John Smith, had been responsible for the short-lived Balmoral Two.

The style chosen by Smith was what has come to be known as Scottish Baronial. Ivor Brown has put up a spirited defence of this romantic style, which resurrected the stone-and-mortar manner of real castles that first and foremost had to be defended before they could be lived in.

'Had Smith insisted upon, and had his royal clients accepted, a Scottish country mansion in the style of the brothers Adam, he would have been equally antique,' says Brown. 'A Neo-Palladian Balmoral would have pleased many critics rather more than does the Neo-Baronial one, but it must be remembered that the classical style, while admirable in Edinburgh or amid the parks of a Border landscape, is not in tune with the scenery or the tradition of the Highlands.'

This skilful apologia overlooks the intrinsic values of the

two styles. Adam and his associates created from their study of the Palladian villas of Italy a homogeneous style immediately recognizable as their own, both satisfying in itself and a subtle reflection of the new humanism of their age. But Smith and the other architects like him who emulated the royal example on a smaller scale all over Scotland created a style which had neither homogeneity nor integrity, reflected only an inability fully to assimilate past influences, and was furthermore extremely ugly. Today only vandal-dominated local authorities counsel the destruction of Adam buildings; but Neo-Baronial castles, so huge and inconvenient and hideous that they cannot be adapted to suit modern living conditions, are being abandoned, de-roofed and blown up all over Scotland.

Victorian economic expansion resulted in the exploitation of the Highlands as a sporting playground, and the abandonment of fine old castles in favour of grander-seeming Neo-Baronial new ones; this at a time when Scotland was very much under the influence of the Romantic Revival, stimulated by Sir Walter Scott. It was unfortunate that when interest in the past and the craze for rebuilding were both at their height, Scotland (indeed, Britain) should have been in an architectural doldrums, the builders unable to assimilate the influences whose original products they so senselessly copied. No matter what the nature of the surrounding scenery, architectural pastiche can never really be justified.

Queen Victoria arrived at her new Highland home in a tartan-decorated barouche. She caused Balmoral to be liberally furnished with tartan curtains and furniture covers, many of them in weaves of her own devising. The kilt which the present Duke of Edinburgh sometimes wears when at Balmoral is of the Balmoral tartan—black, red and lavender on a grey background—designed by Prince Albert. In the matter of inventing weaves, of course, the queen was merely giving practical approval to a craze which had been begun by the Sobieski Stuarts, publicized by the appearance of George IV in Edinburgh in 1824 dressed in generous tartan trews, and further encouraged by a post-Napoleonic craze for tartan that swept Paris and is reflected in the ballet of that time *La Sylphide* (not to be confused with *Les Sylphides*) where the dancers are tartan clad. Naturally, the newly mechanized weaving industry in Scotland was able and willing to meet the increased demand.

The disease of tartanitis transmogrified to become a mental attitude inspired George Scott Moncrieff to invent the pun-word 'Balmorality'. With its implied suggestion of rather hypocritical stuffiness it is an apt description of that pseudo-patriotic enthusiasm for unessential things Scottish which resulted from Queen Victoria's genuine love of Scotland, an attitude still widely encountered more than a century after she made her happy entry to Balmoral.

'Balmorality' makes a brave show of national fervour so long as nothing of any intellectual, political or cultural significance is involved. It favours the maximum public indulgence in kilt-wearing, and of manifesting Scottishness in such other irrelevant ways as marketing tartan souvenirs (which may very probably be made in Birmingham or Hong Kong, and may equally inappropriately clothe a tea-cosy or a selection of the poems of Burns), Burns Suppers, Clan Gatherings and, of course, Highland Games.

The cult of Highland Games is peculiarly associated with 'Balmorality', although it may have much earlier roots. The main annual event of the kind is now the Braemar Gathering, held in early autumn and frequently attended by members of the Royal Family. Because of their expected presence, the Braemar Gathering has attained the distinction of a major Highland social occasion. It is particularly noticeable that nowadays the natives prefer to wear the 'habit' of the Lowlander, leaving the kilt to visiting aristocracy, whose members have presumably not noticed that native habits change. Though Highland Games have much to be said in their healthy favour, and some ears may genuinely relish the thin and futile sound of massed bagpipes, they frequently foster a pettily savage competitive professionalism which should have no place in what are meant to be demonstrations of native sportsmanship.

There was another curious by-product of Queen Victoria's Scottish enthusiasm: the cult of shaggy landscapes. One of the queen's guests at Balmoral was Sir Edward Landseer, whose canvas 'The Monarch of the Glen' became immensely popular and inspired a whole school of colourful glen-and-benery painting. The method of the glen-and-ben school, which included artists of considerable ability like Horatio McCulloch, was to select the picturesque elements of the Highland scene and con-

centrate on them. Their sentimental representations of Highland cattle standing knee-deep in rivers and lochs, and of stags
at e'en drinking their fill from burns set in impossibly purple
moorland, enjoyed widespread popularity. Time-stained sepia
reproductions of such scenes still adorn the walls of many a
Highland cottage. They projected in yet another form the
romantic view of Scotland with which Scots people have constantly to reassure themselves. But the original work of the
glen-and-ben school has become sadly devalued. Canvases which
would once have fetched hundreds of pounds can now be bought
for a few shillings for the sake of the frame.

In 1954 I was one of a group of people invited by the Farquharsons of Invercauld to organize *Scottish Festival, Braemar*, a
survey of the arts and crafts of Scotland, traditional and modern,
in so far as they could be accommodated in a converted 'Wee Free'
church turned into a little theatre with an apron stage, and
a former public hall become art gallery. The art exhibition,
organized by a senior member of the staff of Aberdeen College
of Art, was made up of work by contemporary Aberdeenshire
painters. A hundred years ago such an exhibition would have
consisted of a preponderance of pictures by the glen-and-ben
painters. In this exhibition, in so far as local subject matter
featured at all, it was the grimly enduring sea-and-hard-land
subjects which interested most of the painters. This reflects not
only the decline of romanticism, at least among Scottish painters,
but the steady Lowlandization of Deeside during the past
century. For all its Highland airs and graces, Deeside is now
Highland only in aspect, for Gaelic has gone from it completely;
and with the decline in upper-class autumn shooting parties
economically it has become more than ever dependent upon the
motoring-tourist trade from Aberdeen. To find the surviving
Highland mental attitudes, it is necessary to travel farther West.

13

The Highlands—atrophied attitudes

ALTHOUGH it is about a thousand years now since Scotland first came together under one king, the people of the Highlands and the inhabitants of the Lowlands have never really fully understood each other. Throughout the Middle Ages the history of the Highlands is a dim record of primitive internecine feuding, the details of which are part hidden from us because of the isolation of the mountainous areas and the consequent absence of reliable testimony. The clan system, which was the Highland version of feudalism adapted to suit the geographical conditions of the countryside, bred a sturdy independence in the Highlander. His living he won from croft and boat; his loyalty he kept ready to rally to the call of his chief without any thought for the rights or wrongs of the causes which he was thus pledged to support.

Highlanders and Lowlanders have regarded each other with suspicion since first the Stuart kings found it necessary to curb the rival power of the Lords of the Isles. When William Dunbar wanted to portray the Devil amusing himself in Hell, he made that worthy call for:

'. . . a Hieland padyane;[1]
Syne ran a feynd to fetch Makfadyane
Far northwart in a nuke;
Be he the correnoch[2] had done schout
Ershmen so gadderit him about,
In Hell great room they took.
Thae tarmagents, with tag and tatter,
Full loud in Erse begouth to clatter,

---

[1] Pageant   [2] Coronach or Highland lament

And rowp lik raven and rook:
The Devil sa deevit was with their yell
That in the deepest pot of Hell
He smoorit[1] them with smoke.'

Scotland's second-greatest poet was not a very subtle man, and all he expresses in these lines is his impatience and dislike for a language he was unable to understand. Although it was probably bad temper which prompted Burns to write his acid lines on being poorly received by the innkeeper at Inveraray, a lackey of the Duke of Argyll, Burns's diagnosis went a little deeper:

> 'Whoe'er he be that sojourns here,
>   I pity much his case—
> Unless he come to wait upon
>   The Lord *their* God, "His Grace".
>
> There's naething here but Highland pride,
>   And Highland scab and hunger;
> If Providence has sent me here,
>   'Twas surely in an anger.'

In an alternative version, Burns sharpened the sting in the first line of his second stanza to:

> 'There's Highland greed, there's Highland pride.'

In our own day satire is largely the prerogative of the journalist, and it was a journalist who described education in the Highlands as 'learning to work the subsidies'.

On the Highland side there have certainly been reasonable grounds for suspicion. The three events which stand out most strongly in the history of the Highlands over the last four centuries have been the Massacre of Glencoe in 1692; the savagely repressive punitive measures which followed the Rising of 1745; and the Clearances of the nineteenth century. Two of these crippling disasters were engineered by a British monarch and his Parliament in London; the third was mainly a consequence of the second.

[1] Smothered

On the Lowland side the state of lawlessness which the Highlanders were able to preserve because of the absence of communications in their countryside inevitably bred suspicion and alarm. Nevertheless, it was a Highlander, the Duke of Argyll, who was partly responsible for stimulating King William's apprehensions to the point where he authorized the Glencoe Massacre.[1]

The mere physical appearance of the Highlands once struck terror into the hearts of Lowland beholders, until easier conditions of travel made a kindlier view possible. The old view is perhaps best summed up by Edward Burt, who knew the Highlands intimately about 1725:

'The Highlands are for the greatest part composed of hills, as it were piled one upon another till the complication rises and swells to mountains of which the heads are frequently above the clouds. . . . The summits of the highest are mostly destitute of earth, and the huge naked rocks, being just above the heath, produce the disagreeable appearance of a scabbed head. . . . There is not much variety, but gloomy spaces, different rocks, heath, and high and low. To cast one's eye from an eminence towards a group of them, they appear still one above another, fainter and fainter according to the aerial perspective, and the whole of a dismal gloomy brown drawing upon a dirty purple, and most of all disagreeable when the heath is in bloom. . . . But of all the views, I think the most horrid is to look at the hills from east to west or vice versa, for then the eye penetrates far among them, and sees more particularly their tremendous bulk, frightful irregularity, and horrid gloom, made yet more sombrous by the shades and faint reflections they communicate one to another.'

The Highland way of life was obviously well adapted to the conditions out of which it arose. Once roads began to be ribboned through the glens, along which passed the force of a broader civilization, the clan system began to crack. It was already exhausted when heritable jurisdictions were abolished after the failure of the second Jacobite Rising. Into the dismantled ruins

[1] The main share of blame rests, of course, upon the reputation of Viscount Stair.

of a civilization that, however crude, has produced noble crosses like those on Iona, and fine jewellery like the Glenlyon Brooch and Monymusk Reliquary, came the officials of the Society for the Propagation of Christian Knowledge, bent on destroying the very language that had held the old system together.

The chiefs who recovered their lands in the 1780s were at least one generation younger than their forbears who had come out for Prince Charlie. Many of the new lairds had been educated in England and had married English wives. When they returned to the Highlands to settle in their rebuilt castles and mansions, they came as landlords whose way of life was very different from that of their tenants and whose interests led them to increase the strength of their new English connections rather than revert to the old ways still followed by the crofters who lived on their lands.

A Lowland historian, John Ramsay of Ochtertyre, writing in old age towards the close of the eighteenth century, saw what was happening:

'It will hardly be possible for the rising generation to form a just notion of the love and affection which subsisted between a powerful nobleman and his vassals and clients before the two last rebellions. Compared with it, modern patronage is cold and unavailing. He was their oracle and champion on all occasions, and his espousing their interest with warmth served as a safeguard against the violence and injustice of private men. They found a kind reception at his house and table, where in his social hour distinctions of rank were laid aside, personal merit being more in estimation than fortune or fashion.'

This relationship bred a spirit of proud independence which, when it came into collision with alien Lowland values in the days of decline, seemed to many merely perversity. Major-General David Stuart of Garth, a Black Watch soldier who died in 1829, wrote pertinently of this collision of attitudes:

'It is not easy for those who live in a country like England, where so many of the lower orders have nothing but what they acquire by the labours of a passing day, and possess no permanent property or share in the agricultural produce of the soil, to appreciate the nature of the spirit of independence which is generated in countries where the free cultivators of the soil constitute the major part of the population. It can scarcely be imagined how proud a man feels, however small his property may be, when he has a spot of arable land and pasture stocked with corn, horses and cows. . . . He considers himself an independent person. . . . His independence being founded on permanent property, he has an interest in the welfare of the state, by supporting which he renders his own property secure. . . .

'Those who wish to see only the two castes of capitalists and day-labourers may smile at this union of independence and poverty . . . But the opposite system is daily quenching the independent spirit of the Highlands.'

The 'independent spirit of the Highlands' resisted as best it could the depredations of the Clearances, when English-educated absentee landlords evicted their tenants, sometimes by burning their crofts, to make way for more profitable sheep. The size of the Gaelic-speaking communities in Canada and Nova Scotia today bear witness to the ineffectualness of the resistance put up by the Highlanders.

It would be pointless to pretend that the clan system could have survived much longer than it did; pointless, too, to suggest that the Highlands could have supported today the population supported not much above starvation level in the immediate pre-Clearance years. But had the inevitable changes come more gradually, and by natural means, less damage might have been sustained by the Highland way of life, less havoc wrought upon the character of the Highlander. The Highlands had not recovered from the thrashing of Culloden and its protracted aftermath when the Clearances swept down. To reassert this is not to become sentimentally tangled with old history, for the Highlands still bear the marks of that double maiming.

Deprived of his practical independence, the Highlander fell an easy victim to the extreme doctrines of Calvinistic Presbyterianism. If he could no longer be lord of his own land, at least he could still be lord of his spirit; a narrow, tyrannical, petty lord filled with self-righteousness that offered some sort of compensation for the hopeless ineffectuality of his earthly position. The bigoted nature of the brand of Christianity which claimed so large a part of the Highlands during the nineteenth century made the task of trying to evolve some kind of workable modern economy an almost impossible one. Lowlanders who attempted to do so, to say nothing of Englishmen like Lord Leverhulme, found the Highlander intractable and impractical, and usually had to give up.

The problem of communications, which faced the Government of George I in a different form, bedevils almost every attempt that is made to set up light industries in the Highlands. At least one passionate enthusiast, John Rollo, succeeded on a small scale, but, because of the high costs involved in transporting raw materials into the Highlands and finished products out again, his highly personal pilot-schemes have not inspired the leaders of the big industrial battalions to follow up his example.

The argument usually put forward by the supporters of plans for industrial development in the Highlands is that transportation costs ought to be adjusted in some way to ease the burden on the more distant users. A parallel is drawn with the Post Office. It is pointed out, conveniently forgetting the telephone service, that a flat rate is charged for letters and parcels no matter how far they may have to be carried. If the flat-rate principle were to be applied to heavier goods, users in other parts of Britain would have to subsidize Highland industry. While direct and indirect subsidies are widely used to prop up the coal, gas and agricultural industries of Britain, producing expensively goods which could be more cheaply produced elsewhere has been considered unsound economics since Adam Smith first pronounced forcefully on the subject.

It may be argued that economic and social considerations ought somehow to be balanced. But balances of this sort are really only feasible where widespread interests are affected. By allowing so much of our Scottish industry and industrial potential to come under English control during the past half-century, we have largely lost the power of sustaining, or where necessary creating, accepted marketing centres for ourselves. There is no valid reason why many things, pottery for instance, should not be exported as effectively from Glasgow as from ports in the North and Midlands of England; and the same is true of motor cars,[1] or would have been true if, when these industries were still

[1] The Rootes Group factory at Linwood and the B.M.C. factory at Bathgate may herald the return of a prosperous motor industry to Scotland.

in their first flush of expansive development, we had not failed to retain them in Scotland. It seems fairly obvious that a country which has surrendered its right to control its own destiny must inevitably suffer, and learn simply to accept, deprivations of this sort, since it has no national incentive to help it fight for the retention of industrial control and no considerable economic case to pit against the interests of the prevailing British majority. The *Sunday Times* correspondent on economic affairs gave a sympathetic Englishman's view of this dilemma when he wrote in an article in the *Scotsman* on 8th July 1960: 'Today there is a strong centralized Government and more than a suspicion of a planned economy, and now we down South are the cock of the walk. The decisions are made here, and more and more the rest of you have to conform. You don't like it and I don't blame you, but you shouldn't have let us get away with it.'

If this is true of the Lowlands it is even more forcefully true of the thinly populated Highlands, whose minority wishes naturally count for very little in the councils of the United Kingdom.

The processes of history are first set in motion by the decisions of individuals. Before the moment of decision, potentialities exist which are afterwards removed further and further beyond the bounds of possibility. Ardent Scottish Nationalists may think otherwise, but to me it now seems too late in the day ever to hope to arrest, let alone reverse, the course of events set in motion when the Treaty of Union was signed in a dirty Edinburgh cellar in 1707.

Recently, an English solicitor, writing in the correspondence columns of a Scottish newspaper, described the Treaty as 'a dead letter'. In so far as the maintenance of Scots Law, the Church of Scotland and the right to issue Scots banknotes are concerned, his assertion was incorrect. Scots Law remains the legal basis of Scottish life, although its powers have been much affected by Orders in Council and other modern devices of British legislation which override national differences. The Church of Scotland successfully resisted incorporation with the Church of England as recently as the 1950s, although it is doubtful if it will have the strength to preserve its national identity to the end of the present century. The issuing of Scots banknotes is still regarded as a cherished right, though the number of them has decreased since

Dundee from Broughty Ferry Road

Drawn and engraved by Joseph Swan, published 1836

Aberdeen: Castle Street

the Second World War, and only one of the Scottish banks, the Royal Bank of Scotland, is still under Scottish control.

But these surviving rights and freedoms belong to the past. Certain courtesy freedoms affecting industrial development also survived into the latter part of the nineteenth century, partly because of the nature of the expansionistic Victorian phase through which the British economy was passing, and partly because of the relatively slow means of communication which preceded the development of the internal-combustion engine.

The idea that we Scots have somehow a right to preferential treatment, that our minority needs and desires should be met regardless of whether or not the resulting outcome is in the best interests of Britain as a whole, is a quaint anachronism many of us fiercely cherish. It may well be impossible for us to reverse the particular process of history which with every year that passes is obliterating more completely our sense of nationhood; but at least we ought to be able to diagnose the nature of the malaise that is crippling us, and adjust ourselves to face its consequences.

One of these necessary adjustments seems to me to relate to the impossibility of ever establishing industries in the Highlands on any significant scale. It is possible to point to a few industries that flourish successfully in the Highland area, notably the British Aluminium Company, which manufactures all the virgin aluminium produced in Britain at Foyers, Kinlochleven and Fort William. The establishment of these aluminium factories depended on the ready supply of cheap power. In the case of the two major factories, that power is produced by the company's own plants which use the pioneer hydro-electric schemes in Scotland. But, although the demand for aluminium steadily grows, the productive capacity of the Highland factories remains tied to the amount of water available to drive the turbines. That amount of water cannot easily be increased, and power from the Grid would be hopelessly uneconomic. So the newest factory for making virgin aluminium has been opened not in Scotland but in Canada.

The one industry which the Highlands can develop without the need for preferential treatment or other assistance is tourism; an industry the potential of which, in the words of a member of the Scottish Tourist Board, 'has only just been scratched on the surface'. The Highlands, it is true, do not enjoy Continental summer weather, but although prolonged heat-waves are comparatively rare the sunshine rate is higher and the amount of summer rainfall lower than is generally supposed, especially on either side of the wet period between the middle of July and the middle of August. The future pattern of Highland holiday-making seems likely to be shaped to the needs of motoring tourists. For them, an occasional shower on a sunny day is not the deterrent rain was to the old-style stay-put holiday-maker for whom dryness was all.

Until recently, the average Highlander barely troubled to conceal his antipathy to tourists, or his deep-rooted dislike of the tourist trade. Even a decade ago the idea of catering for the needs of tourists was all too often deemed to imply a slur upon Highland independence and pride. Independence is an admirable trait, but when one is in a position of economic instability it can be overdone. Highland pride is undoubtedly a survival of the peculiar nature of the old relationship between the clan chief and his vassals. But in the bitter days of defeat, when the clan system had been broken up, the old pride and loyalty went sour, degenerating into arrogant touchiness and a rigid code of narrow values.

On one occasion, while visiting the Loch Shiel countryside, I had to go without food of any kind from seven o'clock in the morning, when I left my hotel, until half past eleven at night, because I had not had the foresight to order in advance: 'You cannot expect us to provide meals if we do not know that you are coming.' There may have been some slight excuse for this insistence on ceremony so far as a full-scale meal was concerned; but there could be no excuse at all for the dour unwillingness even to go to the trouble of making coffee and sandwiches.

More recently, I arrived in an Inverness-shire hotel about a quarter to five in the afternoon, after a long drive from Loch Lomondside. When I asked for afternoon tea, I was informed by a scowling landlady that afternoon tea was at four o'clock, and that it was now quite definitely 'off'. 'Off' it was, and so was I; but not before I had seen a party of American tourists similarly treated.

These were personal experiences. I have heard of countless incidents where tourists have been refused a meal because they arrived after the set dinner-hour; of choiceless, unimaginative menus coupled with highly imaginative prices; of expensive packed lunches consisting of meat-paste sandwiches and dry biscuits; of greeds and grumps and downright discourtesies.

Incidents of this sort are much more likely to occur in hotels in the countryside than in town establishments; but they should not occur anywhere in an area one of whose main assets could be, and should be, tourism. They reflect a curdled pride, just as does the discourteous insistence that when in the Highlands visitors must conform to Highland superstitions, and abstain from doing whatever they may properly want to do on Fast Days and Sabbaths.

The stranglehold of the Free Presbyterian Kirk on many parts of the Highlands has now been broken, and many Highlanders openly laugh at its absurdities.

'D'ye know,' a Stornoway taxi-driver said to me of a Free Presbyterian Kirk minister well known for his fundamentalist views, 'the Reverend Whatsit So-and-So won't eat herring at all nowadays.'

'Won't eat herring? Why ever not?' I asked.

'Ach well, you see, it's like this. The thoughtless little buggers insist on playing on the Sabbath.'

Once, when in an island parish, I made the mistake of calling upon a Free Presbyterian Kirk minister instead of his Church of Scotland namesake. As I was ushered into his study I became aware of a certain air of disapproval, of fanatical intensity, so to clear my doubts I said: 'Your charge is, of course, the Church of Scotland, isn't it?'

'The Church of Scotland?' the minister replied. 'Certainly not. I wouldn't be seen dead in that temple of Satan.' With a hasty apology for my mistake in identification, I left this enthusiastic upholder of intolerance to the pleasures of his pathological gloomings.

Intolerance is never a pretty spectacle, but it wears the aspect of alarming folly when it is used as a holier-than-thou rampart against the most obvious source of livelihood to which the Highlander could turn to bring himself increased prosperity. It manifests itself absurdly in the outbursts of Free Presbyterian Kirk ministers whose attacks on the behaviour of members of the Royal Family receive publicity in the British Press quite out of keeping with their numerical inferiority and the size of their declining following. But their influence, and the influence of others equally narrow in outlook, is reflected in the reluctance of some of the Highland counties to consider any alteration in Scotland's absurd and outmoded Sunday drinking laws;[1] in such instances as the insistence of the Town Council of a West Coast holiday resort that cafés must remain shut until after the evening church service; and in the absolute refusal of many Highland places to allow any sort of Sunday entertainments or amenities to be provided for the tourists whose money the inhabitants are only too glad to take during the week, often by overcharging exorbitantly for inadequate service and attention.

It is not only bigoted quasi-religiosity that stands in the way of the development of tourism in the Highlands. There is in many a Highland heart a deep-rooted conviction that to cater for tourists is in some way degrading.

Writing in *The Piping Times* Seumas MacNeil put forward the theory that catering for tourists necessarily weakens the native traditions and culture. It appears to be his belief that the tourists in some way diminish the purity of the Highland dancing, Gaelic singing and piping which visitors quite openly enjoy. This point of view makes several startling assumptions, the largest of which is that the Gaels themselves strive to preserve the purity of their own culture, a culture that, by international standards, is in any case a very minor one.

Gaelic culture flourished most strongly before the traditional Highland economy had been shattered, when the Highlands were prosperous, according to their own standards. No pipe-music of imaginative significance has been produced since the middle of the eighteenth century. By then its social utility was waning and it was giving place to the fiddle as the instrument of domestic popularity. The technical limitations of the instrument are such too that by then its music had been developed to the limit. The Ceol Mhor, or Great Music—the pibroch, which is a theme with a set of cunningly contrived variations gradually increasing in rhythmic and ornamental complexity—was ousted in popularity by the Ceol Beag, or Little Music—the reels and strathspeys and marches—which found greater favour even before the eighteenth century was out, and which received a considerable and a sus-

---

[1] Since the above was written, the Guest Committee's recommendations give hope that the rear-guard obstruction of a small minority will not be allowed to impede reform.

tained stimulus with the formation of Highland regiments in the British Army.

Strictly speaking, pipe-bands are themselves an impurity; yet, without them, might the bagpipes not have suffered the fate of the clarsach, or of Ireland's Uilleann pipes?

Mr MacNeil, however, does not object to pipe-bands. Doubtless he would object to women pipers, to the 'swinging' of pipe-tunes and to attempts to make pipe-bands play tunes in harmony. I would support him whole-heartedly. A woman in a kilt (which should not be confused with a perfectly proper tartan skirt) wearing a sporran and a kilt jacket is committing no less objectionable an aesthetic offence than a man promenading publicly in a two-piece skirt and jacket. Kilted girls look silly in the way that anything which pretends to be what it is not is silly. In any case, the kilt shows off the female figure to the worst possible advantage. Furthermore, the bagpipes is an instrument demanding a kind of physical prowess which women simply do not possess. I have never heard a really able female piper.

The practice of attempting to make pipe-bands play in harmony had its origin in the Army's schools of piping, and, except through a rudimentary and pointless lapse into passages in thirds and sixths, cannot be done because of the restricted tonality and physical structure of an instrument equipped with drones. As for the 'swinging' of pipe-tunes, the practice is deplorable because it is tasteless. Music by Mozart, Chopin and Tchaikovsky has been from time to time 'swung', and has survived unimpaired long after the 'swung' arrangements have been forgotten. In any case, the visitor to the Highlands is not normally regaled with 'swung' pipe-music played by female pipers, but by individual pipers or municipal pipe-bands performing with the legitimate intention of delighting foreign ears with native folk-music.

So far as Gaelic folksong is concerned, it has become so thoroughly decadent and corrupt during the past hundred years that no one would know where to turn in search of purity. Victorian popular songs and the evangelical harmonies of Ira D Sankey have inhibited the Gaelic musical consciousness to such an extent that the average Highlander is quite unable to distinguish a genuine original folksong from the phonified softened versions of the late Sir Hugh Roberton, or other similar sentimental derangers; a fact which anyone who attends the annual

Mod, or musical get-together, of An Comunn Gaidhealach will quickly discover. At this gathering, considerable emphasis is placed upon ensemble and choral singing, socially beneficial but both alien to the pure Gaelic tradition of folksinging, and, so far as their application to Gaelic folk-music is concerned, entirely nineteenth century in origin. The pure instrument of accompaniment, the clarsach, or small harp, has fallen into almost total disuse, and is certainly never used on community occasions, the Italian accordion having driven out the Italian fiddle. It is therefore difficult to see how the purity of Gaelic folk-music can be menaced by the presence of tourists at Highland Ceilidhs, since its purity began to be sullied as soon as the conditions out of which it grew were subjected to Anglicization after 1746.

If the Highlander can shape his much-vaunted traditional hospitality into an attitude of consideration for those who do him the honour of visiting his majestic countryside as paying guests, there seems no reason why a new prosperity, different from that of the old order, should not come. One thing is certain: the old order has gone, and gone for ever, though its vestiges have lingered on sadly and somewhat inefficiently for close on two hundred years after the events that disconnected their validity.

It is natural scenery of incomparable grandeur and variety that draws tourists to the Highlands. Castles apart, there are scarcely any buildings worth a second glance North of the Highland line, since most of the towns only took shape permanently in the nineteenth century. Even today transportation costs inhibit the Highland architect, and many new buildings have obviously been built with cheapness as the overriding consideration.

At least the Highlander does not have constantly to fight in defence of his stone-and-mortar heritage against the Bumbledomers. Not even the most bigoted local authority has yet discovered how monetary advantage might be gained if Ben Nevis were to be demolished to make way for a car factory, or the waters of the Great Glen were to be drained to allow houses to be built for Glasgow's overspill population.

The pleasures of being in the Highlands are many. There is that sense of time having ceased to matter, exasperating to the Lowlander with business on his mind, yet wonderfully relaxing for those able to slacken the tensions that tie them to a faster-paced cosmopolitan way of life. It is the nearest one can get to a return to the pace of a vanished era. Time in the Highlands is something to think with. Beneath the silent hills, the weight of eternity is imaged with an unconcerned clarity, and while most people today no longer attach any religious significance to their awareness of such heightened sensibilities, it is surely good for all of us to be reminded now and again of our own insignificance.

Then there are the people themselves, though fewer of them each year: gracious and kindly, so long as circumstances do not make them draw back behind the frontiers of their pride, and they are not driven to touchiness by any hint of patronage or superiority.

Their Gaelic tongue is dying so fast that it seems unlikely to have left to it more than another fifty years. Its decline is partly associated with the problem of Highland depopulation. National Service took young men away from the townships and the glens, to the towns for military training, and sometimes to other countries. After such a widening of experience, few of them were prepared to go back to the arduous isolation of lonely croft or farm. In any case, the eldest son may succeed his father. But what are the children to do? In many parts of the Highlands and islands, there is no work of any kind for these young people. In Mull, for instance, depopulation is continuing at a rate which, if it were to be consistently maintained, would leave no one at all on the island in twenty-five years' time.

To the young Highlander it therefore seems obvious that, if he wishes a prosperous place beneath the Southern sun, it is English and not Gaelic that will enable him to fulfil his ambition. In spite of the strenuous and thoroughly praiseworthy efforts of An Comunn to help Gaelic find its self-respect again, only a minority of Highland children now learn the language efficiently, and still fewer take the trouble to maintain it once they have left school.

It is strange that a language in its death-throes should at this late hour have produced two excellent poets, George Campbell Hay and Derrick Thomson, and one poet whom the very few Gaelic scholars there are who have modern minds rate among the most powerfully imaginative writers ever to use the old tongue, Somhairle Mac Ghill Eathain (Sorley MacLean). To be a poet using Scoto-English, with the prospect of being read by only a few hundred people, is frustrating enough; but to be a poet writing in a language in which only half a dozen of its native speakers are sufficiently educated to be able to understand what you have said, let alone appreciate it, must chill both heart and muse.

The cinema, radio and television have played a part in modifying Highland speech. It is no use deploring instruments of social change, and those who are inclined to feel angry over the Anglification of Highland speech may draw some comfort from the equally marked Americanization of English speech which has taken place over the same period. Among the Highland upper classes, the language of speech has for long been a kind of English. A curious legend which maintains that the purest English is spoken in Inverness has grown up. I am not at all sure that I would recognize 'pure' English if I heard it. Inverness English simply carries across from the Gaelic tongue it has superseded pitch variations and soft vowel qualities which are not to be heard either in North Country English speech or in the speech of London and the Southern provinces. To the ears of those who may subconsciously harbour a sense of guilt towards the language of their forefathers which they have abandoned, Inverness English may seem reminiscently pleasant. But it can no more lay claim to purity than can Stratford-atte-Bowe French.

The curious hankering after an abstract purity is almost a Highland hobby. It reflects in yet another way the desire to hold on to the things that are going; and perhaps even, in an indirect way, it reflects the relationship between language and morals. When a language disintegrates, so does morality, or the system of relationships.

The disintegration of relationships has, in fact, been going on in the Highlands throughout the long decline of the Gaelic language. The homogeneity of the Gaelic and the homogeneity of Highland society are now both hopelessly fragmented. There is thus no such thing as standard Gaelic. Like Scots, though without the disadvantages of a shared syntax with English, Gaelic survives only in dialects which differ so markedly that a Gaelic-speaking Lewisman may have some difficulty in understanding a Gael from Skye.

The chief of a Highland clan, recently returned from a tour of Canada and Nova Scotia, told me that the Gaelic-speaking communities out there thought him 'a bit of a fraud', because he did not sound in the least like a Scot. Like most Highland aristocrats, he sounds, in fact, more or less like an aristocratic Englishman. There is no longer any common bond of language between chief or laird, and crofter or fisherman. The Highlands of the lairds is a place which, however dearly it may be loved, comes briefly into its own during the killing times of summer and autumn. No Highland chief or laird would ever dream of allowing his children to be educated locally. Many members of the select fraternity have London homes, or spend the greater part of their time outside of Scotland.

They may stroll around their policies or walk the streets of Inverness or Fort William finely attired in that picturesque but, for modern conditions, hopelessly unpractical dress the kilt; but in most cases it is all romantic play-acting. The ordinary Highlander goes about his skills of loch or hill dressed in a mass-produced suit from an English factory. Probably he does not even possess a kilt.

I neither mean these observations to sound critical, nor to suggest that the chiefs and the lairds are not in many cases deeply concerned with the well-being of the Highlands. Some of them give valuable and distinguished service on County and District Councils and other public bodies. But in speech and outlook they are often transplanted Englishmen in all but name and dress; a quaint anachronism; living evidence of the almost complete break-up of the system of relationships, the morality of the Highands.

A true state of the nation report upon the Highlands would show an even less encouraging position than a similar report upon the Lowlands. Depopulation continues; unemployment figures remain obstinately high; and, since the spread of progress was for long slower among the Highland districts than farther South, the pace of change is now more rapid and its effects constantly more disrupting than in any other part of Britain. Anyone who doubted Scotland's will to continuing nationhood would probably find more to disquiet him in the Highlands than in the Lowlands. Anyone who questioned Scotland's economic ability to be anything other than an erratically populated North British province might well feel after a sojourn in the Highlands that he was witnessing the beginnings of the practical working-out of his theory.

PART THREE

The Spiritual Fabric

14

C. M. Grieve: the poet as leader

HAVING surveyed, so to say, the stonework of the Scottish nation, and found it weathering indifferently, I now propose to examine the mortar that still holds the stones together. This involves a survey of the spiritual fabric of the nation; the media through which its ideas are created and fostered.

Twentieth-century Scotland has produced a very small quota of distinguished men. Most of them have achieved their distinction in one specialized field. I can think of only two men who have achieved, or almost achieved, a greatness that came within measuring distance of altering the destiny of Scotland, the nation. One of these men is Thomas Johnston, Secretary of State for Scotland during the Second World War. His vision of quickening the pulse of Scotland by making it work economically has its enduring monument in the hydro-electric schemes which now harness the force of Highland waters, schemes for the creation of which, with the aid of another man, Sir Edward McColl, he pioneered through years of public indifference.

The other is the poet, C. M. Grieve, whose ruthless questioning of the accepted Scottish values during the 'twenties and early 'thirties might, under difficult circumstances, have jolted Scotland seriously to take stock of her spiritual assets and liabilities.

I first met Christopher Murray Grieve ('Hugh MacDiarmid') one Sunday morning during the latter part of the Second World War, while I was on leave from the Army. Some months before I had fallen heavily under the imaginative spell of his early poetry in Scots, contained in *Sangschaw* and *Pennywheep*; as completely as, at the age of eighteen, I became enthralled by A. E. Housman's *A Shropshire Lad*. Then followed the revelation of *A Drunk Man Looks at the Thistle*, with its restless questioning of long-accepted Scots values, and its remarkable re-creation of the climate of industrial Scotland in the 'twenties. Grieve seemed to me then a giant among pygmies, a prophetic figure whose vision was neither shared nor even acknowledged by his fellow countrymen. His revivification of the fragmented Scots tongue, which he used with such unerring musical mastery in his early poems, stirred in me a passionate interest in the language of my Lowland ancestors, and drove me to master Middle Scots and read right through the complete works of the Makars in a mere few months. Grieve, the inspirer of this enthusiasm, became for me a point of focus for those Scottish feelings and aspirations which had somehow percolated through my rather Anglified education; a symbol of a new and better Scotland. Soon afterwards I wrote a poem in his honour, and sent it to him with a request to be allowed to call on him. 'To Hugh MacDiarmid', still seems to me accurately to portray the way that I, and others of what Eric Linklater called the 'second wind' phase of the Scottish Renaissance, felt about Grieve at a time when the scent of reviving nationhood seemed to be very much in the air.

I

The English see you as an angry eagle
who tears at them with sharp and furious claws:
a mad, persuasive Gael who would inveigle
the Celts to raise their long-abandoned cause.

Sometimes they see you set in Highland weather,
red glens of shaggy cattle, a bleak moor
where game-birds flutter from the fading heather,
dark-scented pine-woods laced with pointed spoor.

Or like the island clansmen in the posters,
meeting the steamer once or twice a day;
or fishing with dour crofters for blue lobsters
to fill the creel-pots anchored in the bay.

They think that in your stern and rocky language
you catch the scudding Hebridean spray,
that words like sparks are only cast to furbish
the violent moods of Scottish history.

Your kilt, and all your gestures of romancing
are quaint; but oh! it's late into the day
to intercept the leisurely advancing
of England on her humanistic way.

And so they smile with unconcerned indulgence,
pay tribute to the temper of your thought,
admire your passion's vigorous effulgence,
but not the cause for which you lived and fought.

II

Foreigners see our country veiled in romance
a land where savages robbed and roved in clans;
our people, slow, unwilling to advance,
soft-spoken Gaelic ghillies, shooting hands
who labour to provide the Autumn sport
of English lairds, but never understand
the conscious English joke or the stock retort.

You have put that contemptuous nonsense back in its
    place,
and are no longer concerned with the rotting shielings
and the dreary, crumbling dust of a vanished race;
but with the steady hands and hearts that are willing
to cultivate the vast and desolate space
two hundred empty years have left behind,
you would cut all cancerous growth from the Scottish
    mind.

For you are not contained by the edge of an age,
easing the sharp, contemporary itch
with a trumped-up tag or a newly polished adage
for the anxious eyes that stare at their own last ditch;
but one who, on Time's only mountainside,
searches the clouds for where the heavens divide.

When my request to call upon Grieve was granted, the poet,
who had recently left his home in Whalsay—one of the smaller
islands in Shetland, where he had spent the latter years of the
'thirties—to come to Glasgow to work in war-geared heavy

industry, was living in furnished rooms in a Partick street. Dressed in a pair of grey flannel trousers and a faded old kilt jacket and waistcoat, he received me with that gentle courtesy and charm which astonishes so many people who know him only as a merciless pen opponent. He sat against the light, his Borderer's shock of hair filling out the window-pane, pulling at his pipe—I never catch a whiff of 'thick black' in bus or train without recalling that scene in Grieve's room—as he talked of his hope for Scotland. He immediately impressed me as one who had the ability to create and to share out a sense of confident patience. Things were moving in the right direction, he urged, slowly but surely, and it only needed time for Scotland to awaken to a renewed consciousness of her nationhood. Eagerly I accepted his sense of certainty, his unwavered confidence in Scotland.

'After all,' he had written in his autobiography *Lucky Poet*, 'I have only been writing in Scots and conducting my anti-English propaganda for a decade and a half. That is not a long time in which to register definite results in trying to arrest and reverse what has been the prevailing course for a couple of centuries.'

He seemed to me to have read everything, and always to be able to lay his hands on some learned authority whose big-gun expertise could be fired off in support of his own views. In un-guarded moments of animation, his eyes took on an intensity that I found almost hypnotic.

Soon after that visit, I began to experiment in the writing of Scots myself, and was soon tacitly enrolled, with other similarly minded young writers, under Grieve's Scots revivalist banner. In the autumn of 1946 Grieve and his followers found themselves engaged in an extraordinary public battle, carried on through the correspondence columns of nearly every daily newspaper and magazine in Scotland. The issue was the propriety under modern conditions of using synthetic or plastic Scots in literary papers, and it was developing into a topic which engaged the enthusiastic attention of Scots folk who ordinarily take no interest in poetry whatever. It was a controversy with reverberations of such con-siderable significance that I have discussed them separately in a later chapter.

It is natural for young writers with similar ideas to band to-gether into movements, especially around a romantic leader like Grieve; and equally natural for such movements to disintegrate

Highland Cottage: the home of MacNab, a blacksmith at Dalmally

Published in Voyage en Angleterre, en Ecosse et aux Îles Hébrides by Faujas de Saint Fond, 1784

Glasgow: an amateur concert

as the developing individualities of those who make it up rack the uniting bonds with differing stresses. Artistic movements provide a protective harbour, behind the walls of which the young artist can trim his craft for the voyage ahead. Those who linger behind the shelter too long find either that its protection ultimately saps the will to sail, or that their craft begins to rot; that, in fact, they have nothing personal to say. The career of every artist is a lonely, private voyage, with at best occasional friendly lights to port or starboard bringing passing comfort.

The issues that finally made me cut loose from the group were Communism and Anglophobia. The first creed Grieve has acknowledged throughout his adult life, during which, except for a period of suspension because of 'nationalist deviation', he has been a member of the Communist Party. The second is described in *Who's Who* as his hobby.

Many Scots dislike certain aspects of the English character in varying degrees. Deep down in the Scots racial consciousness there are doubtless memories of ancient enmities. Never having themselves been conquered in close on a thousand years, the English have developed, gradually and inevitably, a sense of natural domination, an unconscious superiority complex towards the lesser breeds who have been brought under their rule. It is a complex that has not exactly endeared them to the people of the countries which, when British Imperialism's bounds were most widely set, used to be coloured pink on the map. In many of these countries, the English—it is surely absurd to pretend that where the ratio of Britain's population is more than four to one in England's favour the oppressive policies were not predominantly English—relinquished their hold only after repressive measures carried out in the name of Law and Order had failed.

From time to time Scots folk may feel that their affairs are being overlooked by the British Government in Westminster, and will protest vocally against this or that particular fancied injustice. But to present, and expect to be widely accepted, an image of the English as brutal oppressors, contemptible creatures who skim all the cream from Scotland's milk and from whose influence the majority of the people of Scotland are longing to be freed, is not only to indulge in romantic escapism of the wildest sort but totally to misinterpret the feelings of the average Scot. What, therefore, could his compatriots make of Grieve when, in *To*

Circumjack Cencrastus, he defined his 'whole personality and life-story' as being to separate the two countries?

> 'I ken the stars that seem sae faur awa'
> Ha'e that appearance juist because my thocht
> Canna yet bridge the spiritual gulf atween's
> And the time when it will still seem remote
> As interstellar space itsel!
> Yet no' sae faur as 'gainst my will I am
> Frae nearly a'body else in Scotland here,
> But a less distance than I'll drive betwixt
> England and Scotland yet.'

A poet whose purpose—achieving a mere act of separation—was so much at variance with the feeling of his compatriots, could hardly fail to find himself isolated. I do not believe that either force, or hate, can achieve the permanent conversion of men's minds, and sense of nationality is largely an attitude of mind. Anglophobia is thus a fussy tilting at ruined windmills, a romantic gesture of superb but pointless extravagance.

As for Grieve's Communism, that, too, seems to me an excursion into romanticism, for it is a Christ-substitute, Gothi-cized Lenin whom the poet worships in 'At Lenin's Tomb' and in the three *Hymns to Lenin*.

> 'Our concern is with human wholeness—the child-like spirit
> New-born every day—not, indeed, as careless of tradition
> Nor of the lessons of the past: these it must needs inherit,
> But as capable of such complete assimilation and surrender,
> So all-inclusive, unfenced-off, uncategoried, sensitive and
>   tender,
> That growth is unconditional and unwarped—Oh, Lenin,
> Life and that more abundantly, thou Fire of Freedom!
> Multiplying talent and virtue without end,
> Firelike in your purity and Heaven—seeking vehemence,
> Yet the adjective must not suggest merely meteori,
> Spectacular—not the flying sparks, but the intense
> Glowing core of your character, your large and splendid
>   stability
> Made you the man you were—the live heart of all humanity!'

One cannot but admire the sweep of the rhetoric and the splendid sentiments with which this passage from the 'Third Hymn to Lenin' begins. But I find it impossible to believe that anyone who objectively examines Lenin's conduct and the manner in which Communism was established in the Soviet Union would ever be convinced by romantic adulation of that sort.

Grieve has hammered so insistently his belief in the necessity of Anglophobia and the inevitability of Communism, that his public militancy upon these issues has not only overshadowed the magnitude of his genius in the popular mind but helped to increase the sense of isolation about which he frequently complains. It has also prevented him from exerting a comparable influence in his own country to that which Yeats exerted in Ireland. 'A kind of Scottish Yeats', I have heard Grieve called. The operative phrase is 'kind of'. While Grieve at the height of his poetic powers probably had more passion than Yeats, he lacked the Irishman's appreciation of the value of restraint and self-discipline.

It is true that the historic figures who make up the mental fabric which is the nationhood of Scotland were all great romantics—Wallace; Bruce; Mary, Queen of Scots; Bonnie Prince Charlie and Burns. It is also true that most of them were neglected, exiled or executed; certainly safely dead before the lost causes which they championed won the allegiance denied to them when it might have had some practical effect.

It seems not unlikely that fifty years hence, if Scotland survives that long as an entity, Grieve may well be seen in retrospect as one of that company. By then, such personal matters as the echoes of other people's writings which sound through his later verse and much of his prose, and his ruthless epistolary savaging of anyone who dared to utter a word of adverse criticism of his work or his crusadings will have been forgotten. The boulder-strewn high places of the prose poems of his later days, and the raging torrents of his copious and quotation-laden prose, will have been charted and sign-posted. The imaginative force of his earlier Scots poems will no longer be shadowed by the prejudices he has engendered in the process of trying to bludgeon Scotland along directions she has no desire to go. He will take his place as one of the most considerable literary figures Scotland has produced, second to Burns only because, in the long run, the poet who loved his fellow men and sympathized with their faults and failings is inevitably a fuller human being than the poet who preferred to ridicule and castigate them.

In 'Talking with Five Thousand People in Edinburgh', Grieve wrote:

'For I am like Zamyatin. I must be a Bolshevik
Before the Revolution, but I'll cease to be one quick
When Communism comes to rule the roost. . . .'

Some day a full study of Grieve and his work may reveal the reasons and causes that made of Scotland's greatest potential leader in the end merely a psychological rebel, an excitable pamphleteer.

Yet I would not have it thought that I underestimate him. Even his most illogical outpourings make rewarding reading; not only because of the always present possibility that at any moment the deluge of interesting but frequently ill-digested opinions of others may give place to a passage of pure poetic genius which is indubitably himself, but because, even at his crankiest, the un-flagging zest of his mind at work is a fascinating spectacle. Though he has failed to become a national leader—to realize the symbol he seemed to me potentially to be when first I met him—and though, when I could no longer remain an uncritical follower, my share of castigation was bitterer than most, I salute the man and love him.

15

Scottish Nationalism: dampness in the heather

IT IS difficult for a small nation to hold its head up without an occasional prideful toss. Big nations need have no inhibitions in the matter of pride. They may rant and boast of their achievements, real or fanciful, and the others must perforce accept their demeanour, whether they like it or not. But when a small nation indulges in even a modest bit of head-tossing it finds itself condemned for chauvinism. In the two-power world of our later twentieth century, nationalism is only an offence against cosmopolitan decency if it is practised by a small nation.

I have never been able to understand the popular set of values which ordains that it is absolutely right and proper to be self-consciously British, and even more right and proper to declare awareness of a Commonwealth affinity, yet simply narrow-minded to be proud of being a Scot. It is almost as if we Scots, stricken for more than two and a half centuries with a deep feeling of inferiority, try to compensate ourselves by being outrageously British, although the result of our efforts is simply a different kind of narrowness. The bluff anti-European pro-lowbrow British-at-any-price propaganda barked out every other day in staccato journalese through the leader columns of the *Daily Express* is to the liberal mind surely just as offensive and absurd as the propaganda of the extreme nationalist groups in Scotland, and a good deal more dangerous?

I was aware of being a Scot from an early age. In later years I have come to regard myself as a Scot and a European, the intermediary British stage being more than anything else an acceptable matter of administrative convenience. Such a position seems perfectly logical. The influences of location and environment have conditioned my Scottishness. The traditions of European culture, including the English traditions, have influenced the development of my mind. There is, in fact, no such thing as a British tradition. More than two and a half centuries of union have not yet entirely eradicated the persistent doggedness of those mental qualities, physical conditions and social circumstances which shaped and preserved the old Scotland. Similarly, the passage of the years has not made the English feel any less English or more willing to describe the United Kingdom as *Britain* if they can get away with calling it *England*.

Yet somehow I have never been able to allow myself to become politically involved. There has to be fanatical Scottish Nationalism, as there have to be herds of pure Highland cattle if the virility of the crossbreeds is to be maintained. But many of the ways in which this concentrated Scottish Nationalism expresses itself are apt to seem ridiculous. Those who annually gather upon the field of Bannockburn on the fourteenth of June, to commemorate Robert the Bruce's victory over Edward I, usually have their fervour warmed by romantic addresses which seek to align the twentieth century with the fourteenth, although the times are so far out of joint that no useful parallel can possibly be drawn.

I was once persuaded to assist a Scottish Nationalist candidate who was contesting a Lowland seat in a Parliamentary by-election. Not being a political person in the party sense, I lent my services out of curiosity rather than conviction. Passionate political enthusiasts, like poets, never accept defeat, no matter how hopeless the odds may be against them. Unfortunately, they are usually, at best, indifferent organizers, and thus suffer a double handicap. I turned up to address one local meeting where the audience consisted of two people. One was the local organizer, the other the village idiot. Undeterred, my companion-in-oratory conjured up the shades of Wallace and Bruce in an impassioned address, and then went on to enumerate alleged facts (which could neither be proved nor disproved on the spot) in support of discriminatory economic manœuvres which, he claimed, were part of England's wicked and perpetual machinations against Scotland. To a duet of applause he stepped down from the platform, mopping his brow as he made way for me. But I was overcome by the ridiculousness of the whole affair, and fled ignominiously from the hall.

Much of the candidate's propaganda effort was directed at the lieges from a car fitted with a loudspeaker. As we made our way through the main street of a busy country town, my companion (poet, scholar and latter-day Admirable Crichton) sat with a microphone in his hand, chanting:

> 'Only a fool
> Likes English rule.'

This he varied with:

> 'Stop the hoary Tory ramp,
> Vote for Bloggs the Scottish champ.'

and:

> 'Put an end to Labour rot,
> Send back Bloggs the progressive Scot.'

Few of the rush-hour shoppers even turned their heads in our direction. When he began to grow hoarse, my companion thrust the microphone into my lap, saying: 'Now you do it.'

I felt my face heating with embarrassment; not because I was out of sympathy with Bloggs, the progressive Scot, but because attempting to settle a district's political destiny in this scatty fashion seemed irresponsible. No doubt every party machine in action at the lowest level is apt to seem ludicrous, since big issues are reduced to trifles, little issues are magnified to absurdity and the truth becomes a commodity that no man knoweth. Anyway, I rolled down the window, hoping that the noise of the traffic would prevent me hearing the sound of my own voice and began:

> 'Only a fool
> Likes English rule.'

I boomed about the heads of the bored and busy people. At the third *da capo*, a police horse, more curious than the pedestrians, shoved its nose through the open window and emitted one of those moist, reverberating snorts which sentimental people assume indicates horse-disapproval. It was certainly a fitting comment upon my performance. The candidate was not successful.

It is not only the unrealistic approach of the Scottish Nationalist Party and the virtual impossibility of producing a sound unscrambled economic blueprint for Scotland which stands in the way of Nationalist candidates achieving practical political results. The Scots disease of dissension-making operates in its most virulent form among the ranks of the patriots. Quarrels lead to divisions and the formation of tiny splinter groups who advocate this or that line of special action. The ultimate result is that none of them are ever in a position to implement any kind of significant action. Even the once-popular Scottish Convention movement which, had it been able in 1951 to secure a nation-wide plebiscite on the question of domestic Home Rule, might very well have persuaded a clear majority of the Scottish people to vote for a Parliament similar in function and organization to the Parliament of Northern Ireland, is no longer a power in the land. Inability to sustain a cause, to carry through the long slow pull, has been proved over and over again to be one of our most unfortunate weaknesses.

But the parties and the organizers must not be blamed too exclusively. With a record of failure going back three-quarters of a century, the cause of Scottish Nationalism itself must obviously now be suspect. If a majority of people want a change in the political conditions under which they live, ultimately they must get what they want. No Scottish party or group has yet succeeded in isolating the issue of Scottish Home Rule from the British concerns of the Conservative, Liberal and Labour parties, and still managed to maintain any significant Scottish following. The vested interests of the upper classes, who have a long tradition of loyalty to the Crown (which, rightly or wrongly, is widely presumed to be opposed to any change in the governmental arrangements within the United Kingdom), inhibits one stratum of Scottish society from giving support to any measure which might strengthen Scotland's sense of nationhood by political means. The centralization of the Trade Union movement has ensured that there is little likelihood of support from that section of the community whose leaders once made it a cardinal issue and where the quality of Scottishness survives most strongly in speech and affection. In between, the middle classes have altered in character, being no longer mainly made up of professional people and *rentier*, but now also containing men and women who have risen to managerial or executive status from the factory floor. Having altered their calculated loyalties accordingly, quite naturally they are strongly opposed to speculative change.

In the end, the validity of Scottish Nationalism becomes a matter of personal attitude. Whenever the question of Home Rule for Scotland comes into a conversation, many people reveal a curious lack of trust in themselves as Scots. Highlanders assert that a Scottish Parliament would merely be a paradise for Edinburgh lawyers; that nothing less than a Parliament in Inverness would be of any use to the Highlands; and that since a Highland Parliament is obviously out of the question things had best be left as they are. Lowlanders declare that Scotland simply could not produce enough men of distinction to provide a Scottish Parliament, and that she would therefore find herself ruled by glorified local councillors, since the few able parliamentarians would sooner or later seek transference to Westminster. Partisan persons are sure that a Scottish Parliament would be Labour-dominated; Conservative-ridden; a breeding-ground for Roman Catholicism; or a means for prolonging the officious power of Presbyterianism. Trade Unionists insist that the industrial affairs of the two countries are now so completely interwoven that separation of any kind could only have harmful effects on the Scottish economy and depress still further Scotland's chronic unemployment rate. Business men see visions of Border barriers and possible discriminatory action against Scottish goods, such as an English Government once threatened when it looked as if Scotland was going to resist the terms of the Union of 1707. Others believe that all nationalism (except, of course, the British variety which came into prominence at the time of the Suez crisis) is harmfully retrogressive.

All these good people may be right. But they remind me of the man who went to see a psychiatrist because he was obsessed with a deep-rooted feeling of inferiority. The psychiatrist gave the patient a long and searching examination before pronouncing his verdict: 'I'm afraid the trouble with you, sir, is that you *are* inferior.'

16

Lallans and all that

WHEN a nation relinquishes its language the defences surrounding its nerve-centre come down. From that point in history when medieval Scotland emerged as a political entity out of the darkness and divided confusion of the preceding three or four centuries, Scotland has had two languages of her own: Gaelic, once apparently the language of most of the country; and Scots, which shared common Germanic roots with English, and which the early Makars even called 'Inglis' to distinguish it from Gaelic. It gradually drove back the older tongue from the Lowlands into the Highlands. For the purposes of learning, Latin, although never in any real sense a live language in Scotland, held considerable sway until about the middle of the eighteenth century. By this time the after-effects of the Union of 1707 had alerted the ears of the Scottish upper classes to English as it was then profitably spoken in and around the Court of St James. Thereafter English gradually began to edge out Scots, as Scots had edged out Gaelic five hundred years before.

Yet throughout the nineteenth century, Scots clung on tenaciously, surviving as the language of the country folk and of the poorer classes in the towns. It even managed to influence the kind of English spoken, and written, by Scots people. But it was fighting a losing battle, in spite of its spirited counter-attack as a powerful literary medium in the hands of Ramsay, Fergusson, Burns and others. By 1887, when Robert Louis Stevenson's *Underwoods* was published, he was moved to lament in his preface: 'The day draws near when this illustrious and malleable tongue shall be quite forgotten, and Burns's Ayrshire and Dr MacDonald's Aberdeen awa' and Scott's brave, metropolitan utterance will be all equally the ghosts of speech.'

The same presentiment of doom was echoed more clearly by Andrew Lang in 1900 in the introduction he provided to Charles Murray's *Hamewith*: '. . . the poems beget a certain melancholy . . . from a world that is dead or dying, the world of Scott and Hogg, the world that knew not polluted streams and railways and motor-cars, and worst of abominations, the gramophone.'

Fifteen years later, John Buchan, in his preface to Violet Jacobs' *Songs of Angus*, prophesied: '. . . pure Scots is a tongue which in the changes of the age is not widely understood, even in Scotland. The various accents remain, but the old words tend to be forgotten, and we may be in sight of a time when that noble speech shall be degraded to a northern dialect of English.'

In view of the prevailing conditions when they were made, none of these prophecies seems in any way unreasonable. Apart from the works they themselves heralded, little or nothing of any significance had been produced in Scots since the deaths of John Galt and Lady Nairne. It had become a medium used only by talentless versifiers hiccupping and nudging themselves over trivial parochial concerns in obscure corners of local news-papers.

The first talkie cinema in Scotland opened its doors in 1929, thereby letting in a new and devastating influence: Hollywood American, which has now begun to edge out English in some quarters. But in 1925, two years after the establishment of broad-casting in Scotland, a remarkable thing happened. C. M. Grieve, in the guise of Hugh MacDiarmid, published his first book of lyrics, *Sangschaw*, which was hailed, very properly, as a notable achievement; a fact which surprised no one more than the poet himself, according to his life-long friend and one-time school-master Francis George Scott. From the files of Grieve's magazine *Scottish Chapbook*, where some of the *Sangschaw* lyrics first appeared, it seems fairly obvious that Grieve was then trying out many styles, including the affected heavily mannered style of his Georgian elders.

In the *Underwoods* preface, from which I have already quoted, Stevenson admitted:

'I simply wrote my Scots as well as I was able, not caring if it hailed from Lauderdale or Angus, from the Mearns or Galloway; if I had heard a good word, I used it without shame; and when

Scots was lacking or the rhyme fitted I was glad—like my betters
—to fall back on English.'

Sangschaw also carried a preface by John Buchan, who now
found cause to applaud a development which clearly he had not
foreseen when he wrote the *Hamewith* preface twenty years before.
In 1925 Buchan wrote:

'My friend, the author of this book, has set himself a task
which is at once reactionary and revolutionary. . . . He would
treat Scots as a living language, and apply it to matters which have
been foreign to it since the sixteenth century. Since there is no
canon of the vernacular, he makes his own, as Burns did, and
borrows words and idioms from the old masters. He confines
himself to no one dialect, but selects where he pleases between
Aberdeen and the Cheviots. . . . I welcome the honest hope and
faith which inspire the experiment.'

Burns, of course, confined his linguistic amalgam more or less
to the dialects of Ayrshire and Galloway. He had no need to
augment his vocabulary from the language of his predecessors,
for the living language was then still adequate for his needs. But,
like Stevenson later, he did not hesitate to 'fall back on English'
when it suited his purpose, or to achieve special effects of contrast
or social characterization.

Grieve's revolution, however, as Buchan had hinted, was not
confined simply to the restoration of the Scots tongue. He
restored intelligence to Scots verse, a restoration already carried
out in English literature by T. S. Eliot a few years earlier. Scots,
in Grieve's hands, was to be made capable of handling any
material, physical or metaphysical, which a man of lively intelligence might want to write about. The theory seemed an admirable
one; but what happened in practice?

Grieve produced a second book of splendid lyrics, *Pennywheep*,
in 1926, following this up two years later with his lyrical and
satirical masterpiece, *A Drunk Man Looks at the Thistle*. Thereafter the intellectual content of his verse grew gradually bulkier
and the Scots grew thinner; until, by the early 'thirties—less than
a decade after his first book was published—he threw Scots over-
board. Although he has never stopped assuring his admirers that

one day he intends to go back and rescue it again, no one, possibly not even himself, now takes that promise seriously.

Grieve's success produced few imitators, because it is not easy to imitate the sort of startling originality of imagery that was the product of Grieve's youthful muse. But it produced one able disciple during the 'thirties, the Perth poet William Soutar. It was a reading of *A Drunk Man Looks at the Thistle* that directed Soutar's energies into the writing of Scots verse. For the greater part of his adult life he was a bedridden invalid, living in a book-lined room which looked out upon the flower-garden of his father's house at Perth. A great deal of Soutar's energy went into the writing of decidedly flat English verse, much of it couched in humdrum hymn stanzas preaching his belief in the necessity of Pacifism. When he used Scots he became a master of the humorous character-sketch in verse which, because of its ironic pointing and implied human sympathy, often strays naturally over the tenuous boundary line between verse and the realm of poetry. He was also a master of vividly imagined children's poems, which he called 'bairnsangs' and which, like most of his Lallans work, were written in a language firmly rooted in the Scots of his native Perthshire, but on to which he occasionally grafted Scots words from other airts as and when he required them.

Had Soutar been in the full possession of his physical faculties, he might perhaps have come to closer grips with the problems of contemporary Scottish life. As it was, he sang sweetly and softly of the world and its ferlies, of the moon and its mysteriousness, and of the uncertainties of human life. In Soutar's work there is always a keenness of observation, a simpleness of structure (for he believed rather too whole-heartedly in the communicative efficacy of the old ballad stanza), an innocent humour and an all-pervading kindness which, blended with his sense of acceptance and resignation, gives to many of his poems a feeling of withdrawnness, of other-worldly calm.

When the 'thirties closed stormily with the world at war, it could not have been said that the Scottish Renaissance (as the late Professor Dennis Saurat dubbed the revival of interest and purpose in Scots literature) was making much progress on a wide front. In the ranks of the poets only Soutar marched with Grieve. True, Lewis Grassic Gibbon (J. Leslie Mitchell) had achieved an original and impressive Anglo-Scots 'speak' in prose, and had used it to depict the rural and urban life of the North-East in *A Scots Quair*; while in *Morning Tide*, *Highland River*, *Young Art and Old Hector*, and other books, Neil M. Gunn had looked at the Highlands with a new and unsentimental integrity. Eric Linklater, too, had cut a vigorous Norse caper or two from his Orkney stronghold in *White Maa's Saga*, *Men of Ness* and *Magnus Merriman*, before allowing his talents to rove more cosmopolitan fields; and Sir Compton Mackenzie (as he now is), already a great British rather than a Scottish novelist, was cheering romantically from the wings. But this was hardly the kind of revival envisaged by Grieve, the national Renaissance hailed by Saurat.

The movement got what Linklater called its second wind during the war. Emotions were perforce kept more tightly strung than normally. Poetry enjoyed a boom. Out of the war there emerged the New Apocalypse movement and the group of writers who became known as the Lallans Makars.

The writers of the New Apocalypse included in their ranks four or five Scots. J. F. Hendry shared the leadership with the Welshman Henry Treece, and G. S. Fraser was well up in the van. Norman McCaig was an enthusiastic supporter, and Tom Scott's work appeared frequently under the Apocalypse banner. I was myself associated with the group, though much less directly.

The whole thing was, in fact, a revolt through literature against the authoritarianism which necessarily prevailed in war-time, and against the political follow-my-leader attitude of the Auden-Spender-Day Lewis group who, in the 'thirties, naïvely embraced Communism as the panacea to cure the world's ills (though happily not to the extent of impairing their considerable talents). Fraser set forth the aims of Apocalypticism in an essay, 'Apocalypse in Poetry', which appeared in *The White Horseman* (1941), the first of the movement's three anthologies.

'The New Apocalypse,' he wrote, 'derives from Surrealism, and one might even call it a dialectical development of it: the next stage forward. It embodies what is positive in Surrealism. . . . It denies what is negative—Surrealism's own denial of man's right to exercise conscious control, either of his political and social destinies, or of the material offered to him as an artist by his subconscious mind.'

Unfortunately, most of the poems in the three anthologies seemed to suggest the very absence of control against which

Fraser took his stand; thus Norman McCaig, who has since become a good poet, could perpetrate lines like these:

'I brought you elephants and volcano tops
and a eucalyptus tree on a coral island,
I had them in baskets. You looked with surprise,
And went away to pick weeds out of the
ground.'

—on the whole a remarkably restrained reaction to such an unusual offering.

By the time the third Apocalyptic anthology *The Crown and the Sickle* appeared, the accent had changed, and was now upon what was openly called 'personalism'. A significant feature of the New Apocalypse was the fact that most of the writers who subscribed to its credo were Scots, and of those who were not more than half were Welsh.

The 'second wind' Lallans Makars drew their energy from the same source as the writers of the Apocalypse: from the urge to assert the value of the individual in a social situation which reduced individuality to a kind of anti-social nuisance; and an extension of this principle, the desire to assert the value of the traditions of small nations, in particular Scotland, their own nation. These basic motives were not perhaps formulated so insistently as the motives of the writers of the Apocalypse, but none the less they had considerable urgency.

The focal point, so far as Scotland was concerned, at which the writers of the two movements came together was the series of four anthologies called *Poetry Scotland* which I edited (in the case of *Poetry Scotland* in collaboration with 'Hugh MacDiarmid') between 1943 and 1949, and the anthology *Modern Scottish Poetry: An Anthology of the Scottish Renaissance, 1940–1945*. It was a review of this anthology in *The Glasgow Herald* which touched off the Lallans controversy. The reviewer wrote: 'There are times, one feels, when the deliberate use of Scots is a hindrance to the complete expression of the modern poet; he is attempting to express himself in what is really an unfamiliar language, in that it is not his ordinary mode of speech.'

Basically, of course, the reviewer was right, so far as his strictures on the viability of the language were concerned. But he was wrong in his inference that there could be no achievement in Lallans. Apart from the considerable early achievement of Grieve, Sydney Goodsir Smith's *Under the Eildon Tree* seems to me to be a masterpiece by European standards; and Smith and at least half a dozen other writers have produced between them a body of about thirty shorter poems which have continuing validity as literature. The fact that they happen to be in Lallans is incidental.

The controversy which broke about the heads of the Lallans poets swelled the correspondence columns of *The Glasgow Herald* and *The Scotsman* for several months in 1947, overflowing into many other newspapers and journals. People who normally had no great interest in contemporary literature entered into the fray with astonishing zest, and not only on the side of those who attacked Lallans. But the predominating character of the controversy was hostility towards the Lallans Makars. 'To be a poet in Scotland nowadays,' Robert Kemp remarked on the day a particularly unpleasant verbal assault appeared, 'you really need to be endowed with the stamina of a professional boxer.'

'D'ye see that awful man Maurice Lindsay's got another letter in the *Herald* today?' said one Glasgow matron to another in a West End post-office queue of which I was also a member.

'Oh, has he?' said the other, standing beside me. 'Him and his Lallans. He's a terrible man. He beats his wife.'[1]

Lallans offered to Scotland the sort of vigorous challenge to her nationhood that a young second wife might present to the once virile but now ageing manhood of her husband. Scotland was impotent to accept the challenge, and with a troubled conscience furiously rejected it. Although it did not seem so to me at the time, no other course was open. The social forces whittling away Scotland's sense of nationhood—which one may lament but against which it is pointless to rail—had produced circumstances which made a successful revival of Lallans similar to the revival of Landsmaal in Norway, a dream without any possibility of realization. The syntactical heart had been carved out of Lallans two hundred years ago. Scholarship, poetic ability, industry, even passion, were powerless to concoct an artificial one.

In the introduction to his interesting anthology, *New Lines*,

[1] Footnote by Mrs Lindsay: 'He does not!'

published in 1958, Robert Conquest, with that understanding which has made the English beloved all over the world, wrote:

'In the 1940s the mistake was made of giving the Id, a sound player on the percussion side under a strict conductor, too much of a say in the doings of the orchestra as a whole. As it turned out, it could only manage the simpler part of melody and rhythm, and was completely out of its depth with harmony and orchestration. This led to a rapid collapse of public taste, from which we have not yet recovered. . . . Poets were encouraged to produce diffuse and sentimental verbiage, or hollow technical pirouettes: praise even went to writers whose verse seemed to have been put together, from the snippets in the "Towards more Picturesque Speech" page of the *Reader's Digest*. Residual nuisances like the Social-realists, the Lallans-mongers, the church-furnishers and the Neo-Georgians were able to maintain themselves.'

So far as the writers of the Apocalypse were concerned, Conquest's charges might have been thought reasonably founded, were it not for the fact that by 1958 many of the Apocalyptics had long since outgrown their wartime confusions and written clearly and well. Some of G. S. Fraser's pieces, for instance, would not have seemed out of place even in *New Lines*, to which, indeed, they would have lent distinction: and Norman McCaig has developed into one of the finest poets writing in Britain today.

So far as the sneer against the 'Lallans-mongers' is concerned, the inference that they were insincere is utterly unwarranted. All of them are known to me personally and their sincerity of purpose at the time of the Lallans dispute is beyond question. Poets who produce even one good poem apiece, in a language which an Englishman finds difficult to understand, may well seem to him to be 'residual nuisances'. A similar attitude is adopted by some Russian critics who feel their colonizing instincts to be affronted by the mere existence of the nationalist cultures of the fringe Soviet Republics.

Nevertheless, whatever may have been the achievement of the Lallans poets between 1940 and 1954—and it was far from negligible—from the moment the inevitability of the rejection of Lallans by the small section of the Scottish public seriously concerned with contemporary literature became obvious, its impetus flagged and it quickly began to wither. Ridiculous muscle-bound excesses—the failed experiments of writers who achieved success with a thinner Scots—became the linguistic basis of a popular front mode in the hands of a group of left-wing versifiers whose aims were always more political than poetical. Imitation Sydney Smiths disclosed themselves in their borrowed clothing in the pages of the Scottish University magazines. One or two parish-pump bores simply went on shouting the invalidated slogans of yesteryear, obstinately manufacturing Lallans verse which bore no relation to present-day Scots life, and by way of justification arguing tediously a case for the inevitability of Scots. This argument runs along worn-out lines. It is not necessary for the language of literature to be the spoken language of the people. After all, Keats did not write in the language of the people—and so on, building up from that neat little piece of verbal deception an imposingly logical structure. Alas for argument! Keats most certainly wrote in the language of the people, though he made use of some words which not every Cockney of the day included in his vocabulary. To use a live language like English in a more profound manner than it is normally employed in conversation is one thing; to employ an atrophied language which only survives through a number of ever-thinning dialects is another.

It is sometimes said that the future of Lallans really lies in the theatre. While it is true that spoken Lallans is more acceptable to the public than Lallans on a printed page, the language presents a problem to the dramatist that no writer has been able completely to solve. If he writes realistic drama, he must confine himself to dealing with happenings affecting Scottish society prior to about 1800. If he wishes to depict a modern scene, then he finds himself forced into the comedy genre, or into situations relating to what our Victorian ancestors called 'the working classes'. Even there his position is a hopeless one, because Lallans is steadily de-generating to a mere matter of dialect everywhere.

The dramatist who might want to deal with avant garde ideas, could not possibly use Lallans, since avant garde ideas do not normally reveal themselves among the least-educated sections of a community.

Poetry and drama must be concerned with people; with places that are living entities; with the human dilemma. Since we are all Anglo-Scots nowadays, whether we like it or not, the future of

Scottish literature must lie with English, albeit English roughened in texture by its contact with the remnants of Lallans and of the traditions that fashioned Lallans seven hundred years ago: English as distinctively the work of a Scot as the English of Yeats and Higgins and Patrick Kavanagh is distinctively Irish both in sound and feeling.

Scotland has relinquished Lallans—though it is surely to be hoped that at least enough knowledge of the language will somehow be preserved to enable future Scots to enjoy the work of Dunbar, Henryson, Burns, Scott, MacDiarmid and the lesser contributors to the Lallans heritage—as it is in the process of relinquishing Gaelic. Languages so far abandoned are most unlikely to generate any further creative impulse that might energize our dwindling sense of nationhood. The significant Anglo-Scots poetry and prose of the future will presumably reflect a nation's *ethos* in decline, and will almost certainly be as much influenced by European and trans-Atlantic trends as are the daily lives of all but a tiny isolated minority of the people of Scotland.

17

Scottish Education: system for yesteryear

ONE of the most keenly treasured of Scotland's boasts is her frequently repeated assertion that her educational system is, and has been for four centuries, the finest in the world. It does not take the inquiring traveller in Europe long to discover how doubtfully such a claim stands up to comparison with the modern Scandinavian and German systems, which not only make more contemporary demands upon their school-children but also insist upon a touch of breadth and liberality in the training of their technologists. As it was the Scottish educational system which once played a considerable part in the moulding of the national character, it is pertinent to consider here why that influence can apparently no longer sustain it, and what prospects, if any, there are of the old strengths and virtues being applied in a new guise to the task of girdering up our sense of nationhood.

In medieval times education in Scotland was almost entirely in the hands of the clergy. Indeed, it was Catholic priests who were responsible for founding Scotland's three fifteenth-century universities of St Andrews, Glasgow and Aberdeen. Poor men, however, had little or no chance of getting enough education through the pre-Reformation schools to have much prospect of benefiting from the knowledge available at these seats of classical learning.

John Knox is usually given the credit for having laid the ground plan of the Scottish educational system in his *Buke of Discipline* of 1560. His aim was a school in every parish under the surveillance of the Reformed Church, with help to be given to the poorer students to pursue their studies. In spite of the Scots enthusiasm for learning, the learned Scots of Knox's day, all of whom were what would now be regarded as upper class, were not particularly keen on paying out money, either from their own estates or from the money recently plundered from the Catholic Church, to help to educate people who were much more easily controlled in an uneducated condition. Indeed, it was not until the end of the religious wars of the seventeenth century and the establishment of the Church of Scotland in 1696 along its Presbyterian lines that Knox's blueprint began to be translated into a practical reality.

While the peculiar character of the Scottish educational system thus owes much to Knox, it is quite wrong to imagine that the Reformer was concerned with some abstract concept of education for its own sake. Knox indicated that ideally he would have liked his teachers to be angels, but, since this was impossible, the mortal teacher's prime duty was to give his pupils learning enough to enable them to understand religion: Knox's religion. After a secondary education, those able to benefit from a higher education were to be encouraged to go to a university; the rest were to learn a trade 'provided always that they have the form of knowledge of the Christian religion'. In other words, education was to Knox first and foremost a means of buttressing the Reformed faith, and in the event a good deal less liberal, though more widely available, than the teaching the Catholic Church had been able to impart.

The Church of Scotland retained the controlling interest in Scottish education until, weakened by schisms and breakaways, it was no longer able to do the job adequately and in 1872 gave place to the State. School Boards were elected in every parish. They functioned until 1918 when they in turn were supplanted by Local Authority Education Committees under the centralized administration of the Scottish Education Department.

The kind of schooling which Knox envisaged, and his successors realized, did well enough in its day. It bred the Scottish dominie, a pedantic character beloved by his pupils. The dominie patiently hammered home the fundamentals of knowledge, mainly designed to enable his pupils to advance themselves to the respected position of being able to 'wag their heids in the pulpit'. John Galt and Sir Walter Scott have both portrayed eighteenth-century dominies in their novels. Burns's teacher William Murdoch stands still more realistically before us, because several of his letters have been preserved. Typical of his kind, he rarely used a single Anglo-Saxon word if a Latinized phrase could be devised in its place. Thus, relating the occasion of his employ-ment, he wrote: 'In the ninth of May following, I was engaged by Mr Burns and four of his neighbours, to teach, and accordingly began to teach the little school at Alloway, which was situated a few yards from the argillaceous fabric above mentioned.' The 'argillaceous fabric' was, of course, William Burns's cottage and the birthplace of the poet.

The traditional Scots educational system flourished from about the middle of the sixteenth until the beginning of the twentieth century, in spite of the administrative changes that overtook it. During that time it produced a more widespread desire for education than existed in England, and it turned out thousands of ministers of religion, countless numbers of shrewd hard-headed men of business and enough schoolteachers, some of them no doubt 'stickit ministers', to perpetuate itself. But it also had another, and much more remarkable, effect.

In an article on 'The Output of Scientists in Scotland, 1600–1950', published in *The Eugenics Review*, R. H. S. Robertson demonstrated that the number of Scots who were Fellows of the Royal Society (founded in 1660 by Charles II), and who made major contributions to scientific knowledge, showed a steady increase from the year 1750, reaching a peak in 1875 then falling sharply, with minor fluctuations, from the year 1900 to half the peak figure in 1955.

It seems reasonable to suppose that, apart from eugenical con-siderations (Edinburgh and the North-East seem to have been productive of the largest percentage of men of science in the eighteenth century, Edinburgh sharing the distinction with Clydeside in the nineteenth), the two factors which most influ-enced this uprising of native ability were the Scots educational system and the comparative poverty of the country. Scientific discovery in the eighteenth and early nineteenth centuries often had fairly immediate beneficial effects. The spur of poverty and the obviousness of the country's practical needs, particularly in the earlier half of the period, must have been a continual stimulus to inventive effort.

There was also the certainty that Scotland would be able to employ her most brilliant sons. That certainty wavered somewhat towards the close of the nineteenth century, as the last borrowed phase of rational energy began to spend itself, and collapsed altogether during the early decades of the twentieth. Mr Robertson pointed out that more than a million Scots emigrated between 1900 and 1950, a loss sixteen times greater than the loss by emigration from the far more densely populated territories of England and Wales. The loss of such a high proportion of Scotland's best 'stock' over so long a period can hardly have failed to weaken the nation's intellectual resources.

However, the odd thing about the Scots educational system is not so much that having been devised to sustain a particular form of religious worship it produced a high proportion of men of science (to say nothing of large numbers of engineers), as that it produced so few major artists. In a sense it can claim Burns and Scott and Stevenson, although of the three only Scott underwent a normal course of education.

It may well be that the Scots got the system best suited to their national character; that the ability to handle facts rather than sustain the imaginative and creative faculties is the true Scots genius. If this is so, then surely it is a secondary genius?

On the other hand, with few exceptions, no country which whole-heartedly embraced any form of the Protestant faith made a major contribution to the arts from the seventeenth to the nineteenth centuries. Among the national exceptions one thinks of the Dutch painters; but their main concern was with the members of the family. Thus, however great of its kind, Dutch painting was first and foremost essentially domestic art. The few individual artists like Bach, those proverbial exceptions that prove the rule, manifested their gifts in countries which came under the Lutheran rather than the Calvinistic influence.

The European artists who most vigorously challenged and incomparably enriched the spirit of man, during the centuries when the Scottish educational system flourished, were, most of them, the products of the Roman Catholic system which Knox and his Reformers drove out of Scotland. The European heritage of the imagination—which provides us with all of the past that endures—is a Roman Catholic heritage from full participation in which the Knoxian system to some extent helped to isolate us.

In spite of its failure latterly to move with the times, and for all its limitations, the Scots system did instil the practical virtues of thrift and endurance. It also instilled some knowledge of Scottish history and, in a rudimentary way, a limited acquaintanceship with Scottish literature. In this manner it played some part in keeping alive the sense of nationhood in the nineteenth century.

The educational system which exists in Scotland today differs in many respects from the old system. No scholar nowadays has to starve his way through term on a sack of meal. Physical conditions, encouragements and opportunities are better than they have ever been before. But the emphasis has shifted from concentration on the able few to the improvement in some degree of the many. In spite of the advantages, this broadening of the educational effort has inevitably led to some diffuseness, and has tended to bring Scottish education much more nearly into line with English educational practice. In other words, while striving to achieve modernity and freedom from religious bigotry, somewhat late in the day, the good aspects of the Scots influence have gone down the drain along with the bad.

In 1946 an Advisory Council on Education in Scotland made recommendations designed to remedy this state of affairs. They felt that 'in the higher classes of primary school—say in the last three years—a short but definite weekly period should be set aside exclusively for Scottish traditions and language, including the reading and recital of verse and prose, telling of stories and discussion of typically Scottish words, phrases and proverbs'. 'Familiarity with the world of homely Scots,' they thought, 'would be a suitable introduction to the study of Scottish literature, which should have a definite place in every secondary school.'

Typically, however, the then Secretary of State for Scotland avoided any possibility of action by countering the Advisory Council's recommendation that 'a separate period in the primary school' was necessary with an alternative proposal that 'the various elements that go to make up the traditional Scottish culture find their appropriate place in the ordinary subjects of the curriculum', a proposal which is quite meaningless, demands no action, and has therefore been largely ignored.

In 1953 the Saltire Society published the Report of an Education Sub-Committee which it had charged with the task of finding out how the Secretary of State's proposal could be implemented.

They made it plain that in their view 'future teachers cannot rely on learning much about Scottish culture in their own years at school. Scottish history will probably have been treated as a subject of interest only to junior pupils. They may have learned very little about Scottish literature. Unless they come from one of the comparatively few schools where Gaelic is taken seriously they will probably have learned next to nothing of either Scottish language. Whether their schools have provided them with any real knowledge of Scottish songs, legends, dances, art or cooking is a matter of accident.'

To remedy this lack and arrest the decline of Scottish content in education, the Saltire Society made a number of recommendations. They suggested, among other reforms, that the examination system should be altered so that evidence of some slight knowledge of Scottish history, the Scots language, Scottish architecture, painting and, where appropriate, Gaelic, should be mandatory; and that the universities should ensure that students studying history, literature, economics, philosophy 'or any other subject to which Scotland has made a distinctive contribution', should receive instruction in the Scottish aspect, 'whether they are studying for Ordinary degrees or for Honours'.

These are in no way outrageously nationalistic demands; yet there is no evidence whatsoever to suggest that they are ever likely to be accepted or implemented in responsible quarters.

Ideally what is wanted is the combination of the liberal European conception of education with some knowledge of the best of our Scottish traditions, a knowledge which can now only be safeguarded and passed on if it is implanted in teachers as well as pupils.

The Saltire Society Report concludes with a blunt warning.

'. . . Unless changes of the kind we propose are wholeheartedly applied during the next few years, Scottish education is likely to lose nearly all its distinctive qualities, and the Scottish people to reach a level of cultural indigence far below that of its neighbours and of its own recent past. In that case we must expect either a root and branch reform of the whole national system of education, or its replacement by an organization and methods borrowed directly from England, or perhaps from the United States.'

Quite apart from the qualitative problem of the thinning of Scottish influence, Scottish education is also facing an acute quantitative crisis. Since the school-leaving age was raised to fifteen—a very proper half-measure towards the ultimate aim of making sixteen the earliest age at which children should be allowed to cease trying to develop their potentialities in order to earn a living—the system has increasingly suffered from a shortage of teachers. There simply are not enough young people willing to enter the profession to meet the demand. Obviously, teaching is not as attractive a profession to Scots boys and girls as society expects it to be.

The remedy seems to lie in society's own hands. I once conducted brief street interviews with about fifty Glasgow University students to try to find out the nature of the unattractiveness of teaching. Four-fifths of the young men and women I spoke to were either determined to avoid teaching at all costs, or willing to enter the teaching profession only as a last resort if they could find nothing better to do. Some of them felt that the monetary rewards were insufficient. The majority complained that nowadays the teacher no longer had what they called status.

In country districts the village teacher is often as much a respected leader of the community as was the dominie before him. Even in small towns teachers frequently play an active part in the running of local affairs, and the number of teachers, particularly headmasters, who become provosts compares favourably with the number provided by other occupations. The majority of teachers, however, have to work in the big urban agglomerations, where they enjoy neither the civic opportunities nor the social standing of their rural colleagues.

Some of the reasons for this may be traced to the workings of the democratic machine. In many urban areas, local-authority government has degenerated into a party-political dog-fight, with the prevailing party determinedly running local affairs not in the fairest interests of the community as a whole but along doctrinaire party lines. Many of the representatives on Local Authority Education Committees are themselves poorly educated. Often their attitude to the teachers in their employment is pettily irksome. Teachers are treated in a way no other professional people would be expected or prepared to tolerate. I have heard many educationalists—among them the Principal of Aberdeen University, Sir Thomas Taylor, addressing a conference of the Educational Institute of Scotland—suggest that Scotland's educational difficulties will never be satisfactorily solved until education is taken out of the hands of local authorities and put under a central professional body. This may seem a dangerous notion to those who believe that local government is still a democratic affair. But, in fact, very few councillors in the urban areas of Scotland are voted into office by a majority of those whom they officially represent. While they certainly defeat their opponents, they still completely fail to win majority support in any real sense. Thus it would appear that throughout industrial Scotland local government has become discredited in the eyes of the electorate.

Under circumstances so generally discouraging, it is difficult to see how the children passing through Scotland's schools in the second half of the twentieth century can be expected to enter adult life with even as much of a sense of Scottishness as their parents possess. Those who are able to absorb higher education will naturally find the pressure upon them to become scientists or technologists considerable. Unfortunately, the mastering of the devices and calculations of man's ingenuity does not often include an acquaintance with those liberal values without the benison of which living withholds much of its grace and savour. Those who pursue the arts, accepting the prospect of far less enticing rewards, may systematically study Scottish literature at only one Scottish University: Glasgow—where there is a lectureship but no chair—but may also, if they wish, more or less sidestep any serious study of Scottish literature or history and still emerge at the end of their academic years fully fledged de-Scotticized cultured Scots.

18

Scotland's Churches: a waning influence

THE processes of history-in-the-making seem to be such that they tend to coalesce individualism into conformity. The system of free-enterprise capitalism, on which our democratic Western way of life is based, is gradually altering its character. Industrial take-overs are constantly removing opposition and creating monopolies or near-monopolies, the larger gobbling up the smaller. Trade Unions charged with the task of securing reasonable working conditions for their members tend to develop into unwieldy organs of block power, capable of forcing a kind of continuous running warfare upon society.

Internationally, similar pressures are gradually making themselves felt. But however close the collaboration of the Continental nations involved in the European trade associations, none of the countries concerned are likely to suffer a change of personality as a result of closer contact with their neighbouring countries.

Scotland, however, is suffering just such a change of personality. She has lost so much confidence in herself, and has for so long been without a cause which could provide a rallying force to revive her failing sinews, that she is ill equipped to face up to the 'winds of change'. There was a time when patron saints possessed the powers of rallying flagging loyalties, and for many years the British Broadcasting Corporation believed it to be its duty to mount an annual evening's radio pageantry on 30th November in honour of St Andrew. But in most European countries patron saints have long been out of fashion. In Scotland St Andrew is almost unknown, except to churchmen and Scots who have lived abroad and who have become aware of his name-day as one of the two occasions when exiled Scots feel impelled to demonstrate to each other the fervour of their emotional links with the home country.

A few years ago I stood in a busy sector of Glasgow's Sauchiehall Street, holding a microphone and a recording machine. It was a cold November morning, the bad breath of a dawn fog lingering on to foul the taste of the thin sunlight. The idea was that I should stop a random selection of passing Glaswegians and ask them the simple question: 'What does next Saturday mean to you?' 'Next Saturday' was, of course, 30th November.

'Celtic plays Hibs,' said a man with a ladder on his shoulder.

'Er . . . nithing et all, ectually,' a middle-aged lady with an over-clipped poodle admitted.

'A'm vera sorry, surr, but a'm a postman, and we ceevil servants are no' allowed tae express poleetical opeenions,' said a round-looking, well-weathered man.

'Git oot o' ma wey or ah'll knoack yer paan in,' leered a bloated pin-striped representative of the new aristocracy as he stepped from a Rolls-Bentley by the kerbside.

'Tee-hee-hee,' twittered two 'teenage girls, clutching each other's arms and eyeing my microphone as if it in some way postulated a threat to maidenhood.

'Sir, I am a Pole, who has learned, sir, the kindness of your people, sir. So, sir, I do not take a part in their—what you call?—poleetis sings. You see, sir? Yes? No?' explained a shoulder-shrugging fiftyish man carrying a suitcase labelled 'John Mackintosh'.

'Why of course; St Andrew's Day. In Persia we used to have a whale of a do every year out there on November thirtieth. You know—kilts and Scots songs, and haggis specially flown out from Edinburgh,' a professional-looking type in tweeds reminisced happily. 'I often think it's a pity we don't celebrate St Andrew's Day at home, because it's certainly a great thing among Scots abroad.'

If St Andrew is of no further use as a rallying force, what power remains with the Church of Scotland, which makes heraldic use of his cross?

The best way to gauge the Church's temper, if not its influence, is to attend a session of its General Assembly. The Assembly is held during May in the impressive nineteenth-century pseudo-Gothic Assembly Hall which stands halfway up Edinburgh's

Mount, and where visitors to the Edinburgh Festival saw *The Three Estates* and other plays. In the courtyard a larger-than-life-size statue of John Knox presides, his hand raised in argumentative assertion, a dour Scottish scowl on his stony face. An unbeliever like myself—albeit a 'wistful agnostic' to borrow the late Professor C. E. M. Joad's phrase—finds himself at something of a disadvantage listening to Assembly debates, because at frequent intervals the course of the argument is diverted into the troubled waters of theological disputation. Theology is somewhat curiously defined in my dictionary as 'the science of the relationship between God and man', though how it can claim to be a 'science', since it does not deal in facts capable of empirical verification, I fail to understand. In its Scottish form, at any rate, theology is largely the ferment of argument and counter-argument around the interpretation of words and phrases which there is neither historical nor scientific evidence to suggest were ever intended to carry a precise or literal meaning. Scottish theology thrives on its own disputatiousness. It has never recovered from the attentions of David Hume. Most of the so-called post-Hume Scottish philosophy of the eighteenth century is in fact little more than theological disputation. Except to the participants and their supporters such disputation bears little or no relation to modern life.

The session of the General Assembly which I attended discussed many issues, some of them of purely ecclesiastical interest. Others related to major international problems of the moment. The debates which had most potential significance for Scotland seemed to me to be related to Sabbath observance, and to family planning.

Since the distraction-seeking 'twenties, Sunday has increasingly become the day of the week devoted, at least in part, to pursuits out of doors. The roads carry a heavier volume of pleasure traffic on Sundays than on Saturdays, and the demand for Sunday golf and similar facilities steadily increases. Recently the members of the Church and Nation Committee decided that the time had come to re-examine and declare the Church's attitude to Sunday recreation. The Committee's proposals amounted to the acceptance of the situation as it is; so they drafted a declaration that, provided the duty of worship was fulfilled—obviously a prime consideration if one professes to be a Christian—there was

no reason why men and women should not thereafter seek the
healthy recreation of mind and body.

When the proposed recommendation (or deliverance, to use
the quaint official parlance) had been moved and explained, a
fierce debate broke out. Fiery-tongued ministers from the Highland glens or with Highland blood in their veins ranted prolixly
and tediously. Over and over again they thundered forth the
iniquity of any relaxation of the Scottish Sabbath as it was
devised four centuries ago. They were supported by lay backwoodsmen, some of whom grew almost hysterical as they pleaded
that the deliverance should be thrown out and the Church go on
pretending that the puritanical Sabbath which once was, still is.
They carried the day. The realists among the Scottish churchmen,
the men with liberal, modern minds, were out-voted. The Church
of Scotland seemed once again content to have elected to remain
out of touch with conditions as they are; with fact.

The debate about the Church's attitude to the use of contraceptives threw light from a different angle upon the Church's
apparent inability to accept the fact that Puritanism—the denial
of the potentialities of man to serve the narrow ends of emotional
bigotry—is dead and done with.

It is perfectly obvious that the over-populated countries of
the world have no hope whatever of achieving a reasonable
standard of living unless some form of birth control is introduced
and practised. The attitude of the Roman Catholic Church to
this problem is hardly logical, since it allows birth control by
so-called natural means but condemns it when artificial aids
are employed. Hitherto, the Church of Scotland has avoided
formulating its views on this issue, though it is obviously a
matter of practical concern to a large number of people in
Scotland.

In this debate the enlightened element of the Church supported the practice of birth control, with certain reservations.
In spite of an impassioned attack from the Highlanders and
the lay backwoodsmen, the moderates prevailed. But their
reservations were revealing. For the deliverance condemned the
use of contraceptives 'from such motives as indulgence, luxury,
or to avoid the sacrifices which a family inevitably entails'. The
third ground of objection is clear, and surely valid; the first, if
far from clear, is at least valid if it relates to the imposition of one

of the partners against the will of the other. But what does the
second objection mean?

It reminds me of the decent young Highlander who was
married late on a Saturday evening. Before consummating the
union he called on his minister to ask if it would be all right to do
so, in view of the fact that in a mere matter of minutes the Sabbath
would be upon them. He was assured that the consummation
would be quite in order, provided he did not enjoy it. In other
words, the old Puritanical beast that distrusts the senses and finds
safety only in their denial still seems to stir uneasily, if perhaps
subconsciously, even in the Church of Scotland's more modern
minds.

The fact of the matter is that neither the Church's ruling on
Sabbath observance nor its condemnation of contraception as a
luxury are likely to have any influence whatever on the Scottish
way of life in the second half of the twentieth century. Churches
will be no more crowded, roads no less busy on Sundays, and the
families of most young Scots, Christian or otherwise, are unlikely
to assume larger proportions than the present national average;
for the decisions of the Church are obeyed by only a minority
even of its own members. To what extent, therefore, may
the Church of Scotland really still be considered a national
force?

In 1959 there were 1,306,661 members on the Church's rolls,
of whom 932,456 communicated at least once during the year.
Once-a-year communication hardly suggests a very high standard
of devotion, or a radically forceful church influence. However,
accepting these figures, which are the Church's own, about a
quarter of Scotland's inhabitants over twenty years of age—
Scotland had an adult population of 3,500,300 in 1959—took
communion in their national Church at least once during the year.
Even adding in the Roman Catholic Church's claim of a practising half-million Scots,[1] the Episcopalian Church's 56,000 and the
180,000 or so attached to various splinter-sects, the picture that
emerges is of a Scotland with rather less than half its population
over the age of twenty regularly practising organized worship
according to the form of any of the recognized Churches. These
figures take no account of the 'teen-agers, about three-quarters of
whom have no regular church connection. By the elementary

[1] Which it is impossible to verify.

head-counting laws of democracy, it would therefore seem that no churchman has any longer the right to claim that Scotland is still a Christian country. This reflection may well arouse a most unchristian feeling of irritated intolerance in many a professedly Christian bosom; but all I am concerned with here is whether or not the Church of Scotland—which, by virtue of its establishment, its associations and its numerical superiority over the other Churches in Scotland, must still be regarded as the national Church—is any longer likely to be able to exert a decisive influence which could arrest Scotland's declining sense of nationhood.

In his excellent survey of the raw materials of that nationhood, *Scotland Past and Present*, J. M. Reid wrote: 'It was chiefly to safeguard the national Church of Scotland that the liquidation of the national State was accepted two centuries and a half ago. This gives the Church a peculiar place in Scottish history.'

Indeed it does. Just how peculiar was demonstrated when, in 1959, a scheme for union with the Church of England which involved the acceptance of bishops was debated and thrown out by the General Assembly. What was truly astonishing was not so much the overthrowing of the union proposals by the churchmen themselves—though one might have thought that the spirit of Christianity would have inclined them towards union—but the fierce 'No Bishops' campaign conducted by several daily newspapers, and vigorously supported by readers through the correspondence columns. A Scots scientist, well known for his convinced atheistical views, remarked to me how strongly he opposed the introduction of bishops to the Church of Scotland. 'But surely,' I said, 'you're an atheist?'

'Yes, I am,' he snapped back. 'But I reserve the right to be a Presbyterian atheist.'

It was largely over the bishops issue that the dreary wars of the seventeenth century were fought; wars which certainly produced the sturdy defiance of the Covenanters, but which nevertheless kept Scotland isolated in that parochial and cultureless wilderness to which the violence of her Reformation had condemned her in the previous century. Inevitably, these wars have been romanticized, and the petty brutalities of both sides have been glossed over according to the particular persuasion of the writer of the moment. That they should still be able to evoke so passionate a partiality in the minds of people who do not ordinarily feel moved to support any Church in its work of worship, seems to me yet one more piece of evidence of our Scots inability to free ourselves from the irrelevancies of a romanticized past. Surely no one with a modern mind could possibly think that in relation to the human dilemma which faces us all—the still unanswered question of whether or not man will learn to control his technological discoveries before they destroy him and his world—doctrinal details of the precise formula to be employed in the worshipping of a God, in whom apparently less than half the population believes, can any longer be a matter of fundamental significance?

19

The Scottish Press: less and less Scottish

BRITISH newspapers periodically assure us that the British
Press is the finest in the world. The claim may be justified,
though I find it hard to understand how such an assertion
can be seriously sustained by anyone not possessing command of
a multitude of languages and an inexhaustible passion for somewhat pointless research. Until comparatively recently the newspaper was the principal organ of communication, and, as such, of
immense importance. Radio and television have considerably
lessened the influence of the Press; but, together, all these media
of communication now keep up a more insistent barrage against
men's minds than ever before. No one seriously concerned with
the state of Scotland's nationhood can therefore fail to take into
account the effects of that influence.

Scotland's daily newspapers fall into two categories: those
which are Scottish owned, and those which, though printed in
Scotland, are English owned. In 1946, when Duncan Ferguson
published his candid survey *The Scottish Newspaper Press*, the
former group was still sizeable. Since then, unfortunately, Scotland has lost control of some of its newspapers, while others have
ceased publication. *The Scotsman* has passed out of the hands of
its Scottish owners into the vast newspaper domain of Roy
Thomson, the Canadian business man who has also acquired the
Kemsley newspaper interests. Happily, however, it has retained
its Scottish orientation and considerably livened up its comment.
While it has thus so far remained faithful to the interests of the
readers it serves, and is still indispensable to anyone seriously
concerned with Scottish affairs, it is surely a sad reflection upon
the state of Scotland that the control of its leading daily newspaper has passed out of Scottish hands?

Its complement (or rival, depending upon how you look at things), *The Glasgow Herald*, necessary reading for the Glasgow business man, is still Scottish owned, though the opinion it reflects is usually broadly British rather than specifically Scottish in orientation. It was the *Herald*'s lively little brother, *The Bulletin*, that in 1960 went out of existence after a 'life' of forty-five years. Over many of these years *The Bulletin* held to a markedly Scottish line. Indeed its decline, though no doubt accelerated by the development of commercial television, dated from its abandonment of a pro-Scottish policy in favour of no particular policy at all. Its loss leaves in circulation only one major Scottish-owned daily apart from the *Herald*—the *Dundee Courier and Advertiser*. Vigorous if sometimes a trifle eclectic, it is in many ways a large local daily rather than a national Scottish newspaper. The *Paisley Advertiser*, a daily evening, is unique, though hardly a major paper.

Competing against two Scottish-owned morning papers and one which, though not Scottish owned, is still thoroughly Scottish in outlook, are Beaverbrook's *Scottish Daily Express*, published in Glasgow; Rothermere's *Scottish Daily Mail*, published in Edinburgh; the *Daily Record*, which since it passed from the Kemsley group into the empire of Cecil King has come to look increasingly like its English counterpart the *Daily Mirror*; and the *Aberdeen Press and Journal*, now in Roy Thomson's hands.

The *Mail* seems to preserve in Scotland a reasonable reputation for reliability. The *Express* and the *Record* are apt to vie with each other in exploiting human privacies, and in overblowing local information to sensational proportions; the one with a strong bias towards the Right, the other invariably leaning heavily in the direction of the Left.

What emerges from all this? Simply that the morning newspapers which now go into the majority of Scottish homes are no longer owned by Scots. Though printed in Scotland, their outlook and comment must necessarily be predominantly English in feeling and understanding.

This situation might not be so serious if Scotland possessed one independent weekly or monthly magazine to provide a forum for second thoughts, and for the exchange of informed opinion and comment on Scottish affairs. Since the demise of the *Scots*

Review, a decade ago, no paper has appeared even to attempt to meet this need.

True, evening papers still maintain large local circulations, although they have been quite seriously affected by the advance of television. In Glasgow the *Evening News*, which once numbered among its contributors the novelist George Blake and the essayist William Power, and among its editors Neil Munro, has been a post-Second World War casualty, leaving the Outram-owned *Evening Times* and the Beaverbrook-controlled *Evening Citizen* to fight it out. In Edinburgh the London-owned *Edinburgh Evening News*, a paper with a long Liberal tradition behind it, has a clear and apparently secure lead over *The Scotsman*'s junior relative, the *Evening Dispatch*. Aberdeen has a Thomson-owned evening paper, while Dundee and Greenock still manage to support Scottish-owned products of the kind.

Traditionally, evening papers in Scotland have always been lightweight affairs compared with the morning papers. Rightly or wrongly it seems to me that if evening papers are to compete with growing competition from television they will have to provide their readers with more Scottish news, and far more thoughtful comment on local and national affairs than most of them at present offer. In this respect the *Edinburgh Evening News* is much in advance of the other city evening papers. There ought also to be a return to authority in the reviewing of books, concerts and plays. Was not Corno di Bassetto, alias George Bernard Shaw, the most entertaining music critic of them all, an employee of a London evening paper?

Even among local weekly newspapers there have been heavy casualties. The value of the local newspaper in reporting local-authority business cannot be overestimated. It is therefore disturbing to note the number of local newspapers that are being taken over, either by Scottish-owned dailies or by newspapers controlled from south of Scotland.

So far as major Scottish issues are concerned, it is still possible to read full straightforward reports, distorted neither by bias nor by the interlacing of disguised comment, in *The Scotsman* and *The Glasgow Herald*. In these papers, fact and comment are kept scrupulously apart, so that it is possible to accept the one and reject the other. But this sort of fundamental honesty of purpose is not always to be met with in all the popular papers. The cut-throat competition which now whets the energies of the London-owned dailies presumably discourages straightforward reporting. Apparently there has to be a measure of distortion to make the story more arresting, more readable. This distortion may take the form of sensationalizing a minor happening; of altering the emphasis of events; or of grossly overblowing a story in an attempt to make it seem to carry an importance it simply does not possess. Often, too, a patronizing twist is introduced into Scottish stories designed to find their way into English editions. In addition, we in Scotland are also subjected to the general pressures. In Scotland, as elsewhere in Britain, trivial happenings are constantly elevated to the status of major stories, while the really important news is often printed in a position of insignificance; and in this way our sense of values is constantly jeopardized in the interests of large circulations and big profits.

There is neither protection nor redress from this sort of treatment. The Press Council, a predominantly English body which even in England has no real authority and is boycotted by one of the most powerful of the newspaper tycoons, takes a very humble view of professional standards, and often seems more anxious to defend members of the journalistic craft from their accusers than to protect the public.

Not that the public seems much perturbed by any assault upon its sense of values, or even by slanted reporting, provided the slant is towards sexy sensationalism. A majority of readers buy the most sensational newspapers because they are thus enabled vicariously to enjoy an element singularly lacking in their own lives.

Fortunately, the popular Press appears to have been tumbled from its high estate during the last quarter of a century by its own readers, a fact which may be responsible for the hysterical self-congratulation over circulation figures practised by some newspapers. 'It must be right; it's in the papers,' was a remark often heard on the lips of the unthinking during the 'thirties. Now, their touching faith in the accuracy and honesty of newspapers has been somewhat shaken, and, 'It mayn't be right; it was only in the papers,' seems to be the reaction on a similar level of thoughtlessness today.

The reason for this change lies partly in the growth of the British Broadcasting Corporation's reputation for accuracy and integrity during the Second World War. Statisticians concerned with audience reaction know that, whenever a cloud of international crisis darkens our dangerous skies, listening figures for the B.B.C.'s news programmes show a sharp increase. Not even the excellent service provided by the Independent Television News studios seriously challenges the B.B.C.'s authority and supremacy of world-wide coverage during a crisis: and this in spite of its day-to-day obsession with rockets and royalty.

An instrument of such great power must obviously have exercised some influence on Scotland, where it has been functioning since 1923. By its very nature, broadcasting inevitably helped to destroy that isolation on which the survival of many old customs of speech and manners depended. The old ways would ultimately have gone in any case, even without the shouldering pressure over the air. But broadcasting struck above all at speech; at Scots and at Gaelic, already in decline and so desperately vulnerable.

Although officially the B.B.C. has always obstinately regarded Scotland as a region, provision was made in the original charter for the safeguarding of regional ways of life. Whatever conscious view, if any, of Scotland may have been taken by the London hierarchy in the early days, the view taken by those operating the service in Scotland has always been that they are providing a national service. Consequently, during the years of monopoly, the years of sound broadcasting, the B.B.C. in Scotland contributed substantially to the buttressing of Scottish culture, and carried it to a wider audience than had known it before.

Nowadays culture has become almost a dirty word, suggesting cartooned long-chinned blue-stockings and youthful bearded fringes. I use the word to denote the literature, music and dancing which, with painting, are the only permanent living records of the past which can be fixed and preserved for all time. So far as music is concerned, from its excellent series 'The Foundations of Scottish Music', which cleared the way for later research that has resulted in, among other publications and discoveries, the *Music of Scotland* volume of the *Musica Britannica* series, to its regular broadcasts of Scottish dance music, which touched off a nation-wide revival of practical interest in Scottish country dancing, the B.B.C. in Scotland has exercised a stimulating influence.

Literature has been no less comprehensively served. From the novels of Scott and Galt, adapted dramatically for the more effective telling over the new medium, to the work of the Lallans Makars in the post-Second World War years, the 'Scottish Heritage' series, and magazines like 'Scottish Art and Letters' and that redoubtable discursive forum of criticism 'Arts Review', the B.B.C.'s range of activities has been immense and beneficial alike to the artists and the public.

If the same cannot be said about the influence of broadcasting on Scottish drama, that is hardly the fault of the Corporation. Broadcasting is not a form but a means of communication. A work of art cannot be conceived purely in terms of radio, although obviously certain practical adjustments must be made to suit the technical demands and limitations of the medium. But a symphony, a poem or a play must stand or fall by its own intrinsic merits. The best that broadcasting can do for a bad play is perhaps to give it a glossy appearance of betterment, as the camera can sometimes bestow handsomeness upon an unhandsome man. The camera does not, in fact, leave its subject more handsome than he really is.

The B.B.C. in Scotland has never been without its critics. There are those who have kept up a running ungrammatical fire against 'the Scottish B.B.C.' because it is not a separate Scottish body. Yet a Scottish Broadcasting Corporation, financial considerations apart, could hardly be a feasible proposition politically without a Scottish Government. The people of Scotland have so far shown no serious desire to have a Government of their own, even along the limited lines of the Government of Northern Ireland (which, incidentally, does not maintain an independent broadcasting corporation).

There are others who think the B.B.C. harbours mediocrities and fosters those civil-service habits, fatal to any artistic enterprise, of passing the buck and playing safe whenever possible. In his autobiography *A Life in the Theatre*, Sir Tyrone Guthrie deplored the monopolistic tradition of the B.B.C. on the grounds that 'it rendered the officials at once complacent . . . the conditions attract the prudent, rather than the daring, men and women; once in, there is every incentive to play safe and none to stick your neck out. Artistic achievements are only to be had by sticking your neck out as far as ever it will go.' This may be so. But at the end of the day—and the day of supremacy of the B.B.C.'s policy of benevolent idealism ended with the establishment of commercial television—it is the achievement that matters most. Thirty years of broadcasting is a sufficient period for some sort of judgment to be made. Although the introduction of 'cats' whiskers' crystal sets into Scottish homes invisibly carried the enemy of Scots and Gaelic over the threshold, the B.B.C. has, in my view, contributed immeasurably to the dissemination of Scottish culture during its first thirty years.

It is perhaps too soon fairly to assess the impact of television on Scotland, but the portents are not encouraging. Television is London-centred to a far greater extent than sound broadcasting ever was. The officials of the B.B.C. in Scotland have to ask permission from London if they wish to opt out of the network programme in order to present a Scottish programme. So far as Scotland is concerned, the competition offered to the B.B.C. by commercial television during the first few years of its existence has been on such a consistently low intellectual and cultural level that mass-audience figures and, on the commercial side, profit, would seem to have become the main criteria of successful operation. Results are now measured quantitatively, and quality has no place in the calculation.

In the days of the supremacy of sound broadcasting, one was always aware of the existence of a serious-minded conception of public service. However faithfully lip-service may still be paid to the old conception in B.B.C. circles, 'The Industry' is now the term in common use. Since it is impossible to serve both God and Mammon, and Mammon enjoys the closer proximity, the standard of home entertainment is much less Scottish in content, and much less comprehensive in intellectual range[1] than in pre-television days.

It would be absurd to pretend that television has not made a considerable contribution to the enrichment of our lives; but it would be equally absurd to pretend that, so far as Scotland is concerned, either side has so far expended enough time or money to reflect adequately the variety of Scottish life, or to cater reasonably and consistently for the interests of the more intelligent minorities. In Scotland, the B.B.C. has presumably to make the best of whatever money London may choose to give it. Scottish

[1] This was written before the establishment of the Border and Grampian Television stations.

Television, however, earns substantial profits, and should have more freedom of choice.

One other channel of communication remains to be considered, that of book publishing. Scotland has behind her a long and honourable tradition of fine printing. Two major publishing houses with international connections have their main printing works in Scotland. There are also a number of smaller firms, who no doubt do what they can for Scottish authors. Books useful and useless, books beautiful and hideous, drop in their thousands month by month from the Scottish presses. While a few of these books do deal with aspects of Scottish life, hardly a single creative Scottish writer of any distinction regularly publishes his work in his native land. Imagine a comparable situation whereby the creative writers of, let us say, Holland, were forced to publish their books in Germany because the Dutch publishing houses took virtually no interest in Dutch writing.

It is not wilful perversion that makes the Scots author look to London, but simple necessity. He has to look to London if he wants his manuscript to be sympathetically considered and, if accepted, thereafter efficiently and widely distributed. Obviously there must be novels and poems which, like the delightful wines of Austria, do not carry well, and which it would be unfair to expect an English publisher to import. Awareness of this problem makes it difficult for a Scots author any longer to address himself wholly to a Scots audience, should he wish to do so. It also makes virtually impossible the reissue of Scots classics with a purely national appeal—the poems of Robert Fergusson and all but one of Galt's novels come into this category, to say nothing of delightful minor masterpieces like D. M. Moir's *Mansie Wauch*— since most English publishers naturally expect to sell at least a proportion of their books by Scots authors outside Scotland.

20

The National Character

'I LOVE every rock and stone of Scotland,' an exasperated
patriot once burst out; 'but I loathe the creatures that crawl
over her surface.' The 'creatures' were, of course, his fellow
Scots. A shocking sentiment, really; for has not Burns firmly implanted in the Scots consciousness the assurance that one day all
men 'shall brithers be for a' that'? 'A' that' takes in not only
differences of intellectual rank which no amount of political
dogmatizing shows any sign of levelling out—indeed, the steady
trend towards a new élite of university graduates in the key posts
both of this country and of England suggests that the division is
widening itself—but also the differences that make up national
character. The temperamental differences which divide, let us say,
a German from a Chinaman, are obvious and enormous. The
differences which distinguish a Scot from an Englishman are less
obvious, and are becoming less marked with every generation.
But they still exist. Scottish national character now lives on mainly
in the lower and lower-middle classes. It has been virtually
eliminated among the upper classes.

In some ways it is possibly misleading to speak of 'the national
character', as if the great divide between Highlands and Lowlands
had never existed. There are really two national characters: the
majority or Lowland character, and the minority or Highland
character. The minority character has long been supplanted for all
practical purposes by the majority one. Because of this, Highlanders often harbour a deep-seated resentment against their
Lowland brothers, sometimes even betraying them into co-opera-
tion with the English rather than with their fellow Scots. The fatal
weakness for schism common to both characters, combined with
this Highland-Lowland dichotomy, has time and again produced

203

disastrous consequences, and left Scotland virtually without a national voice.

The thrust, the drive, the restless energy of the Scot at home and (alas! more frequently) abroad during the past four centuries, have mostly come out of the Lowlands. We read of the sixteenth-century Scot being famed for his fieriness, his desire for action, his impetuosity, his 'dash' and his intellectual energy; a very different version of the national character from the canny, douce, dour, penny-counting sentimentalist familiar to us all as the popular image today.

From the Middle Ages to the Reformation the Scot seems to have been a formidable fighter. When wars were still largely a matter of local dirty business, Scots fighting men hired themselves out to whoever was willing to pay for their services, whatever the cause. Probably it was not so much the money as the love of fighting that induced the Scots mercenaries to attach themselves, as opportunity arose, to warring European princelings. Though the fighting activities of the Reformers and the Covenanters were carried out officially under the banner of the Prince of Peace, the hymns and psalms which these craggy men drummed into our heritage deal extensively and enthusiastically with snares and fowlers and 'bloodie cruelties'. It was therefore a wise move when George II's London Government harnessed the old Scots love of fighting to the British Army by the formation of new Scots regiments. The fighting traditions of the Scots regiments have twice in this century inspired fresh generations of young Scots to do battle with the old determination, fortunately for European civilization, but, especially in the First World War where Scots losses were disproportionately heavy, with disastrous eugenical results for many a lonely little village.

However necessary the ability to fight may have been in the days before science rendered it an unprofitable and therefore pointless occupation on an international scale, it is not usually an attribute that contributes much in the way of constructive energy to a civilized national life. During the Second World War, when I was a young student at the Staff College, I said something to this effect during a debate on: 'Ought Regimental Traditions to be Abolished?' For the purposes of the exercise, I submitted that they were completely outmoded; placed a false emphasis on history; drew their strength entirely from a base primitivism; and should most certainly be abolished. To my dismay there arose to speak in defence of regimental tradition, not the fellow student whose name had been selected in the draw, but the Commandant of the Staff College, Major-General Douglas Wimberley, who had commanded the Highland Division during the North African Campaign. Possibly he feared that my purely theoretical eloquence —I had no real interest in the issue, one way or the other, not myself being by nature a fighting man—might do some damage to morale. At any rate, he quoted from his own practical experience with such telling effect that when the vote was counted I sustained a crushing defeat.

A fondness for fighting, for brawling, or for arguing in a manner likely to lead to one or other of these consequences, has long been a prominent Lowland characteristic, particularly in urban areas. It does not appear to be confined to any one stratum of society, and even finds its way into local affairs whenever some fiery Scot suffers a surge of ancestrally charged blood to his head. As I write this very day, a report of one such outburst appears in *The Scotsman*.

The scene is a budget meeting of Glasgow Corporation. A Councillor William Samuels has questioned 'items in the police account', and there have been shouts of protest.

'River Bailie Tom Fulton accused Mr Samuels of "talking a lot of rubbish". Mr Samuels tried to go on, but when Councillor Dr Maurice S. Miller commented: "You are wasting our time," he swiftly retorted: "I have shot better than you before breakfast."'

At this extraordinary revelation, the proceedings seem to have become still more animated, several people talking at once. The report goes on: 'Mr Samuels, addressing several Labour members who were speaking, said: "If you want a bear garden, I will give you one, and if you want a fight I will take you on individually or collectively outside."'

No doubt on this occasion the atavistic instincts of Mr Samuels were satisfied by the mere utterance of the threat. But argumentativeness on this level, even if not carried to the extreme of action, does suggest some deficiency of imagination. Remarking on the supreme importance of replenishing and satisfying the imagination, John Davidson once suggested that there was, in fact, 'no other enjoyment'. National imaginations, like those of individuals, are satisfied at different levels, the Scots imagination at a comparatively low level.

The Scot is a man of action, and men of action are always suspicious of men of dreams. The Scot mistrusts visions, unless the visionary can provide a practical appendix to his vision, relating it stage by stage to the proposed expenditure and likely source of the bawbees. Dundee, a city that made a great many bawbees in its hey-day, and whose public men sometimes talk as if they bore a grudge towards a world that no longer allows them their profitable monopoly in jute, recently refused to increase the annual civic grant to the Scottish National Orchestra; a grant the size of which—unlike the pay packets and dividend envelopes of most of Dundee's citizens—had not been increased over a period of five years. 'We ought to pull out of this thing altogether,' one Councillor was reported to have said. 'There's absolutely no prospect of it ever paying.'

The Scot derives almost his supreme satisfaction out of making things pay, a kind of satisfaction in which he is perhaps rivalled only by the Swiss. It is, of course, very necessary to make most things pay, but surely somewhat unimaginative to elevate the business to that of a higher ecstasy? The Scot also gets enormous satisfaction out of making things work. Obviously it is better that things should work, and work well, than that they should work indifferently. But other races who exhibit at least a comparable engineering aptitude do not find that building ships and locomotives and industrial machinery absorbs the major proportion of the national imagination.

The noblest, or at least the most ostentatious, buildings put up in most Scottish cities and towns during the last hundred years have been banks and insurance offices. Even the traditional Scots interest in religion—though, as we have seen, neither as intense nor as widespread as once it was—could be interpreted as an extension of the canny Scots principle of laying by for the future, and, so to say, insuring against eternity.

Such a remarkable degree of concentration upon practical results in this world, and straightforward prospects in the next, betokens a kind of nagging uncertainty. So does the Scot's peculiar modern respect for Authority which, however much he may bristle at it, he really does not like to gainsay.

To be able to enjoy un-selfconsciously the subtler and more

rewarding satisfactions, the imagination needs assurance. Perhaps only once in her disturbed history did Scotland enjoy the stability and material prosperity out of which the necessary assurance could have grown. That was in the second half of the nineteenth century, by which time the Scots had already started to sell out on themselves.

So Scotland has produced few visionaries; few poets or painters who count for much in the European scene; and not a single major composer. But she has sent forth bankers and business men to stand with both feet firmly planted on the ground, and explorers to discover more ground for them to stand upon; heids o' depairtments to carry out the boss's orders, and accountants to tally up the profits and losses of others; colonizers and controllers, grave, worthy and wise; men of pomp, few words, and less imagination.

Wherever in these severely practical walks of life the Scot has won leadership, the image he has left of himself is limned by words like 'dour', 'canny' and 'hard-headed'. As often as not his dourness has merely reflected the absence of anything to say, his canniness his inner uncertainty, and his hard-headedness his lack of imagination.

In a word, the Scot is comfortably and contentedly dull. He actually enjoys his dullness as the poet John Betjeman enjoys grotesque Victorian buildings, and he views with suspicion and contempt any foreigner who has the temerity to rail against it or to use it as a butt for humour.

'Where there is no vision the people perish,' an ardent young Scottish Nationalist used to assure me from my own doorstep whenever he wanted the use of a bed. I was never quite certain whether he meant that if I refused him nocturnal facilities I personally would perish, or that the entire Scottish race would be afflicted because of my lack of vision. And I never found out, because I always gave him his bed. The quotation with which he won his rest is so much a cliché, and so frequently heard on the lips of unctuous do-gooders, that the hard core of meaning encased in it is apt to be overlooked. The visionary looks forward. But people who do not look forward look backward, there being no other positive direction to engage their attention.

The Scot is a sentimentalist. The difference between sentiment and sentimentality is that while the one involves the play of strong

active feelings the other implies nostalgia for feelings that have
ceased to be active. The constant application to adult people and
sizeable things of the word 'wee', often in conjunction with the
diminutive 'ie' (as in 'Annie', 'duckie' or 'dearie') is one indication
of the Scots habit of thinking small. The perpetually unsatisfied
yearning after an antiseptically romanticized past is another. I am
all for holding fast to the past, so long as that past is being constantly added to from the present. But the past of the average
Scot has scarcely been added to at all for more than a hundred
years. Consequently, the Scots are living on their traditional
capital. Living on capital is certainly a legitimate way of arranging
things so long as your capital lasts. In Scotland's case it can hardly
last much longer.

In a searching poem, 'Scotland, 1941', the gentle Edwin Muir
(whose influence on Scottish letters has been far more pervasive
than is generally recognized) touches upon just this matter.

> 'Now smoke and dearth and money everywhere,
> Mean heirlooms of each fainter generation,
> And mummied housegods in their musty niches,
> Burns and Scott, sham bards of a sham nation?
> And spiritual defeat wrapped warm on riches,
> No pride but pride of pelf . . .'

Whatever one may think of the nature of the Scots character,
few have called in question its granite-like qualities of toughness
and courage (although, in the poem from which I have just
quoted, Muir described it as 'courage beyond the point, and
obdurate pride'). Scotland does not breed a high proportion of
chronic neurotics. Her suicide rate is comparatively low. While
her illegitimacy rate has shown regional increases from time to
time (particularly when religious revivalism has broken out in an
area; it was once reputedly high in the Covenanting country of
the South-West), at the moment it compares favourably with that
of the Scandinavian countries. The Scots character has always had
the stolid, unimaginative stability associated with the extrovert
temperament. It might perhaps be described as a sort of Northern
stoicism. It is reflected in the Scottish face.

Some years ago C. M. Grieve declared that the Scots face had
deteriorated. He instanced the character-studies of Sir Henry

Raeburn, and the impressive series of callotype photographs of later nineteenth-century worthies by the pioneer Scots photographer D. O. Hill. Where in Scotland today, he asked, could features of such strength and originality be found?

There were squeals of protest from outraged face-fanciers, who claimed that the same sort of faces were still to be seen in the same towns and villages where they had always been seen. From my own casual observation I should have thought that, in fact, people with craggy sculptured features had declined in number, even since the days of my boyhood.

Not that in any case I can bring myself to feel very enthusiastic about the features of many of Hill's hirsute gentlemen. The 'character' they are supposed to display often suggests the aftermath of a lifetime of dourness and intolerance. I find that I am not unsupported in this view. R. B. Cunninghame Graham also seemed to think that religion was a powerful wrinkle-forming agent when he described the Scottish face as 'a wet cloak ill laid up' or 'the new map together with the augmentation of the Indies', for he comments: 'Ethnologists have not remarked if the features of . . . those districts . . . which have remained Catholic are as repellent as those of the more essentially Protestant cantons of Scotland.'

For my part, the face that delights me is the mobile countenance, swift to match the thoughts or the speech of its possessor; the kindly communicating face of the liberal mind, rather than the jagged features of the self-ravaged Calvinist, sure in righteousness and of the iniquity of everyone who disagrees with him.

In any case anthropologists, who can relate a living man to, say, the Gallovidian Picts by a glance at the shape of his skull, would surely dismiss any suggestion that a national face, if such there be, could alter significantly in fifty or even a hundred years.

Fascinating as Grieve's speculation is, therefore, it is really something of a diversion. Look after the habits, one might say, and the faces will take care of themselves.

The most obvious defect of the Scottish character is surely its parochialism. The book-readers, the playgoers and the gallery promenaders are apt to prefer sugared confections made with the stale ingredients of yesteryear to the stronger-tasting recipes of today. Scottish design is hopelessly dated, while the men who pay

our architectural pipers usually insist upon calling a tune that is
nothing more than safe pastiche.

Ultimately, these things depend upon people, and therefore
upon the Scottish character. A century ago the Scots were still
in the vanguard of development where the heavy industries were
concerned. The drive that kept them there has long since
slackened. Scotland no longer has enough people present at that
forward point of contact where new ideas are generated and where
the elements of new creativity are constantly being formed. It is
almost as if, during the past fifty years, the Scots character had
begun to slip gear with time, and was now faltering and falling
farther and farther behind.

21

The Death of Scotland?

I**T IS** a good day; a summer day; a good day in which to round off this rambling gallimaufry, as I lie in the garden watching the torn scraps of cloud that are scattered about the sky. Every now and then some of them are stirred, as bits of paper on the ground are stirred, like fledgling seagulls; but by a wind that does not reach down to the level of the lawn where I lie writing. At irregular intervals the distant background of bird-noise in the trees and bushes is obliterated by the quick growing and diminishing sound of passing cars. On a day like this Scotland seems a fine country to live in, and Loch Lomondside an uncommonly pleasant part of it.

More than most people perhaps, poets enjoy lying in the sun, letting the warm sounds of summer seep into their senses. On a day like this, it is easy to accept life at its immediate face value; easy to blame our discontents upon the advent of middle age or the usual prevalence of distempered weather. Yet the weather has really nothing to do with it; for even in the locked cold of a Scottish winter Loch Lomondside can delight with the contrast between its humid brown softness, when the fields seem to be drawing in upon themselves, and the polished brilliance of its sunny frosts.

I ask myself, therefore, if my reading of the pulse of Scotland is not in some way a false one; if I am allowing purely subjective considerations to overset my judgment? People who know nothing of the craft of criticism sometimes allege that a bad dinner beforehand can sour a drama critic's views of a play. Can I be sure that I am reasonably free from the digestive or ingestive disturbances of my own ego?

I once sat in the class of an English master who firmly

instilled in the heads of his pupils the maxim that to get the most out of life it is necessary to harbour what he called 'good, honest prejudices'; by which he really meant enthusiasms. I absorbed his advice, and have held fast to it ever since.

It would not be unreasonable to describe my interest in Scotland over the past fifteen years or so as a long-drawn-out love affair. At the height of the sweet fury, passion completely blinds the lover to the defects of his beloved; but in the ensuing cooler climate of the affections, the virtues that once gave un-alloyed delight may assume the proportions of intolerable short-comings. So I ask myself: Can this be what has really happened between me and Scotland?

The statistician might say that I have allowed my poet's method of making sense-judgments hopelessly to mislead me. The people of Scotland, he might claim, have never been better off financially than they are today. Their cars and television sets and washing-machines testify to their prosperity. The standard of liv-ing for all but the unemployed is higher than it has ever been before (and, by the standards associated with unemployment, even the workless are less poorly off than their predecessors three decades ago). New factories are going up in the industrial estates. Diseases like tuberculosis and rickets, once the scourge of Scotland, have been almost completely obliterated. Infant mortality has been reduced to a new low level, and fewer Scottish mothers die in childbirth. Housing standards have improved; schools are airier and brighter; Burns Clubs continue to increase in number; and more people own kilts than ever before. Haggis is now tinned and sent abroad. There are two Government Ministers at the Scottish Office instead of, as formerly, only one. International football and rugby matches still arouse virile demonstrations of pro-Scottish fervour. According to the politicians, and the more extrovert popular newspapers, the Way Ahead is bright and shiny. So what possible right has a minor poet, a mere commentator on men and affairs, to suggest that the pundits and the prophets, and the men and women whose anonymous chair-borne public services are properly rewarded with honours and decorations, are wrong, and that all is not right in our officially Presbyterian Scots heaven? Today, is there not plenty; and for tomorrow, rich promise? Let the gloomsters be silent. Here's tae us: wha's like us!

I do not think my sense-judgments are wrong. If I had continued a good Presbyterian, I should have believed in the existence of the soul, and might have been tempted to coin some highly original phrases like 'the soul of the people' to describe that indefinable entity which holds a country together and keeps alive its sense of nationhood. For this is where the sickness lies.

I am not for one moment suggesting that in the foreseeable future the machinery of Scotland will cease to work, and that town and countryside will grind to a desolate stand-still. I am, however, convinced that if the watering down of the Scottish character continues at the rate the dilution has occurred during the last twenty or thirty years, then Scotland the Nation must eventually cease to exist—probably within the next half-century. As Colin Walkinshaw has remarked: '. . . the final and permanent destruction of a nation once fully established and conscious of itself will be something unique in the records of Western Christendom.' In Scotland's place, at long last, there will be North Britain, the realization of the early Unionists' dreams.

What sort of North Britain would fill the vacuum created by the death of Scotland? In my blacker moments, I envisage the consummation of the thought-trends of many of our present-day politicians and planners.

Sometimes I imagine a minor slave state in which the population will be compulsorily crammed and concentrated in the Central Lowlands, busily engaged during cyclic boom periods in operating the former Anglo-American branch factories. To the South of this industrial subtopia will lie a sparsely populated no-man's-land; and to the North an almost uninhabited mountainous area where screened foreign tourists willing to rough it will still be able to enjoy a strictly organized pioneering holiday, walking, shooting and fishing, provided they make their own administrative arrangements and do not trespass upon the secret sites where rockets were made before the Labour Party decided that defence was morally indefensible and the Russians flew in and took over.

In less gloomy moments, I can at least visualize English-speaking mastership: the Anglo-American factories still in Anglo-American hands, and those who live in the overcrowded industrial belt all owning cars. These they will be unable to use in the sprawling central area, because of the static traffic problem. In the more distant rural areas villages will have been torn in half, to make the cheapest possible way for fast-travel roads, and the inhabitants of the surviving half-villages will have to live out their lives behind protective cages, as the residents of Harthill, on the road between Glasgow and Edinburgh, do now. The North British local authorities will have overridden the regulations relating to National Parks tardily made by their Scottish predecessors, and blocks of concrete cells like giant soap-powder packets will tower in serried ranks about the banks of Loch Lomond and the shores of the Firth of Clyde. Everyone will have more leisure, and no one will have the least idea what to do with it. Eyesight will deteriorate, because of the breakfast-to-bedtime television craze; the art of reading will be lost, and the crime ratio will shatter all previous records. Sentimental lip-service will still occasionally be paid to those former Scottish deities, Mary, Queen of Scots; Bonnie Prince Charlie; Burns; and the Hydro-Electric Board; but only by the older generation. Burns suppers will still be held, but in a streamlined form. Since none of the participants will understand the Scots tongue, readings of the National Bard's work will be generally regarded as boring and pointless. The kilt will be a museum piece, quaint relic of the days of barbarism, and social historians will lecture on transvestism among the vanished race of Scots with the confidence that now inspires their dissertations on homosexuality among the Ancient Greeks.

Unless there is a rapid and radical departure from the present Scots determination to indulge in national self-destruction, and to allow the best Scots brains to be lured South of the Border in a manner and on a scale almost amounting to genocide, I do not see how a recognizable Scotland can long survive. The outward formalities may seem to be carrying on as usual. The Establishment will wear a suitably complacent look on its poker face, as Establishments do everywhere. But behind the façade of pomp and pretence the sense of nationhood will dwindle down to an ever-fainter murmur, and ultimately to extinction.

Many perfectly sincere people would probably regard this as a good thing, holding the view that nationalism is at all times an evil force, and that in the long-term best interests of mankind nations should gradually merge their identities. I respect, but do not entirely share, their view. Yet it may be that some sort of process of coalescing is inevitable. So far as the internal economy is concerned, the natural working out of the capitalist principle of the greater swallowing the lesser may bring about monopoly conditions where competition and variety are virtually eliminated. If the same principle were to operate among nations, the outlook even for the larger countries of the Western World would be grim indeed.

I cannot bring myself to believe that nationality, those physical and intellectual conditions which nations evolve to provide the environment in which the temperaments of their peoples can develop most naturally and freely, is an outmoded conception, and that the future of mankind lies in the successful domination of one powerful nation over all the others.

At the dawn of the present century, the historian Lord Acton was able to declare that 'where absolutism reigned, by irresistible arms, concentrated possessions, auxiliary churches, and inhuman laws, it reigns no more; that commerce having risen against the land, labour against wealth, the State against the forces dominant in society, the division of power against the State, the thought of individuals against the practice of ages, neither authorities, nor minorities, nor majorities can command implicit obedience'. Until about the middle of the century, Lord Acton's declaration could hardly have been challenged. He would be a foolhardy prophet indeed who, however strong the seeming evidence of its impending refutal might presently be, would maintain that the events of little more than a decade are likely to overthrow it utterly and finally.

I believe in the ultimate survival of the Nation State, adapted to fit into a pattern of living where international rivalries, except of the civilized sort, no longer have meaning or therefore place. The obliteration of nationality in general, in my view, would be as disastrous for the human race, and as impossible to achieve, as the obliteration of individuality.

Other nations may co-operate with each other increasingly, yet still retain their identity. Scotland, however, is alone in her sickness. Assuming, therefore, that some shift in the effectiveness of the deterrent does not bring about a nuclear war; that the absorption of the lesser by the greater is not an inevitable process against which resistance is useless; and that attempted world tyranny will falter and fall back at some stage on its course; can anything be done to reverse the decline of Scotland? It is not easy to formulate an encouraging answer, because the basic requirement for any attempt to stimulate the sense of nationhood is lacking: the will of the Scots themselves to survive as a modern nation. Were it not lacking, there would be no decline.

In his perceptive study of this very problem, *The Future of Scotland*, written almost thirty years ago, Dr James A. Bowie thought that 'the first step, and a necessary step whatever the political future, is to engender a common will'. This, he realized, would be 'a slow, difficult process, involving the creation among the people of the consciousness of a problem, a knowledge of the relevant facts, the putting forward of alternative solutions, discussion, argument and research in comparing them, and finally the decision by a majority that one of the alternatives is preferable to all others'.

The years have passed since Dr Bowie diagnosed a possible cure, and there have been no such discussions, except, perhaps, in private, among passionate minorities. Dr Bowie, a practical economist and at that time Principal of Dundee School of Economics and Commerce, suggested reasons which might account for this particular failure:

'Mainly this is due to the fact that young Scots are kept culpably ignorant of what concerns them most—the position of their own country—and incipient leadership is encouraged to become the mercenary of other interests. The result is that the pulse of Scotland beats feebly, and with every blow to her fortunes she becomes less able to breast the times, to think clearly and act vigorously for her own salvation.'

He may have been right, but the phrase 'young Scots are kept culpably ignorant' suggests a sinister 'they' to whom blame can be conveniently transferred. No such 'they' exists.

The root of the trouble is that intelligent young Scots, and middle-aged ones too, are no longer able to visualize Scotland as a modern economic and political entity. They are aware that the popular image of a be-tartaned, romanticized Scotland is slightly ridiculous, and show embarrassment when they are publicly confronted with it. When Sydney Goodsir Smith's play *The Wallace* was performed at the Edinburgh International Festival of 1960, a group of well-meaning but misguided Scots patriots made political use of the emotional excitement created by the dramatist, and at the end of some of the performances tried to induce the audience to rise to its feet and sing 'Scots wha hae wi' Wallace bled'. As there were always in the audience more Scots wha haena, the reluctant and self-conscious singing straggled to a much diminished, word-fumbling close.

Incidentally, it is unfortunate, but significant, that Scotland has no real national anthem. 'Scots wha hae' has a limping dirge of a tune. Even if Francis George Scott's triumphal setting were to be generally adopted, no one really wants to 'lay the proud usurper low'; and, if anyone did, the 'usurper' is no longer standing high to engage their ferocious attentions. Nor is 'Auld lang syne', with its harping upon the pleasantness of past associations, a substitute. The only other song which comparatively modern wont and usage qualifies to some extent for consideration is 'Scotland the Brave', a music-hall ballad with a jaunty 'wha's like us' tune and words that exhibit the feeblest-minded aspects of Scotland's be-tartaned past-fixation.

The Scotland of the Edinburgh Military Tattoo, the March of the Pipers along Princes Street, the Braemar Gathering, the wearing of tartan tammies at football matches, and so on, no doubt has its value in making tourists feel that they are getting good Scotch satisfaction for their money. We may, if we wish, share our visitors' simple pleasure. But these things are survival relics, belong to an idea of Scotland that has no living reality—I do not dispute their commercial reality!—and provide no basis for the construction of a viable image of a modern state with a complete and rounded national personality.

There are some Scots who find it possible to accept the idea of the death of Scotland, but who maintain that isolated fragments of her influence will survive of their own accord; that bagpipes and haggis and Sabbatarianism, the Burns cult and whisky will keep alive all that is worth preserving of Scotland the nation. The poetry of Burns and whisky no longer belong solely to Scotland. As for the rest, such an elevation of unessentials represents nothing much more than the half-hearted armchair evasion of the realities of the situation, as I have tried to suggest in this book.

What Scotland desperately needs is a new beginning, drawing

strength from the facts and precedents of her history, but creating out of them a national entity of significance by European standards.

How could such a reborn Scotland be midwifed into being? C. M. Grieve asked a similar question in the concluding chapter of his *Scottish Eccentrics* as long ago as 1936.

'If . . . Scotland is to survive, where is the impetus to come from, what invisible reservoir secretes such a startling potentiality? No glimpse of anything of the sort is to be found in the conception of the Scottish character almost universally accepted today; certainly nothing seems to be further from the minds of the vast majority of Scots themselves. So far as they are concerned the long centuries of Scotland's national life have long ago been brought to nothing. . . .'

It is still the case that the health of Scotland's nationhood is not of the slightest interest to the average Scot. He likes to feel that a Scottish nation is there, warm and docile, somewhere in the background, a reassuring pretence upon which he can fall back occasionally over issues of no serious importance. Probably he will be genuinely distressed when one day he discovers that even the pretence has disappeared.

The case of Ireland is sometimes hopefully cited in relation to Scotland's plight. Ireland appeared to be in danger of losing her identity many times during the last four hundred years. But there is no real parallel. Unlike the Scots, the Irish never allowed their *virr*, their national character, to be gelded. Consequently, when the Irish poets of the Anglo-Irish Renaissance became Shelley's 'trumpets that sing to battle', there was a popular follow-up. Trumpeters by themselves cannot win a single encounter, let alone a battle. So, in Ireland, the poets were successful in rebuilding at least three-quarters of a nation. In Scotland, the poets may blow their trumpets till they burst, but the 'army' will continue its retreat.

There was a time, even in Scotland, when poets were able to play a direct part in influencing affairs. Such intervention was possible because there then existed generally accepted beliefs, public confidences, so to say, upon which the poet's insight operated more acutely, giving him a certain practical social value.

In early Stuart times Bishop Gawain Douglas of Dunkeld, translator of Virgil's *Aeneid* into Scots, did his best to play a vigorous political hand. True, he proved himself to be a trifle inept against the seasoned professionals; but he was still a force to be reckoned with in his day. Sir David Lyndsay was much more successful in influencing the movement for the reform of the Catholic Church; a movement which no doubt went far beyond Lyndsay's modest dreams to explode itself in the holocaust of the Reformation. Indeed, Scott thought that, after Knox himself, Lyndsay's contribution to the Reformation was more considerable than that of any other single man.

Burns's early satires did much to break the imposition of church tyranny in Scotland. Scott made at least one successful sally into the political arena when he managed to overthrow the intention of the Government of the day to deprive the Scottish banks of their cherished right to print their own banknotes.

Today, however, there are no generally accepted beliefs. The poet can, and must, still comment upon the absence of beliefs, but he has become, for the moment, something of an anachronism. C. Day Lewis has gone so far as to ask if the poet can 'survive in the modern world except as a kind of village idiot, tolerated but ignored, talking to himself, hanging round the pub and the petrol pumps, his head awhirl with broken images, mimicking the movements of a life in which he has no part'.

He is very much in the position of an onlooker who watches the movement and confusion of a street corner from the quiet of an hotel window. He has a room with a view, from which he may see what goes on, but he cannot influence the action.

'A single bed, a wash-hand basin, a wardrobe,
an armchair by the window—a cheap hotel
where travellers retreat from the sense of travelling
and self to itself's the one thing left to sell.

A room with a view. I pull back the dingy curtains.
Slanted below me, the corner of a street,
a sagging stave of telegraph wires ruled through it,
cancelling out the angle where people meet,

exchanging dissatisfactions, fervours or favours
till their stock runs dumb, and they turn away and are passed
through the corner's arms from the frame of the window-
                                                    picture;
a repeating detail singled out from the vast

entanglement of possibilities
that fills the telegraph wires' continuous hum.
These are the men of our times, and the women, enacting
what shapes our times on the frontiers of time-not-become;

the heroes of indecision whose gentle gestures,
tender or foolish, conjugate their own
unhappiness to tenses that relate
in the *now* of history where no one's so alone

as the lonely poet, sensually aware
of the casual conjugations, the empty page
on which the huge necessities are written
as he scrawls in the margin his pity or his rage.'

That poem refers, of course, not to Scotland's problems, but
to the problems of humanity; so grave and complex that the poet
who would turn his back on them to concern himself with the
plight of a country that is dying mainly because it no longer has
any real desire to live, would be guilty of a terrifying irresponsi-
bility.

So for me the love affair is over. The fervour, the obsession
with Scottishness for its own sake, the strongly emotional
response to whatever carried even the faintest Scottish overtone,
all these things have faded to a gentle but regretful affection; an
affection, however, which, I fancy, will persist to the end of my
days.

Index

ABERDEEN, 125–37
Aberdeen Press and Journal, 196
Aberdeen University, 127, 131, 180
Acton, Lord, 215
'Address to Loch Lomond, The',
    quoted 56–7, 58–60
Albert, Prince Consort, 44, 45, 132,
    134, 135
Alloway, 100, 102, 182
An Comunn Gaidhealach, 150, 151
ancestor worship, 11–12
Anglophobia, 161–2, 163
'Annie Laurie', 62, 63
'Apocalypse in Poetry', quoted 174
architecture, Scottish, 89–91, 105
Argylls, 25, 28, 36, 48, 50
Arran, 26, 33, 42

BALLADS, Border, 112–13
Balloch, 38, 41, 44, 79
Balmoral Castle, 134–6
Barbour, John, 54, quoted 55, 128
Barrie, Sir James, 108, 119, 120
Ben Lomond, 33, 37, 39, 40, 42, 43, 44,
    53, 57, 59–61, 63, 64, 65–6
Ben Nevis, 42, 150
Binyon, Laurence, 70 fn.
Blake, George, 117, 121, 197
Bliss, Sir Arthur, 98, 111
Bonnie Prince Charlie, 62, 121, 123,
    141, 163, 214
Border country, 111–13
Boswell, James, 34, 35, 104
Bowie, Dr James A., 8, quoted 216
Bridie, James, 108, 122
British Broadcasting Corporation, 188,
    198–201
broadcasting in Scotland, 198–202
Brown, George Douglas, 129
Brown, Ivor, quoted 134
Bruce, George, quoted 131–2
Bruce, Robert, 11, 12, 24, 25, 44, 54, 55,
    163, 166
Buchan, John, quoted 171, 172
Buchanan, Janet, 47, 52
Buchanans, 26, 50

Bulletin, The, 196
Burns, Robert, 38, quoted 56–8, 72,
    100–2, 107, quoted 115, 119, 121,
    123, 136, quoted 139, 163, 170,
    172, 179, 181, 182, 183, 214, 217,
    219
Burt, Edward, quoted 53, 140
Bute, 26, 42
Byron, Lord George, 72, 128

CALVINISM in Scotland, 70, 96, 111, 142,
    183
Camden, William, quoted 33 fn.
Carlisle, 24, 61
Catholicism, 98, 107, 183, 191
character, Scots national, 203–10
Charles I, 28, 91
Charles II, 26, 182
Churches, Scottish, 188–94
Clearances, 139, 142
Cochrane, William, 48 fn.
Coleridge, Samuel Taylor, 38, 39
Colquhoun, Lady Helen, 35
Colquhoun, Sir Humphrey, 28–9
Colquhoun, Sir James, 29, 34
Colquhoun, Sir James (eleventh baronet),
    quoted 66–7
Colquhoun, Sir John, 28
Communism, 161, 162–3, 164, 174
Conquest, Robert, 8, quoted 177
Convention movement, Scottish, 19,
    168
Cririe, Dr James, quoted 58–60
Crockett, Samuel R., 119, 120
Cunninghame Graham, R. B., 209

DANTE, quoted 70
Darnley, Lord, 26
Davidson, John, 205 (quoted)
Defoe, Daniel, 33 fn.
Dibdin, Charles, 37, 38, 41
Dibdin, Rev. Thomas Frognell, quoted
    41–2
Donne, John, 47, 72

drama in Scotland, 107, 110, 121–4, 200
Dryburgh, 30, 116
Dumbarton, 24, 28, 35, 41, 42
Dunbar, William, quoted 126, 127, quoted 138–9, 179
Dundee, 117–22, 197, 206
Dunoon, 99, 100

EDINBURGH, 25, 29, 63, 85, 98, 103–16, 122, 134, 135, 144, 169, 182, 189–90
Edinburgh Castle, 42, 85, 104, 164
Edinburgh International Festival of Music and Drama, 106–11, 190, 216
education, Scottish, 180–7
Edward, I, 24, 166
emigration, Scottish, 183

FARQUHARSONS, 134, 137
Faujas de Saint Fond, B., quoted 35–6, 37, 38
Fintry, 21–2
folk-music, Gaelic, 149–50
Ford, Robert, quoted 62
Franck, Richard, quoted 127, 128
Fraser, G. S., 8, quoted 130–1, 174, 177

GAELIC tongue, 151–2, 170, 185, 199
Gaels, 96, 148–52
Galt, John, 114, 171, 181, 200, 202
Gartocharn, 21, 22, 47, 49 fn., 76–80, 85
General Assembly of the Church of Scotland, 189–90, 193
Gibbon, Lewis Grassic, 128, quoted 129–30, 173–4. See also Mitchell, J. Leslie
'Gil Morrice', quoted 112
Glasgow, 17, 18, 20, 41, 50, 80–1, 85–102, 105, 110, 111, 117, 118, 121, 122, 143, 150, 159, 189
Glasgow Herald, 175, 176, 196, 197
Glasgow University, 46, 47, 180, 186, 187
Glen Fruin, 28, 45, 63
Glencairn, Earl of, 25
Glencoe, Massacre of, 139, 140
Grants, 28–9
Grieve, C. M., 118, 157, quoted 158–9, 160–1, quoted 162, 163, quoted 164, 171, 172, 173, 174, 176, 208–9, 218 (quoted). See also MacDiarmid, Hugh
Guthrie, Sir Tyrone, 107, 200 (quoted)

HALDANE of Gleneagles, Sir John, 25, 27
Hammerton, Philip Gilbert, quoted 65–6
Helensburgh, 18, 29, 34
Highlands, 138–53
history, Scottish, 23–9
holiday resorts, Clyde-coast, 99–100
Holloway, John, quoted 131
Home Rule, Scottish, 168, 169
'Home Town Elegy', 8, 130
housing in Scotland, 80–1
Hume, David, 104, 105, 190

INCH Tavannach, 38, 45
Inch-laverack, Isle, 33, 34
industry in Scotland, 92–3, 115–16, 118, 125–6, 143–4, 145
Innellan, 18, 20, 99
Inveraray, 32, 36, 139
Invercauld, 134, 137
Inverness, 152, 153, 169
Inversnaid, 43, 45
Irish colonizers, 17–18

JACOBITES, 49, 61, 120, 140
Risings, 139, 140, 141
James I (of Scotland), 25
James III, 25
James V, 25, 30
James VI, 26, 28, 103
'Jamie Telfer o' the Fair Dodhead', quoted 112
Johnson, Dr Samuel, quoted 34–5, 38, quoted 54

KAILYARD movement, 119–22, 129
Kemp, Robert, 107, 108, 123, 176
Kilmaronock, 47–8, 76
Knox, John, 123, 124, 180–1, 183, 190, 219

'LADY of the Lake, The', 23, 42, quoted 63
Lallans Makars, 174, 175–9, 200
Lang, Andrew, quoted 171
Leaves from the Journal of a life in the Highlands, 43
Leckie, Rev. Thomas, 47–8, quoted 49–52
Lenenru, Marie, quoted 70
Lenin, 162–3
Lennox, 20, 21
  location, 23
  earls of, 24–9
  history, 24–9
  reactions of travellers to, 30–46

Lewis, C. Day, 219 (quoted)
Lindsay, Maurice
  ancestry, 17–18
  influence of Ted Verschoyle in
    boyhood, 17–18
  wartime service, 18–19
  caravan life, 20–1
  finds a home in Scotland, 22
  poem, 68
  his village, 76–80
  Glasgow childhood, 85
  meeting with C. M. Grieve, 157–60
  experience of Scottish Nationalism,
    166–7
  associations with New Apocalypse,
    174, 175
Lindsay, Mrs Maurice, 8, 21, 176 fn.
Linklater, Eric, 108, 123, 158, 174
literature, Scots, 114–15, 118–21, 128,
    151, 157–64, 170–9
Loch Lomond, 13, 21, 23, 24, 25, 28,
    47, 80, 98, 214
  legends, 30–2
  first tourist, 31
  fish, 31
  observers' impressions, 31–46
  Lake Poets, 38–40
  first steamboats, 40–1
  Queen Victoria's reactions, 43–5
  lochside diary, 47–52
  in verse, 54–68
  most famous poem, 61
  proposed National Park, 79
  'Loch Lomond', 63
London, 19, 72, 86, 125, 152, 153, 201
Luss, 28, 32, 33, 35, 36, 38, 40, 42, 45,
    62–3, 67–8
Lyndsay, Sir David, quoted 27–8, 107–8,
    219

McCAIG, Norman, 174, quoted 175, 177
MacDiarmid, Hugh, 8, 54, 129, 157, 158,
    171, 175, 179. See also Grieve,
    C. M.
Macfarlanes, 27–8
McGonegal, William, 118–19
McGregors, 28, 32, 44
Mackintosh, Charles Rennie, 90–1
'MacLaren, Ian', 119, 120
McLellan, Robert, 108, 123
MacNeil, Seumas, 148, 149
Malcolm, Earl of Lennox, 24–5
Maldwin, Earl of Lennox, 24, 28
Mar, earls of, 49, 133
Mary, Queen of Scots, 26, 121, 123,
    163, 214
Matthew, Earl of Lennox, 25–6
Meldrum, William, 27–8
Miller, Hugh, quoted 45–6, 63

Mitchell, J. Leslie, 128, 173. See also
    Gibbon, Lewis Grassic
Muir, Edwin, 8, 208 (quoted)
Murdoch, William, 181, quoted 182
music in Scotland, 106–7, 109, 111

NATIONAL Parks, 79, 214
nationalism, Scottish, 29, 144, 165–9,
    214–18
New Apocalypse movement, 174–5, 177
Nicoll, Sir William Robertson, 119, 120

PENNANT, Thomas, 26, quoted 32–4, 38
Perth, 121–2, 173
Pin, Patrice de la Tour du, quoted 71,
    74
pipe-music, Highland, 148–9
Pliny, 33 fn.
poems on Loch Lomond, 53–68
poet and society, 69–75
Press, Scottish, 195–8
pugnacity, Scots, 204–5

RAEBURN, Sir Henry, 208–9
Ramsay, John, quoted 141
Reformation, 91, 108, 109, 180–1
Reid, Alexander, 108, 123
Reid, J. M., 121, 193 (quoted)
religion in Scotland
  Calvinism, 70, 96, 111, 142, 183
  in Glasgow, 96
  Catholicism, 98, 107, 183, 191
  in the Highlands, 147–8
  in Reformation times, 180–1, 183
  present-day, 188–94
Rob Roy, 49, 52
Robertson, R. H. S., 182, 183
Rossdhu, 29, 34, 35, 63
Rowardennan, 42, 44, 45, 60

ST ANDREW, 188–9
Saltire Society Report, 184, quoted
    185–6
Saurat, Professor Dennis, 173, 174
'Scotland, 1941', 208 (quoted)
Scots Review, 196–7
Scots tongue, 97, 170–9
Scotsman, 144 (quoted), 176, 195, 197,
    205 (quoted)
Scott, Francis George, 171, 217
Scott, Sir Walter, 23, 38, quoted 63–4,
    65, 100, 113–15, 127, 135, 170, 179,
    181, 183, 200, 219
Simpson, Archibald, 132 fn.
Smith, Ian Crichton, quoted 67–8

Smith, Sydney Goodsir, 108, 176, 216–17
Smollett, Tobias, 38, 40, 44
Soutar, William, 122, 173
Southey, Robert, 39, quoted 40, 72
Staffa, island of, 35, 37
Stair, Viscount, 140 fn.
steamboats, 40–1, 99
Stevenson, R. L., 97, 105, quoted 170, 171–2, 183
Stirling, 25, 98
Stronachlachar, 43, 45
Stuart, Major-General David, quoted 141–2
Swave, Peder, 30–1

TARBET, 36, 39, 40, 41, 42, 45
tartans, 135–6
Taylor, John, 132, quoted 133
Tennyson, Lord Alfred, 71, 72, 75
Thomson, Roy, 195, 196, 197
tourism in Scotland, 100, 110, 111, 145–7, 148, 150

Union of the Parliaments, 92, 144, 169

VERSCHOYLE, Ted, 17–18
Victoria, Queen, quoted 43–5, 132, 134, 135, 136

WALKINSHAW, Colin, 213 (quoted)
Wallace, Sir William, 12, 24, 108, 163, 166
Wars of Independence, 24–5
Watson, Rev. John, 119
Waverley Novels, 115
Wimberley, Major-General Douglas, 205
Wordsworth, Dorothy, 38, quoted 39
Wordsworth, William, 38, 39, 58, 71, 72, quoted 100

YEATS, William B., 18, 74, 163, 179
Young, John, quoted 67
Young, William, 89